TACITUS
ANNALS XV

TACITUS
ANNALS XV

EDITED BY N.P. MILLER
FORMER READER IN LATIN,
ROYAL HOLLOWAY COLLEGE
UNIVERSITY OF LONDON

PUBLISHED BY BRISTOL CLASSICAL PRESS
GENERAL EDITOR: JOHN H. BETTS
(BY ARRANGEMENT WITH THOMAS NELSON & SONS LTD)

First published by Macmillan Education Ltd in 1973

Reprinted by arrangement with Thomas Nelson & Sons Ltd. in 1994, 1995 by
Bristol Classical Press
an imprint of
Gerald Duckworth & Co. Ltd
The Old Piano Factory
48 Hoxton Square, London N1 6PB

A catalogue record for this book is available
from the British Library

ISBN 0-85399-434-0

Available in USA and Canada from:
Focus Information Group
PO Box 369
Newburyport
MA 01950

Printed in Great Britain by
Booksprint, Bristol

Contents

Preface

THIS edition is intended primarily for Sixth Formers and undergraduates, and I hope that it provides the information necessary for an understanding of the text, and pointers toward further reading. I have tried to be as brief as possible: but Tacitus' *Annals* are neither short nor simple, and a commentary on them cannot, if it is to be helpful, be too compressed. Students, whether at school or university level, who are old enough (and who know enough Latin) to read Tacitus, should not be expected to accept an editor's statements as pronouncements *ex cathedra*, and I have therefore tried to include as many references as possible both to ancient sources of information, and to modern books and periodicals where problems which are important for the book and its author are discussed.

The edition is not a 'critical edition', but I have necessarily considered the text. With the exception of readings at 13,2 and 41,2, the text used is that of C. D. Fisher's Oxford Classical Text, with the more convenient section numbering of the Teubner text. I have not commented on readings where they are generally accepted or obviously correct. But textual problems cannot be isolated from problems of interpretation: ancient texts do not spring fully armed even from the presses of Messrs Macmillan, and the problems raised by their production are not so esoteric as is commonly imagined. Meaning, Latinity, Tacitean usage, and applied common sense, are the basic issues, and I have discussed some textual problems on those lines.

Purely linguistic exposition is kept as short as possible. But the workings of the language are important, and have repercussions far beyond the ' purely linguistic ' sphere: students are recommended to consult E. C. Woodcock, *A New Latin Syntax* (London, Methuen, 1959). Literary analysis is also important (as well as fashionable), and I have tried to indicate some of the methods by which Tacitus produces his literary effects, and to suggest that students consider how the literary presentation may affect the historical content of the work.

In preparing the edition, I have consulted especially the editions of the *Annals* by E. Koestermann (Heidelberg, 1968) and H. Furneaux (Oxford, 1907), and Sir Ronald Syme's *Tacitus* (Oxford, 1958). Other books and periodicals used are acknowledged at appropriate points in the commentary. Any translation provided is usually my own, and is intended to be explanatory rather than elegant.

To two friends, I wish to record my warmest thanks: to Dr J. P. Bews, for allowing me to use some valuable and unpublished material from her thesis on *Virgil and Tacitus*: and to Professor H. Tredennick, who read my typescript and made most valuable comments on its form and content. For the final version of both form and content, I am alone responsible.

N. P. M.

Introduction

Cornelius Tacitus[1] was born about A.D. 56,[2] and lived at least to know (*A.* 2,61) the Eastern boundary of the Roman Empire as it was between A.D. 115 and 117. He was probably the son of a Roman *eques* who governed Gallia Belgica (Pliny, *N.H.* 7,76), and his family perhaps (to judge from his friends and his interests) came from Gallia Narbonensis, the hinterland of the bay between Marseilles and Perpignan. By A.D. 88 (*A.* 11,11) he was praetor, and already holding an important religious office. In 77 (*Ag.* 9) he had married the general Agricola's daughter, and they were both away from Rome (*Ag.* 45) from 89 to 93: during this period Tacitus would, according to normal Roman practice, be commanding a legion, or holding some civil office, in one of the provinces. In 97, under Nerva, he was consul (Pliny, *Epp.* 2,1,6), and soon afterwards, in the early years of Trajan's principate, he was speaking eloquently in court (Pliny, *Epp.* 2,11). A fragment of an inscription (OGIS 487) records that he was proconsul of Asia (one of the ' plums ' of provincial office) in A.D. 113.

Such is the evidence: it presents a man who had personal knowledge of Imperial Rome and its government, from the

---

[1] His *praenomen* is uncertain. Sidonius Apollinaris (*Epp.* 4,14 & 22) says Gaius, the best MS has Publius.

[2] This is a reasonable inference from Pliny's indication (*Epp.* 7,20,3-4) that he is a little younger than Tacitus, and from the known date of Pliny's birth as A.D. 61/2 (*Epp.* 6,20,5).

reign of Nero to the reign of Trajan, a man following a public career which combined some of the functions of a modern member of Parliament, a barrister, a civil servant and a senior diplomat. For the historian, such a background was valuable, because it provided access to information, and experience against which to assess it. For the man, public service under emperors in general and Domitian in particular, created a frustration and bitterness which is obvious in all his writings.

Of these writings, all but one are, in some sense, historical. The *Dialogus de Oratoribus* discusses, in dialogue form and the ' Ciceronian ' style appropriate to such a work, the reasons for the decline of oratory in Tacitus' own day. It was probably, like the next two works, written in the last years of Domitian's reign and published after 96: but its date cannot be certainly established. The *Agricola* and *Germania* were both published in 98 (*Ag.* 3: *G.* 37): the *Agricola* is a biography of his father-in-law, which in its account of the campaigns in Britain, comes close to historical treatment, and in its picture of a provincial in public service, indicates the problems which faced men of intelligence and integrity in the Roman Empire. The *Germania* is more technical: a monograph on a country, its peoples and its customs, based mainly on literary sources, it belongs to a recognised literary type: but it also suggests, sometimes, the historian's view of his own people in comparison (or conflict) with the Germans, and perhaps also his reflections on the political and moral issues of such conflict.

Tacitus' first major historical work was what we call the *Histories*, an account of the years A.D. 69–96, which was certainly being written about 106/107 (Pliny, *Epp.* 6,16 & 20). Of this work, only Books 1–4 and part of 5 survive, but it must originally have contained twelve to fourteen books: Jerome[1] tells us that the *Annals* and *Histories* together formed thirty books, and the *Annals* obviously contained at least sixteen. These *Annals* (*Ab excessu diui Augusti*) are Tacitus' last and perhaps unfinished work. They covered the period A.D. 14–68 (death of Augustus to death of Nero) in sixteen to eighteen books, of which 1–4 and 12–15 survive, together with parts of 5, 6, 11 and 16.

Since they were rediscovered in the fourteenth and fifteenth centuries, the historical works of Tacitus have been variously received. They have encouraged revolutionaries and disgusted dictators,[2] they have been praised as art and dismissed as biased. Biased they certainly are: an historian's business is interpretation, and that is inevitably influenced by his character and circumstances. A thinking man who had seen at close quarters what an absolutist emperor could do and how helpless others (himself included) were in face of such terror, was likely to take a jaundiced view of imperial power and those who wielded it. He was also, if a realist, likely to be aware that to imperial rule there was at the moment no real alternative, and that most forms of opposition achieved little but a useless martyrdom. It was a very real dilemma, and it colours Tacitus' attitude to all his material.

His historical sources for that material were various. For the later *Histories* he must have used primary sources; for the period of the *Annals* both documentary and literary evidence existed. The theory that Tacitus used only one major literary source for each period, and simply turned it

---

[1] *Comm. in Zach.* 3,14.
[2] See J. von Stackelberg, *Tacitus in der Romania* (Tübingen, 1960), 36–55.

into Tacitean Latin, has long since been exploded.[1] The careful recording of detailed information, the quality of judgement which compares so well with that exhibited by, e.g., Suetonius and Dio, the inquiring mind which sees and investigates the puzzling piece of evidence, these belong to an historian and not to a literary charlatan. Ancient historians' methods, preconceptions and interests were different from our own: they did not always think it necessary to re-examine primary sources, or to explain institutions which everyone took for granted, or to consider the socio-economic implications of their narrative: they seldom cited their sources, and they were very much concerned with the literary quality of their work. But they were, according to their lights, just as much concerned to record and interpret as is a modern historian (who has his own prejudices and preconceptions): and it is perhaps reasonable to remind ourselves that literary history is not necessarily worthless because it is well written.

For the period of Nero's reign, and for *A.* 15 in particular, Tacitus seems to have used a variety of sources, some of which he mentions in the narrative. The Elder Pliny's *History* (53,3 and n.) was written by a man who, while not a senator, had experience of public life in Rome and the provinces and who, to judge by his extant *Natural History*, was an assiduous accumulator of information, but often naïve in his judgement of its quality and value. Fabius Rusticus (61,3) was a friend and protégé of Seneca's (*A.* 13, 20): he was probably a literary and not a public man, but he may have got some interesting information from Seneca, and he is likely to have been hostile to the Emperor who killed his patron. Cluvius Rufus (*A.* 13,20) was not only a

[1] See Goodyear, pp. 25 f.: Syme, pp. 298 f.

consular, but a member of Nero's court circle (Suet. *Nero* 21): whatever his attitude to Nero, he was clearly in a position to know and to hear many things. Other literary sources (the *auctores* of 38,1) may lie behind the *ferunt*, *constitit* etc. (of, e.g., 10,4: 16,1: 23,4: 45,3) with which Tacitus often hedges a statement for whose accuracy he is not prepared to vouch. Among subsidiary sources may be counted such works as Corbulo's Memoirs (16,1 and n.), and probably also written accounts of the last hours of great men driven to death by various emperors: such accounts are mentioned in *Ag.* 2 and by Pliny (e.g. *Epp.* 5,5,3: 8,12,4), and may have provided some of the details for the death scenes of the Pisonian conspirators. Apart from literary sources, Tacitus as a senator would have access to the *acta senatus*, the official record of the senate's meetings, and in *A.* 15 we have (74,3) his sole specific reference to its information. His presentation of senatorial proceedings, however (20,1 n.) and of certain information (22,2 n.: 73,3 n.) suggests that he used the records more frequently than that.

It is clear that Tacitus could look critically at his sources, and assess their reliability, in the light of their authors' sympathies and qualifications, of the other evidence available, and of general probability. He so discusses Corbulo's Memoirs (16,3), the conflicting evidence for the Fire (38,1) and the Pisonian Conspiracy (73,1–2), the varying tradition about Seneca's place in that conspiracy (56,2) and a statement of Pliny's (53,4) which he finds incredible. The careful articulation, too, of those involved in the conspiracy suggests a critical collation of several sources, to make a coherent narrative.

Tacitus is a serious historian, and should be taken

seriously: he is not a perfect one. His account of Nero's reign has never been under the same attack as his presentation of Tiberius, but some of the same techniques are apparent. He will recount a rumour which he does not credit, in order to point a character or an incident (e.g., 15,2: 39,3: 65): he will insinuate discreditable motive in various complex ways (e.g., 38,7: 46,2): he will use his considerable literary resources to weight an interpretation (e.g., 6,1: 56,2). But neither here nor in the earlier work does he suppress or distort the facts: he is, as we all incline to do, stating as forcefully as possible something he believes to be the truth. Tacitus' jaundiced view of emperors and of human nature tends to lead him to believe the worst when there are several possible explanations: in Nero's Rome, the worst is quite often true.

The historical writings of Tacitus are incomparably our best source of information about the period: they reflect, too, a mind and a personality full of interest and quality: and their information is presented in Latin as fascinating as it is complex.

2 THE LANGUAGE OF TACITUS

Tacitus writes a concentrated and closely wrought Latin, which is both an impressive literary style, and an effective instrument of historical interpretation. From the Silver Latin of the early Empire, which was neatly turned, epigrammatic, deliberately 'interesting' and striking, he created his own version, which has all these qualities, but also a sustained intensity of expression and feeling, which gives it quality and depth. The style is designed to attract attention, to the subject matter and to the interpretation of it that the style itself suggests. His vocabulary is selective and evocative, his sentence structure economical and varied, his syntax often bold and experimental. The combination of these elements can be extremely effective, and is worth examining in detail:

A. 15,5,3. *Vologesi uetus et penitus infixum erat arma Romana uitandi, nec praesentia prospera fluebant. inritum obsidium, tutus manu et copiis Tigranes, fugati qui expugnationem sumpserant, missae in Armeniam legiones, et aliae pro Syria paratae ultro inrumpere: sibi imbecillum equitem pabuli inopia: nam exorta uis locustarum ambederat quidquid herbidum aut frondosum.* The two halves of Vologeses' motive are dislocated in structure: his over-riding interest is suggested by the position of his name, and his first motive is emphasised by the alliteration (*uetus . . . uitandi*) which picks up its initial sound, and by the striking syntax of *uitandi* (5,3 n.). The second motive is presented (with its own alliteration) by a change of construction which shifts the sentence from imputed motive to stated fact: and the basic fact is further emphasised by the detail of the following sentence. The first set of troubles – the futility of the siege, the safety of Tigranes, the rout of the besiegers and the movements of the Roman legions – are presented in a series of clauses, each starting with the participle which carries the point: the participles vary in number and gender, and the clauses vary in length and structure: the apparent afterthought (*et aliae f.*) is also a climax, hinting at a possible invasion of Parthia. Vologeses' next concern – lack of fodder – is (as the initial *sibi* makes clear) in indirect speech, so that we see it through the mind and as part of the motive of the king. The importance of this motive is emphasised by the explanation added by Tacitus, in a clause which contains three words which appear only here in his works. Locusts were rare and interesting, and so therefore is their name: *frondosus* is a word much commoner in poetry than in prose: *ambedo* is both poetical and rare (5,3 n.): together they evoke an image of a distant and desolate countryside.

The striking vocabulary and syntax of this passage, the dislocation produced by sudden change or variation. of construction, the concentration and significant juxtaposition effected in the second sentence by the total ellipse of the verb *esse*, attract and direct attention. Although variation of construction may often be simply a literary craftsman's device for presenting in palatable form a necessary catalogue of facts (e.g., the list of laws in 20,3 or of military forces in 26,2), it can also be a pointer to an historian's opinion of the relative importance of two possible explanations (e.g., *non utilitate publica sed in saeuitiam unius* 44,5: *gloriae eius non aduersus, simul amore, ne sibi unice dilectam ad iniurias relinqueret* 63,2): and it can insinuate an idea for which there may be little hard evidence (e.g., *siue ut raptus licentius exercerent, seu iussu* 38,7: *clades rei naualis accipitur, non bello . . . sed certum ad diem in Campaniam redire classem Nero iusserat* 46,2). It should always be considered with careful reference to its context.

The vocabulary of Tacitus makes its own contribution to the total effect. He uses archaism (e.g., *non ibo infitias* 2,3: *diu noctuque* 12,4: *mercimonium* 38,2) and Sallustian vocabulary (sometimes itself archaistic, cf. *diu noctuque Jug.* 38,3: *aequabilius atque constantius* 21,4: *aduersa . . . declinans* 26,3 etc.) not only to give colour and the authority of tradition to his work, but to add emphasis to the contexts where the words appear. Like most Silver Latin writers, too, he uses poetical, especially Virgilian, expressions (e.g., *Oceano abusque* 37,2: *squalenti litore* 42,2: *agrestibus pomis* 45,3): these provide epic

associations and therefore colour, and sometimes imply a
more specific comment, as when Lateranus (53,2) is described in a phrase whose Virgilian context suggests that he
is heroic, but doomed. Words exotic (e.g., *megistanas* 27,3)
and rare (e.g., *prodigentia* 37,1 : *deprecabundus* 53,2 : *sesquiplaga*
67,4) are carefully placed where their quality will add to the
effect of their context – *prodigentia* points Nero's outrageous
behaviour, *deprecabundus* a crisis in the Pisonian Conspiracy,
and *sesquiplaga* the horrors of the executions which followed
its discovery. More ordinary words, too, can by careful
placing convey extra significance: e.g., *cupido dominandi* 53,4
produces, in Tacitus' comment on human nature, a whole
complex of associations and reflections.

Tacitus wastes neither words nor structure. By compression he concentrates his sentences and the reader's attention
on their content. His complex use of allusion and association
is often akin to a poet's. And by his choice of vocabulary and
careful use of structure he often suggests an interpretation
of the historical evidence. The style of this literary historian
should not be studied in isolation from the content of his
narrative.

3 THE EMPEROR NERO[1]

The name of Nero has for so long been equated with
Monster, that it almost automatically and universally evokes
associations of cruelty and debauchery. The evidence for
these associations, though from an obviously hostile tradition and very obviously embroidered, yet contains a hard

---

[1] See Genealogy, p. xviii. There is a good modern account of Nero and
his reign in B. H. Warmington, *Nero: Reality and Legend* (Chatto &
Windus, London, 1969).

Some Julio–Claudians

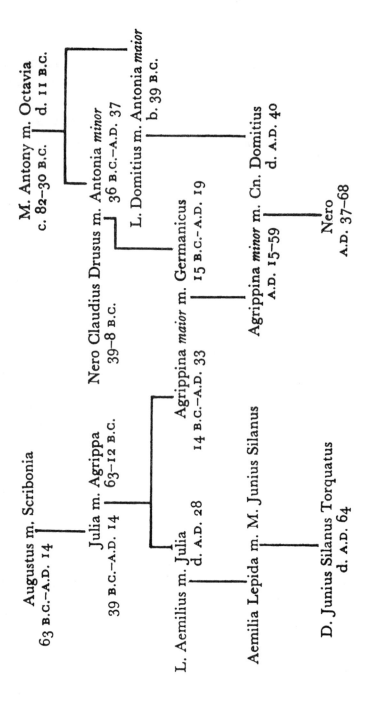

core that looks factual and cannot be ignored. And yet Nero has importance: he was titular head of the Roman world for fourteen years, from A.D. 54 to 68, a period which is not without interest: he was the last of the Julio–Claudians, and perhaps the first whose reign was both blatant enough and long enough to demonstrate the unpalatable fact of the ruler's very real power – with Nero, the *princeps* was seen to be an emperor.

The evidence suggests that Nero was unfortunate both in heredity and environment. The Domitii Ahenobarbi, his father's family, had a reputation for violence (Suet. *Nero* 1–5), and his mother, the younger Agrippina, was a ruthless intriguer for power (*A.* 12–14): his father died and his mother was exiled when Nero was about three years old (Suet. *Nero* 6), and he was for some time brought up by an aunt: with his mother's return, and her increasing influence with and eventual marriage to the Emperor Claudius, Nero became a member of the imperial household, and a pawn in its power politics. He was adopted by Claudius in A.D. 50, when he was about twelve years old (*A.* 12,25) and during the next four years he had a fair amount of publicity. In 53 he married Octavia, the Emperor's daughter (*A.* 12,58), and when Claudius died (perhaps with the assistance of Agrippina) in October 54, the proclamation of Nero as his successor was carefully engineered (*A.* 12,68–9). In his seventeenth year, he had become Emperor of Rome.

At first, all went reasonably well. Seneca and Burrus (*A.* 13,2) acted as his advisers on the business of empire, while Nero enjoyed the power. They were united in opposition to Agrippina's attempts to become the power behind the throne: ' dynastic ' murders, belonging to the accepted pattern which controlled palace intrigue and possible civil war, were kept to a minimum: co-operation with the Senate was promised, and a good general appointed to deal with the trouble in Armenia (*A.* 13,1–9). But gradually Nero's desire for self-gratification, and his resentment of anyone who interfered (or might interfere) with it, increased. The murder of his mother in 59 (*A.* 14,1–12), the divorce and murder of Octavia in 62 (*A.* 14,60–64), his increasing pre-occupation with public performance and display, the death of Burrus and the waning of Seneca's influence (*A.* 14,51–6), all led naturally to a situation where conspiracy against Nero was to be expected, and where his increasing tendency to execute on suspicion was equally predictable. Much of *A.* 15 is concerned with this situation.

The last three years of Nero's reign were marked by three major events. A revolt of Jews in Judaea turned into a major war (Jos. *B.I.* 2,284 f.): Nero had a triumphal tour of Greece and its Games in 67 (Suet. *Nero* 23): and a revolt in Gaul (Dio 63,22) eventually led to the proclamation of a new emperor. Nero was abandoned by all except a few slaves and freedmen and finally, with assistance, committed suicide in a suburban villa, on 9 June, 68. He was thirty-one.

Nero was not really suited to the business of government. What he took seriously was his art, and he seems to have had a (perhaps excessive amount of) genuine artistic tempera-ment. That, combined with a thirst for praise and a lack of any real sense of responsibility (both probably native to the man, but enhanced by his early upbringing) made him an unfortunate ruler. The one real achievement of his reign, the agreement with Parthia (Introd. 4), was perhaps pro-duced by good advice and good appointments: his inability to meet a crisis on his own is amply demonstrated by his behaviour in 68. He was extravagant, short sighted in his relative neglect of armies and provinces, and alarmingly single-minded in his pursuit of immediate objects. He was foolish, but not a fool: his interest in art and literature was deep, and he was probably a competent practitioner: his imagination could be captured by the possibility of re-building a city, cutting a canal, or draining marshes: and his extravagance of behaviour and liking for display, which alienated the governing classes, won him the affection of the populace of Rome and the Greek East, where for many years after his death, any *Nero rediuiuus* was assured of support.

He was the wrong man for the job. His inability to control the events of 68 led to terrible civil war before eventually the sober, frugal Vespasian took over. Nero as a personality is full of colour and interest: as a ruler of Rome, he was only intermittently successful.

4 ROME AND PARTHIA

During some hundred years of the first centuries B.C. and A.D., for reasons historical, geographical and psychological, these two empires were in intermittent conflict, though rarely in an official state of war. The Parthians, in origin Iranians from the Caspian steppes (see Map, p. xxii), had from about 250 B.C. established and extended their empire by in-corporating in it the Seleucid kingdoms created after the death of Alexander, until in the first century B.C. it extended from the Euphrates to the Oxus, from the Caspian Sea to the Persian Gulf. It comprised, that is, modern Iran, together with the eastern half of Iraq and the northeast corner of Syria. The Parthians were the nobles and overlords of this empire, the Arsacid family providing the ruling house. It was more a conglomerate of kingdoms than a

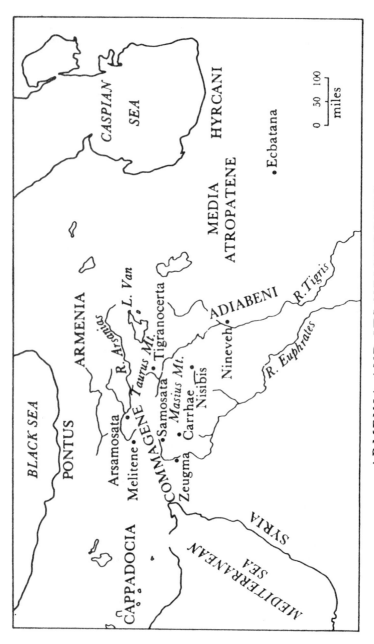

ARMENIA AND ITS NEIGHBOURS

unified empire: provided they recognised the supremacy of the 'King of Kings', the original inhabitants, whether Iranian or Greek, were left to organise their lives as they had done before. The Parthian nobles were hunters and fighters: they fought in armour and on horseback, while their followers provided the archers for which Parthia became famous.

As Parthian interests extended westwards, and Roman interests eastwards, contact between the two powers was inevitable, but need not have been unfriendly. First relations – with Sulla in 92 B.C. (Plut. *Sulla* 5,4) – were in fact cordial, because both empires had the same enemy in Mithridates of Pontus. The river Euphrates provided a natural boundary between the two empires, and both Rome and Parthia recognised this (Plut. *Pomp.* 33,6). Three factors wrecked a possible concordat – Pompey's double dealing with Parthia in 66 B.C., which Parthia never forgot (Plut. *Crass.* 31): Crassus' defeat at Carrhae in 53 B.C., which Rome could not forget: and Armenia.

Armenia, a mountainous country lying to the north of the Parthian empire, was in many ways very like Parthia. It was organised on the same lines, and its rulers were kin to the Arsacids. Early in the first century B.C., it was a powerful and independent country, ruled by Tigranes I. He was a son-in-law of Mithridates of Pontus, which brought him into conflict with Rome, and in 69 B.C. Lucullus invaded Armenia and captured Tigranocerta its capital (Plut. *Luc.* 28–29). Trouble continued during the eastern command of Pompey, and in 53 B.C. the triumvir Crassus, trying to emulate the military glory of his partners, was disastrously defeated at Carrhae: some 20,000 men, including Crassus, perished, and the Roman legionary standards were captured by the

Parthians. The Civil Wars presently distracted Rome's attention from the East, but in 34 B.C. Antony again invaded Armenia, and for two years it became a Roman province. By 30 B.C., however, it was back under Parthian influence, and this was the situation facing Augustus when he tackled the problem of Rome's eastern frontier.

The natural frontier was, as has been said, the river Euphrates. To guard it, Rome had Syria, a first class province with a standing army of four legions (*A.* 4,5), and various protectorates or client kingdoms, which could produce some local levies. The crossings of the Euphrates were the vulnerable points: of these, Zeugma was within reach of the Syrian legions, but Melitene and Samosata were not. To safeguard these, Rome must either station more legions near the frontier (and she did not have such legions), or she must have a friendly Armenia on the farther bank. Armenia was thus important to Rome as a buffer state between herself and Parthia: and Armenia was currently under Parthian control.

There were four possible courses of action, none without difficulties:

(*a*) Rome could annex Armenia and make it a province: but she did not have the soldiers to hold it, and without a garrison it would be very open to Parthian attack.

(*b*) She could establish on the throne of Armenia a client king of her own choosing: but Roman-educated princes were not acceptable to the Armenians, and were equally vulnerable to Parthian attack.

(*c*) She could accept a Parthian nominee, provided he recognised Roman suzerainty over Armenia: but it would not be easy to persuade an Arsacid to do that.

(*d*) She could abandon Armenia – not really a dangerous

course, because Parthia was not aggressive, and not strong or united enough to be a real menace: but the damage to prestige would be great, and the loss of the standards still rankled.

Augustus decided on diplomacy. The Arsacids were, as usual, fighting among themselves, and he had some useful hostages. The standards were returned in 20 B.C. (*RG* 29: cf. Hor. *Odes* 4,15,6: Virg. *Aen.* 7,606), a Roman nominee was put on the Armenian throne, and Augustan coins proclaimed ARMENIA CAPTA (*RIC*, I, p. 63,42: pl. III,58). But the captive broke free in 6 B.C., trouble continued through the campaigns and death of Gaius Caesar in A.D. 2, and when Augustus died in A.D. 14, Armenia had no king and had slipped from Roman control (*A.* 2,4).

Tiberius sent Germanicus to the East, and in A.D. 18/19 he annexed Cappadocia to be a second class province, and made Zeno king of Armenia. Zeno was not a ' Romanised ' monarch: he was acceptable to all parties, and there was peace until A.D. 34, when he died. Then the see-saw from Roman nominee to Parthian nominee and back again restarted, and continued through the reigns of Gaius and Claudius. In A.D. 51, Vologeses, a man of obvious character and ability, became King of Parthia, and in 55 the news that Parthia had again taken control of Armenia presented the young Nero with the first crisis of his reign (*A.* 13,6). He appointed Domitius Corbulo to a special command with responsibility for Armenia. For three years there was little activity, while Vologeses dealt with rebellion and Corbulo with a slack and indisciplined army. In 58 he invaded Armenia, demonstrated Roman power, and advised Vologeses' brother Tiridates (the Parthian nominee) to ask for Nero's recognition. This Tiridates was unwilling to do, so Corbulo captured and destroyed Artaxata, and later took Tigranocerta (*A.* 14,24): he also made punitive expeditions throughout Armenia, and demonstrated the possibility of take-over. Then Nero suddenly reverted to policy (*b*), and sent Tigranes V as a client king: whether this was stupidity or a feint is uncertain, but Corbulo established Tigranes in Armenia, left some troops, and withdrew to his own province of Syria (*A.* 14,26).

The next and final moves are recorded in *A.* 15. Tigranes provoked Vologeses to action, Vologeses threatened Armenia, Nero sent Paetus to annex the country, Paetus was defeated but Corbulo arrived in strength, and finally compromise was reached, with pomp and ceremony to save face on both sides. Corbulo knew that Rome could not hold Armenia: but he successfully demonstrated that Parthia, with Rome against her, could not hold it either. So Tiridates came to Rome in A.D. 66, to receive his crown from Nero's hands: and there was peace for fifty years.

The wisdom of the Neronian solution is confirmed by later events. In about A.D. 111 a new Parthian king deposed the reigning king of Armenia, and put on the throne his own nominee, without the sanction of the nominal overlord, Rome. Trajan decided to settle the Armenian question once and for all (Dio 68,17 & 20), and himself set out for the East. During 114–15 he overran Armenia and established it as a province, and in 115–16 he attacked and captured the Parthian capital. But, inevitably, Parthia and Armenia rose behind him, and desperate fighting followed. Trajan had to modify his plan of conquest, and his successor Hadrian virtually abandoned Armenia to its native inhabitants (H.A. *Hadr.* 5,3: 21,11). It is an interesting and sobering thought, that Tacitus almost certainly wrote his account of Corbulo's campaigns with the knowledge of Trajan's very different ones in his mind.

Fear and pride, distrust and desire for glory, combined (as often) to complicate a situation which was fundamentally not dangerous at all. Given the initial complications, the only solution must be Corbulo's (or was it Nero's?): and credit should be given to the statesman who saw it, and the soldier who carried it out.

5 TACITUS, NERO AND THE CHRISTIANS

The problems of *A.* 15,44, the chapter which records the punishment of Christians as incendiaries, are notorious and complex. They involve questions of authenticity of text and of Roman criminal law, as well as of interpretation of the text that is there. The main issues are these:

(*a*) Is the text Tacitean or interpolated?

(*b*) How is it to be interpreted?

(*c*) Does the interpretation fit with other evidence for the period?

(*a*) If stylistic criteria mean anything at all, the chapter was written either by Tacitus or by a very skilful imitator of his style. The digression on the *auctor*, the resumption of the main theme by *igitur*, the tone of *exitiabilis superstitio f.*, as well as the vocabulary and sentence structure, are most plausibly produced by the historian himself, and not by a later interpolator. Some of the text in its present form was certainly known to Sulpicius Severus[1] in the early fifth century A.D., and it is difficult to envisage a writer of the

---

[1] *Chron.* 2,29: *ut ferarum tergis contecti laniatu canum interirent, multi crucibus affixi aut flamma usti, plerique in id reseruati, ut cum defecisset dies, in usum nocturni luminis urerentur.*

centuries between Tacitus and Sulpicius with either the talent or the motive to produce and insert it: Christian writers would not, even to claim martyrs, refer to their faith in these terms, and the well-intentioned pagan glossers of ancient texts do not normally express themselves in Tacitean Latin. The chapter, with all its difficulties, stands or falls together, and the section from *ergo abolendo* to the end provides a climax for which the earlier section is an obvious preparation. The text has some difficulties, but it is fundamentally Tacitean.

(*b*) A careful reading of it suggests very strongly that Tacitus is presenting Nero as looking for scapegoats to distract public attention from the rumours about his own responsibility for the fire (*subdidit reos*: for the meaning ' substitute falsely ' cf. *A.* 1,39 *quamuis falsis reum subdere*). He chose as victims a sect already unpopular (*per flagitia inuisos*) and beginning to be called by the somewhat contemptuous *-iani* suffix: their crimes were those (like incest and infant cannibalism, cf. Tert. *Apol.* 7) which a lurid imagination attributed to an apparently peculiar and secretive group, and of which members of that group were automatically presumed to be guilty (cf. *flagitia cohaerentia nomini* Pliny, *Epp.* 10,96,2). There was therefore likely to be little popular opposition to their execution, nor would a religion with the origin and development sketched be likely to have influential friends at court.

Once Nero had proclaimed the Christians guilty, all that had to be done was to find Christians and arrest them – a proceeding recently very familiar to the Jews of Nazi Germany. Those who admitted to being Christians (*qui fatebantur*) were first brought in, and from them was extorted (presumably by torture: few of them would be Roman citizens) the names of others. People acquiesced in their conviction, not because they really believed them guilty of arson (*haud proinde in crimine incendii*), but because Christians, with their *flagitia*, were in any case anti-social (*odio humani generis*) and deserved death. Tacitus shares this view (*aduersus sontes et nouissima exempla meritos*), but is moved, as often, by compassion for the victims of an emperor's cruelty.

(c) On that interpretation, Tacitus' account can be considered basically plausible and self-consistent: the textual problems affect details and not the main theme. Various difficulties have been felt and should be considered:

(i) Tacitus alone connects the punishment of Christians with the Fire. Suetonius, e.g., in *Nero* 16 says *afflicti suppliciis Christiani*, and in *Nero* 38 describes the Fire. But Suetonius' arrangement of his biographical material is peculiarly his own: he equally fails to connect the death of Seneca (*Nero* 35) with the Pisonian Conspiracy (*Nero* 36), and that does not seem to have worried anyone. The silence of Christian writers, on the other hand, may be produced by a desire to emphasise the fact of martyrdom rather than its immediate cause. Tacitus may be wrong in his connection: but he makes it quite specifically, and when he is specific, he usually has some evidence to support it: he may have found the information in at least one of his sources.

(ii) The legal procedure under which the Christians could have been tried and convicted has provoked much discussion. It appears to have been a *cognitio extra ordinem* – a ' procedure arbitrary and irresponsible, but perfectly legal and official ': see G. E. M. de Ste. Croix in *Past and Present*, 1963, 6 f.

(iii) The suggestion (by, e.g., J. Bishop, *Nero, the Man and the Legend* (London, 1964), pp. 82 f.) that the Christians either talked of or actively promoted an apocalyptic conflagration to destroy their enemies, is not perhaps impossible, but certainly unlikely. And the text implies strongly that they were *not* responsible for the Fire.

(iv) Various attempts to prove that Tacitus has confused Christians and Jews are equally unsatisfactory. They were clearly distinguishable by the time Tacitus was writing: the text specifically distinguishes and explains the Christians: punishment of Christians by Nero is mentioned by several other sources, pagan and Christian (e.g., Suetonius, *Nero* 16: Tertullian, *Apol.* 5): and to suppose (with e.g., Koestermann in *Historia* 1967, 456f.) that there existed simultaneously Jewish zealots known as *Chrestiani*, is to stretch coincidence rather far.

The bibliography of the subject is vast and multi-lingual: it is not possible to list it, much less summarise it, here. A balanced discussion of it can be found in J. Beaujeu, *L'incendie de Rome en 64 et les Chrétiens* (Latomus 1960, 65–80, 291–311: reprinted as *Collection Latomus* 49, Brussels 1960). The problems are real ones: they spring, in Professor Beaujeu's words, from *concision extrême, mots équivoques, structure douteuse, incertitude même dans l'établissement du texte.* But they have also been exaggerated: ingenious explanations tend to create more difficulties than they solve, and together they smell of the lamp in a way in which, for all its problems, the text does not. It is perhaps time to return to a more conservative view of the chapter and its significance.

Cornelii Taciti

AB EXCESSV DIVI AVGVSTI
ANNALIVM LIBER XV

1. INTEREA rex Parthorum Vologeses cognitis Corbulonis rebus regemque alienigenam Tigranen Armeniae impo-
situm, simul fratre Tiridate pulso spretum Arsacidarum
fastigium ire ultum uolens, magnitudine rursum Romana
et continui foederis reuerentia diuersas ad curas trahebatur, cunctator ingenio et defectione Hyrcanorum, gentis
ualidae, multisque ex eo bellis inligatus. atque illum am- 2
biguum nouus insuper nuntius contumeliae extimulat:
quippe egressus Armenia Tigranes Adiabenos, contermi-
nam nationem, latius ac diutius quam per latrocinia
uastauerat, idque primores gentium aegre tolerabant: eo
contemptionis descensum ut ne duce quidem Romano
incursarentur, sed temeritate obsidis tot per annos inter
mancipia habiti. accendebat dolorem eorum Monobazus, 3
quem penes Adiabenum regimen, quod praesidium aut
unde peteret rogitans. iam de Armenia concessum, proxima
trahi; et nisi defendant Parthi, leuius seruitium apud
Romanos deditis quam captis esse. Tiridates quoque regni 4
profugus per silentium aut modice querendo grauior erat:
non enim ignauia magna imperia contineri; uirorum
armorumque faciendum certamen; id in summa fortuna
aequius quod ualidius, et sua retinere priuatae domus, de
alienis certare regiam laudem esse.

2. Igitur commotus his Vologeses concilium uocat et proximum sibi Tiridaten constituit atque ita orditur: 'hunc ego eodem mecum patre genitum, cum mihi per aetatem summo nomine concessisset, in possessionem Armeniae deduxi, qui tertius potentiae gradus habetur: nam Medos Pacorus ante ceperat. uidebarque contra uetera fratrum odia et certamina familiae nostrae penatis 2 rite composuisse. prohibent Romani et pacem numquam ipsis prospere lacessitam nunc quoque in exitium suum 3 abrumpunt. non ibo infitias: aequitate quam sanguine, causa quam armis retinere parta maioribus malueram. si cunctatione deliqui, uirtute corrigam. uestra quidem uis et gloria in integro est, addita modestiae fama quae neque summis mortalium spernenda est et a dis aestimatur.' 4 simul diademate caput Tiridatis euinxit, promptam equitum manum, quae regem ex more sectatur, Monaesi nobili uiro tradidit, adiectis Adiabenorum auxiliis, mandauitque Tigranen Armenia exturbare, dum ipse positis aduersus Hyrcanos discordiis uiris intimas molemque belli ciet, prouinciis Romanis minitans.

3. Quae ubi Corbuloni certis nuntiis audita sunt, legiones duas cum Verulano Seuero et Vettio Bolano subsidium Tigrani mittit occulto praecepto compositius cuncta quam festinantius agerent: quippe bellum habere quam gerere malebat; scripseratque Caesari proprio duce opus esse qui Armeniam defenderet: Syriam ingruente Vologese acriore 2 in discrimine esse. atque interim reliquas legiones pro ripa Euphratis locat, tumultuariam prouincialium manum armat, hostilis ingressus praesidiis intercipit. et quia egena aquarum regio est castella fontibus imposita; quosdam riuos congestu harenae abdidit.

4. Ea dum a Corbulone tuendae Syriae parantur, acto

raptim agmine Monaeses ut famam sui praeiret, non ideo
nescium aut incautum Tigranen offendit. occupauerat 2
Tigranocertam, urbem copia defensorum et magnitudine
moenium ualidam. ad hoc Nicephorius amnis haud spernenda latitudine partem murorum ambit; et ducta ingens
fossa qua fluuio diffidebatur. inerantque milites et prouisi
ante commeatus, quorum subuectu pauci auidius progressi
et repentinis hostibus circumuenti ira magis quam metu
ceteros accenderant. sed Partho ad exequendas obsidiones 3
nulla comminus audacia: raris sagittis neque clausos ex-
terret et semet frustratur. Adiabeni cum promouere scalas
et machinamenta inciperent, facile detrusi, mox erum-
pentibus nostris caeduntur.

    5. Corbulo tamen, quamuis secundis rebus suis, mode-
randum fortunae ratus misit ad Vologesen qui expostu-
larent uim prouinciae inlatam: socium amicumque regem,
cohortis Romanas circumsideri. omitteret potius obsidio-
nem, aut se quoque in agro hostili castra positurum.
Casperius centurio in eam legationem delectus apud 2
oppidum Nisibin, septem et triginta milibus passuum a
Tigranocerta distantem, adit regem et mandata ferociter
edidit. Vologesi uetus et penitus infixum erat arma 3
Romana uitandi, nec praesentia prospere fluebant. inritum obsidium, tutus manu et copiis Tigranes, fugati qui
expugnationem sumpserant, missae in Armeniam legiones,
et aliae pro Syria paratae ultro inrumpere; sibi imbecillum equitem pabuli inopia: nam exorta uis locustarum
ambederat quidquid herbidum aut frondosum. igitur metu 4
abstruso mitiora obtendens, missurum ad imperatorem
Romanum legatos super petenda Armenia et firmanda
pace respondet: Monaesen omittere Tigranocertam iubet,
ipse retro concedit.

6. Haec plures ut formidine regis et Corbulonis minis
patrata ac magnifica extollebant: alii occulte pepigisse
interpretabantur ut omisso utrimque bello et abeunte
2 Vologese Tigranes quoque Armenia abscederet. cur enim
exercitum Romanum a Tigranocertis deductum? cur de-
serta per otium quae bello defenderant? an melius hiber-
nauisse in extrema Cappadocia, raptim erectis tuguriis,
quam in sede regni modo retenti? dilata prorsus arma ut
Vologeses cum alio quam cum Corbulone certaret, Corbulo meritae tot per annos gloriae non ultra periculum
3 faceret. nam, ut rettuli, proprium ducem tuendae Armeniae poposcerat, et aduentare Caesennius Paetus audie-
batur. iamque aderat, copiis ita diuisis ut quarta et
duodecima legiones addita quinta, quae recens e Moesis
excita erat, simul Pontica et Galatarum Cappadocumque
auxilia Paeto oboedirent, tertia et sexta et decima legiones
priorque Syriae miles apud Corbulonem manerent; cetera
4 ex rerum usu sociarent partirenturue. sed neque Corbulo
aemuli patiens, et Paetus, cui satis ad gloriam erat si
proximus haberetur, despiciebat gesta, nihil caedis aut
praedae, usurpatas nomine tenus urbium expugnationes
dictitans: se tributa ac leges et pro umbra regis Romanum
ius uictis impositurum.

7. Sub idem tempus legati Vologesis, quos ad principem
missos memoraui, reuertere inriti bellumque propalam
sumptum a Parthis. nec Paetus detrectauit, sed duabus
legionibus, quarum quartam Funisulanus Vettonianus eo
in tempore, duodecimam Calauius Sabinus regebant,
2 Armeniam intrat tristi omine. nam in transgressu Euphratis, quem ponte tramittebant, nulla palam causa turbatus
equus qui consularia insignia gestabat retro euasit; hostia-
que quae muniebantur hibernaculis adsistens semifacta

opera fuga perrupit seque uallo extulit; et pila militum arsere, magis insigni prodigio quia Parthus hostis missilibus telis decertat.

8. Ceterum Paetus spretis ominibus necdum satis firmatis hibernaculis, nullo rei frumentariae prouisu, rapit exercitum trans montem Taurum reciperandis, ut ferebat, Tigranocertis uastandisque regionibus quas Corbulo integras omisisset. et capta quaedam castella gloriaeque et praedae 2 nonnihil partum, si aut gloriam cum modo aut praedam cum cura habuisset. longinquis itineribus percursando quae obtineri nequibant, corrupto qui captus erat commeatu et instante iam hieme, reduxit exercitum composuitque ad Caesarem litteras quasi confecto bello, uerbis magnificis, rerum uacuas.

9. Interim Corbulo numquam neglectam Euphratis ripam crebrioribus praesidiis insedit; et ne ponti iniciendo impedimentum hostiles turmae adferrent (iam enim subiectis campis magna specie uolitabant), nauis magnitudine praestantis et conexas trabibus ac turribus auctas agit per amnem catapultisque et ballistis proturbat barbaros, in quos saxa et hastae longius permeabant quam ut contrario sagittarum iactu adaequarentur. dein pons continuatus 2 collesque aduersi per socias cohortis, post legionum castris occupantur, tanta celeritate et ostentatione uirium ut Parthi omisso paratu inuadendae Syriae spem omnem in Armeniam uerterent, ubi Paetus imminentium nescius quintam legionem procul in Ponto habebat, reliquas promiscis militum commeatibus infirmauerat, donec aduentare Vologesen magno et infenso agmine auditum.

10. Accitur legio duodecima et unde famam aucti exercitus sperauerat, prodita infrequentia: qua tamen retineri castra et eludi Parthus tractu belli poterat, si Paeto

aut in suis aut in alienis consiliis constantia fuisset: uerum
ubi a uiris militaribus aduersus urgentis casus firmatus
erat, rursus ne alienae sententiae indigens uideretur in
2 diuersa ac deteriora transibat. et tunc relictis hibernis non
fossam neque uallum sibi sed corpora et arma in hostem
data clamitans, duxit legiones quasi proelio certaturus.
deinde amisso centurione et paucis militibus quos uisendis
3 hostium copiis praemiserat trepidus remeauit. et quia
minus acriter Vologeses institerat, uana rursus fiducia tria
milia delecti peditis proximo Tauri iugo imposuit quo
transitum regis arcerent; alaris quoque Pannonios, robur
equitatus, in parte campi locat. coniunx ac filius castello,
cui Arsamosata nomen est, abditi, data in praesidium
cohorte ac disperso milite qui in uno habitus uagum hostem
4 promptius sustentauisset. aegre compulsum ferunt ut instantem Corbuloni fateretur. nec a Corbulone properatum
quo gliscentibus periculis etiam subsidii laus augeretur.
expediri tamen itineri singula milia ex tribus legionibus et alarios octingentos, parem numerum e cohortibus
iussit.

11. At Vologeses, quamuis obsessa a Paeto itinera hinc
peditatu inde equite accepisset, nihil mutato consilio, sed
ui ac minis alaris exterruit, legionarios obtriuit, uno tantum centurione Tarquitio Crescente turrim, in qua praesidium agitabat, defendere auso factaque saepius eruptione
et caesis qui barbarorum propius suggrediebantur, donec
2 ignium iactu circumueniretur. peditum si quis integer
longinqua et auia, uulnerati castra repetiuere, uirtutem
regis, saeuitiam et copias gentium, cuncta metu extollen-
3 tes, facili credulitate eorum qui eadem pauebant. ne dux
quidem obniti aduersis, sed cuncta militiae munia deseru-
erat, missis iterum ad Corbulonem precibus, ueniret pro-

pere, signa et aquilas et nomen reliquum infelicis exercitus tueretur: se fidem interim, donec uita suppeditet,
retenturos.

12. Ille interritus et parte copiarum apud Syriam relicta,
ut munimenta Euphrati imposita retinerentur, qua proximum et commeatibus non egenum, regionem Commagenam, exim Cappadociam, inde Armenios petiuit.
comitabantur exercitum praeter alia sueta bello magna uis
camelorum onusta frumenti ut simul hostem famemque
depelleret. primum e perculsis Paccium primi pili centuri- 2
onem obuium habuit, dein plerosque militum; quos
diuersas fugae causas obtendentis redire ad signa et clementiam Paeti experiri monebat: se nisi uictoribus immi-
tem esse. simul suas legiones adire, hortari, priorum 3
admonere, nouam gloriam ostendere. non vicos aut
oppida Armeniorum, sed castra Romana duasque in iis
legiones pretium laboris peti. si singulis manipularibus
praecipua seruati ciuis corona imperatoria manu tribuere-
tur, quod illud et quantum decus, ubi par eorum numerus
aspiceretur qui adtulissent salutem et qui accepissent! his 4
atque talibus in commune alacres (et erant quos pericula
fratrum aut propinquorum propriis stimulis incenderent)
continuum diu noctuque iter properabant.

13. Eoque intentius Vologeses premere obsessos, modo
uallum legionum, modo castellum, quo imbellis aetas
defendebatur, adpugnare, propius incedens quam mos
Parthis, si ea temeritate hostem in proelium eliceret. at 2
illi uix contuberniis extracti, nec aliud quam munimenta
propugnabant, pars iussu ducis, et alii propria ignauia aut
Corbulonem opperientes, ac uis si ingrueret, prouisis exemplis pacis[1] Caudinae Numantinaeque; neque eandem

[1] O.C.T. cladis.

uim Samnitibus, Italico populo, ac Parthis, Romani
imperii aemulis. ualidam quoque et laudatam antiquita-
3 tem, quoties fortuna contra daret, saluti consuluisse. qua
desperatione exercitus dux subactus primas tamen littcras
ad Vologesen non supplices, sed in modum querentis
composuit, quod pro Armeniis semper Romanae dicionis
aut subiectis regi quem imperator delegisset hostilia faceret: pacem ex aequo utilem; ne praesentia tantum specta-
ret; ipsum aduersus duas legiones totis regni uiribus
aduenisse; at Romanis orbem terrarum reliquum quo
bellum iuuarent.

14. Ad ea Vologeses nihil pro causa sed opperiendos
sibi fratres Pacorum ac Tiridaten rescripsit; illum locum
tempusque consilio destinatum quid de Armenia cernerent; adiecisse deos dignum Arsacidarum, simul ut de
2 legionibus Romanis statuerent. missi posthac Paeto nuntii
et regis conloquium petitum, qui Vasacen praefectum
equitatus ire iussit. tum Paetus Lucullos Pompeios et si
qua Caesares obtinendae donandaeue Armeniae egerant,
Vasaces imaginem retinendi largiendiue penes nos, uim
3 penes Parthos memorat. et multum in uicem disceptato,
Monobazus Adiabenus in diem posterum testis iis quae
pepigissent adhibetur. placuitque liberari obsidio lcgiones
et decedere omnem militem finibus Armeniorum castella-
que et commeatus Parthis tradi; quibus perpetratis copia
Vologesi fieret mittendi ad Neronem legatos.

15. Interim flumini Arsaniae (is castra praefluebat)
pontem imposuit, specie sibi illud iter expedientis, sed
Parthi quasi documentum uictoriae iusserant; namque iis
2 usui fuit; nostri per diuersum iere. addidit rumor sub
iugum missas legiones et alia ex rebus infaustis quorum simulacrum ab Armeniis usurpatum est. namque

et munimenta ingressi sunt, antequam agmen Romanum
excederet, et circumstetere uias captiua olim mancipia
aut iumenta adgnoscentes abstrahentesque: raptae etiam
uestes, retenta arma, pauido milite et concedente ne qua
proelii causa existeret. Vologeses armis et corporibus 3
caesorum aggeratis quo cladem nostram testaretur, uisu
fugientium legionum abstinuit: fama moderationis quaere-
batur, postquam superbiam expleuerat. flumen Arsaniam
elephanto insidens, proximus quisque regem ui equorum
perrupere, quia rumor incesserat pontem cessurum oneri
dolo fabricantium: sed qui ingredi ausi sunt ualidum et
fidum intellexere.

16. Ceterum obsessis adeo suppeditauisse rem frumen-
tariam constitit ut horreis ignem inicerent, contraque
prodiderit Corbulo Parthos inopes copiarum et pabulo
attrito relicturos oppugnationem, neque se plus tridui
itinere afuisse. adicit iure iurando Paeti cautum apud 2
signa, adstantibus iis quos testificando rex misisset, neminem Romanum Armeniam ingressurum donec referrentur
litterae Neronis an paci adnueret. quae ut augendae 3
infamiae composita, sic reliqua non in obscuro habentur,
una die quadraginta milium spatium emensum esse
Paetum, desertis passim sauciis, neque minus deformem
illam fugientium trepidationem quam si terga in acie
uertissent. Corbulo cum suis copiis apud ripam Euphratis 4
obuius non eam speciem insignium et armorum praetulit
ut diuersitatem exprobraret. maesti manipuli ac uicem
commilitonum miserantes ne lacrimis quidem temperare;
uix prae fletu usurpata consalutatio. decesserat certamen
uirtutis et ambitio gloriae, felicium hominum adfectus:
sola misericordia ualebat et apud minores magis.

17. Ducum inter se breuis sermo secutus est, hoc

conquerente inritum laborem, potuisse bellum fuga Parthorum finiri: ille integra utrique cuncta respondit: con-
uerterent aquilas et iuncti inuaderent Armeniam abscessu
2 Vologesis infirmatam. non ea imperatoris habere mandata
Corbulo: periculo legionum commotum e prouincia egressum; quando in incerto habeantur Parthorum conatus,
Syriam repetiturum: sic quoque optimam fortunam oran-
dam, ut pedes confectus spatiis itinerum alacrem et
facilitate camporum praeuenientem equitem adsequeretur.
3 exim Paetus per Cappadociam hibernauit: at Vologesis ad
Corbulonem missi nuntii, detraheret castella trans Euphraten amnemque, ut olim, medium faceret; ille Armeniam
quoque diuersis praesidiis uacuam fieri expostulabat. et
postremo concessit rex; dirutaque quae Euphraten ultra
communiuerat Corbulo et Armenii sine arbitro relicti
sunt.

    18. At Romae tropaea de Parthis arcusque medio Capi-
tolini montis sistebantur, decreta ab senatu integro adhuc
bello neque tum omissa, dum aspectui consulitur spreta
2 conscientia. quin et dissimulandis rerum externarum curis
Nero frumentum plebis uetustate corruptum in Tiberim
iecit quo securitatem annonae sustentaret. cuius pretio
nihil additum est, quamuis ducentas ferme nauis portu in
ipso uiolentia tempestatis et centum alias Tiberi subuectas
3 fortuitus ignis absumpsisset. tres dein consularis, L. Pisonem, Ducenium Geminum, Pompeium Paulinum uectigalibus publicis praeposuit, cum insectatione priorum
principum qui grauitate sumptuum iustos reditus antissent: se annuum sexcenties sestertium rei publicae largiri.

    19. Percrebuerat ea tempestate prauus mos, cum pro-
pinquis comitiis aut sorte prouinciarum plerique orbi
fictis adoptionibus adsciscerent filios, praeturasque et pro-

uincias inter patres sortiti statim emitterent manu quos
adoptauerant. . . . magna cum inuidia senatum adeunt, 2
ius naturae, labores educandi aduersus fraudem et artes et
breuitatem adoptionis enumerant. satis pretii esse orbis
quod multa securitate, nullis oneribus gratiam honores
cuncta prompta et obuia haberent. sibi promissa legum
diu expectata in ludibrium uerti, quando quis sine sollicitudine parens, sine luctu orbus longa patrum uota repente
adaequaret. factum ex eo senatus consultum ne simulata 3
adoptio in ulla parte muneris publici iuuaret ac ne usur-
pandis quidem hereditatibus prodesset.

20. Exim Claudius Timarchus Cretensis reus agitur,
ceteris criminibus ut solent praeualidi prouincialium et
opibus nimiis ad iniurias minorum elati: una uox eius
usque ad contumeliam senatus penetrauerat, quod dictitasset in sua potestate situm an pro consulibus qui Cretam
obtinuissent grates agerentur. quam occasionem Paetus 2
Thrasea ad bonum publicum uertens, postquam de reo
censuerat prouincia Creta depellendum, haec addidit:
'usu probatum est, patres conscripti, leges egregias, ex- 3
empla honesta apud bonos ex delictis aliorum gigni. sic
oratorum licentia Cinciam rogationem, candidatorum
ambitus Iulias leges, magistratuum auaritia Calpurnia
scita pepererunt; nam culpa quam poena tempore prior,
emendari quam peccare posterius est. ergo aduersus 4
nouam prouincialium superbiam dignum fide constantiaque Romana capiamus consilium, quo tutelae sociorum
nihil derogetur, nobis opinio decedat, qualis quisque ha-
beatur, alibi quam in ciuium iudicio esse.

21. Olim quidem non modo praetor aut consul sed
priuati etiam mittebantur qui prouincias uiserent et quid
de cuiusque obsequio uideretur referrent; trepidabantque

gentes de aestimatione singulorum: at nunc colimus ex-
ternos et adulamur, et quo modo ad nutum alicuius
2 grates, ita promptius accusatio decernitur. decernaturque
et maneat prouincialibus potentiam suam tali modo
ostentandi: sed laus falsa et precibus expressa perinde
3 cohibeatur quam malitia, quam crudelitas. plura saepe
peccantur, dum demeremur quam dum offendimus. quaedam immo uirtutes odio sunt, seueritas obstinata, inuictus
4 aduersum gratiam animus. inde initia magistratuum
nostrorum meliora ferme et finis inclinat, dum in modum
candidatorum suffragia conquirimus: quae si arceantur,
aequabilius atque constantius prouinciae regentur. nam ut
metu repetundarum infracta auaritia est, ita uetita gratia-
rum actione ambitio cohibebitur.'

22. Magno adsensu celebrata sententia. non tamen senatus consultum perfici potuit, abnuentibus consulibus ea
de re relatum. mox auctore principe sanxere ne quis ad
concilium sociorum referret agendas apud senatum pro
praetoribus proue consulibus grates, neu quis ea legatione
fungeretur.

2   Isdem consulibus gymnasium ictu fulminis conflagrauit
effigiesque in eo Neronis ad informe aes liquefacta. et
motu terrae celebre Campaniae oppidum Pompei magna
ex parte proruit; defunctaque uirgo Vestalis Laelia, in
cuius locum Cornelia ex familia Cossorum capta est.

23. Memmio Regulo et Verginio Rufo consulibus natam
sibi ex Poppaea filiam Nero ultra mortale gaudium accepit
appellauitque Augustam dato et Poppaeae eodem cognomento. locus puerperio colonia Antium fuit, ubi ipse gene-
2 ratus erat. iam senatus uterum Poppaeae commendauerat
dis uotaque publice susceperat, quae multiplicata exoluta-
que. et additae supplicationes templumque fecunditatis et

certamen ad exemplar Actiacae religionis decretum, utque
Fortunarum effigies aureae in solio Capitolini Iouis locaren-
tur, ludicrum circense, ut Iuliae genti apud Bouillas, ita
Claudiae Domitiaeque apud Antium ederetur. quae fluxa 3
fuere, quartum intra mensem defuncta infante. rursusque
exortae adulationes censentium honorem diuae et puluinar
aedemque et sacerdotem. atque ipse ut laetitiae, ita maeroris immodicus egit. adnotatum est, omni senatu Antium 4
sub recentem partum effuso, Thraseam prohibitum immoto
animo praenuntiam imminentis caedis contumeliam ex-
cepisse. secutam dehinc uocem Caesaris ferunt qua recon-
ciliatum se Thraseae apud Senecam iactauerit ac Senecam
Caesari gratulatum: unde gloria egregiis uiris et pericula
gliscebant.

24. Inter quae ueris principio legati Parthorum mandata
regis Vologesis litterasque in eandem formam attulere: se
priora et toties iactata super optinenda Armenia nunc
omittere, quoniam dii, quamuis potentium populorum
arbitri, possessionem Parthis non sine ignominia Romana
tradidissent. nuper clausum Tigranen; post Paetum legion- 2
esque, cum opprimere posset, incolumis dimisisse. satis
adprobatam uim; datum et lenitatis experimentum. nec
recusaturum Tiridaten accipiendo diademati in urbem
uenire nisi sacerdotii religione attineretur. iturum ad
signa et effigies principis ubi legionibus coram regnum
auspicaretur.

25. Talibus Vologesis litteris, quia Paetus diuersa tamquam rebus integris scribebat, interrogatus centurio, qui
cum legatis aduenerat, quo in statu Armenia esset, omnis
inde Romanos excessisse respondit. tum intellecto barba- 2
rum inrisu qui peterent quod eripuerant, consuluit inter
primores ciuitatis Nero bellum anceps an pax inhonesta

placeret. nec dubitatum de bello. et Corbulo militum
atque hostium tot per annos gnarus gerendae rei praefici-
tur, ne cuius alterius inscitia rursum peccaretur, quia
3 Paeti piguerat. igitur inriti remittuntur, cum donis tamen,
unde spes fieret non frustra eadem oraturum Tiridaten, si
preces ipse attulisset. Syriaeque executio C. Cestio, copiae
militares Corbuloni permissae; et quinta decima legio
ducente Mario Celso e Pannonia adiecta est. scribitur
tetrarchis ac regibus praefectisque et procuratoribus et qui
praetorum finitimas prouincias regebant iussis Corbulonis
obsequi, in tantum ferme modum aucta potestate quem
populus Romanus Cn. Pompeio bellum piraticum gesturo
4 dederat. regressum Paetum, cum grauiora metueret,
facetiis insectari satis habuit Caesar, his ferme uerbis:
ignoscere se statim, ne tam promptus in pauorem longiore
sollicitudine aegresceret.

26. At Corbulo quarta et duodecima legionibus quae
fortissimo quoque amisso et ceteris exterritis parum habiles
proelio uidebantur in Syriam translatis, sextam inde ac
tertiam legiones, integrum militem et crebris ac prosperis
2 laboribus exercitum, in Armeniam ducit; addiditque legionem quintam, quae per Pontum agens expers cladis fuerat,
simul quintadecimanos recens adductos et uexilla delecto-
rum ex Illyrico et Aegypto, quodque alarum cohortiumque,
et auxilia regum in unum conducta apud Melitenen, qua
3 tramittere Euphraten parabat. tum lustratum rite exercitum ad contionem uocat orditurque magnifica de auspiciis
imperatoris rebusque a se gestis, aduersa in inscitiam
Paeti declinans, multa auctoritate, quae uiro militari pro
facundia erat.

27. Mox iter L. Lucullo quondam penetratum, apertis
quae uetustas obsaepserat, pergit. et uenientis Tiridatis

Vologesisque de pace legatos haud aspernatus, adiungit iis
centuriones cum mandatis non immitibus: nec enim adhuc
eo uentum ut certamine extremo opus esset. multa Romanis 2
secunda, quaedam Parthis euenisse, documento aduersus
superbiam. proinde et Tiridati conducere intactum uasta-
tionibus regnum dono accipere et Vologesen melius socie-
tate Romana quam damnis mutuis genti Parthorum
consulturum. scire quantum intus discordiarum quamque
indomitas et praeferocis nationes regeret: contra imperatori
suo immotam ubique pacem et unum id bellum esse.
simul consilio terrorem adicere et megistanas Armenios, 3
qui primi a nobis defecerant, pellit sedibus, castella eorum
excindit, plana edita, ualidos inualidosque pari metu
complet.

28. Non infensum nec cum hostili odio Corbulonis nomen etiam barbaris habebatur eoque consilium eius fidum
credebant. ergo Vologeses neque atrox in summam et
quibusdam praefecturis indutias petit: Tiridates locum
diemque conloquio poscit. tempus propinquum, locus in 2
quo nuper obsessae cum Paeto legiones erant barbaris
delectus est ob memoriam laetioris ibi rei, Corbuloni non
uitatus ut dissimilitudo fortunae gloriam augeret. neque
infamia Paeti angebatur, quod eo maxime patuit quia
filio eius tribuno ducere manipulos atque operire reliquias
malae pugnae imperauit. die pacta Tiberius Alexander, 3
inlustris eques Romanus, minister bello datus, et Vinicianus
Annius, gener Corbulonis, nondum senatoria aetate et pro
legato quintae legioni impositus, in castra Tiridatis uenere,
honori eius ac ne metueret insidias tali pignore; uiceni
dehinc equites adsumpti. et uiso Corbulone rex prior equo
desiluit; nec cunctatus Corbulo, sed pedes uterque dexteras
miscuere.

29. Exim Romanus laudat iuuenem omissis praecipitibus tuta et salutaria capessentem: ille de nobilitate generis multum praefatus, cetera temperanter adiungit: iturum quippe Romam laturumque nouum Caesari decus, non aduersis Parthorum rebus supplicem Arsaciden. tum placuit Tiridaten ponere apud effigiem Caesaris insigne regium nec nisi manu Neronis resumere; et conloquium 2 osculo finitum. dein paucis diebus interiectis magna utrimque specie inde eques compositus per turmas et insignibus patriis, hinc agmina legionum stetere fulgentibus aquilis signisque et simulacris deum in modum templi: medio tribunal sedem curulem et sedes effigiem Neronis sustine3 bat. ad quam progressus Tiridates, caesis ex more uictimis, sublatum capiti diadema imagini subiecit, magnis apud cunctos animorum motibus, quós augebat insita adhuc oculis exercituum Romanorum caedes aut obsidio: at nunc uersos casus; iturum Tiridaten ostentui gentibus quanto minus quam captiuum?

30. Addidit gloriae Corbulo comitatem epulasque; et rogitante rege causas, quoties nouum aliquid aduerterat, ut initia uigiliarum per centurionem nuntiari, conuiuium bucina dimitti et structam ante augurale aram subdita face accendi, cuncta in maius attollens admiratione prisci moris 2 adfecit. postero die spatium orauit quo tantum itineris aditurus fratres ante matremque uiseret; obsidem interea filiam tradit litterasque supplices ad Neronem.

31. Et digressus Pacorum apud Medos, Vologesen Ecbatanis repperit non incuriosum fratris: quippe et propriis nuntiis a Corbulone petierat ne quam imaginem seruitii Tiridates perferret neu ferrum traderet aut complexu prouincias obtinentium arceretur foribusue eorum adsisteret, tantusque ei Romae quantus consulibus honor esset.

scilicet externae superbiae sueto non inerat notitia nostri
apud quos uis imperii ualet, inania tramittuntur.

32. Eodem anno Caesar nationes Alpium maritimarum
in ius Latii transtulit. equitum Romanorum locos sedilibus
plebis anteposuit apud circum; namque ad eam diem
indiscreti inibant, quia lex Roscia nihil nisi de quattuordecim ordinibus sanxit. spectacula gladiatorum idem annus
habuit pari magnificentia ac priora; sed feminarum
inlustrium senatorumque plures per arenam foedati
sunt.   33-37

33. C. Laecanio M. Licinio consulibus acriore in dies
cupidine adigebatur Nero promiscas scaenas frequentandi:
nam adhuc per domum aut hortos cecinerat Iuuenalibus
ludis, quos ut parum celebris et tantae uoci angustos
spernebat. non tamen Romae incipere ausus Neapolim 2
quasi Graecam urbem delegit: inde initium fore ut trans-
gressus in Achaiam insignisque et antiquitus sacras coronas
adeptus maiore fama studia ciuium eliceret. ergo contrac- 3
tum oppidanorum uulgus, et quos e proximis coloniis et
municipiis eius rei fama acciuerat, quique Caesarem per
honorem aut uarios usus sectantur, etiam militum manipuli, theatrum Neapolitanorum complent.

34. Illic, plerique ut arbitrabantur, triste, ut ipse, prouidum potius et secundis numinibus euenit: nam egresso
qui adfuerat populo uacuum et sine ullius noxa theatrum
conlapsum est. ergo per compositos cantus grates dis atque
ipsam recentis casus fortunam celebrans petiturusque maris
Hadriae traiectus apud Beneuentum interim consedit, ubi
gladiatorium munus a Vatinio celebre edebatur. Vatinius 2
inter foedissima eius aulae ostenta fuit, sutrinae tabernae
alumnus, corpore detorto, facetiis scurrilibus; primo in con-
tumelias adsumptus, dehinc optimi cuiusque criminatione

eo usque ualuit ut gratia pecunia ui nocendi etiam malos
praemineret.

35. Eius munus frequentanti Neroni ne inter uoluptates
quidem a sceleribus cessabatur. isdem quippe illis diebus
Torquatus Silanus mori adigitur, quia super Iuniae fami-
2 liae claritudinem diuum Augustum abauum ferebat. iussi
accusatores obicere prodigum largitionibus, neque aliam
spem quam in rebus nouis esse: quin inter libertos habere
quos ab epistulis et libellis et rationibus appellet, nomina
3 summae curae et meditamenta. tum intimus quisque
libertorum uincti abreptique; et cum damnatio instaret,
brachiorum uenas Torquatus interscidit; secutaque Neronis
oratio ex more, quamuis sontem et defensioni merito
diffisum uicturum tamen fuisse si clementiam iudicis
expectasset.

36. Nec multo post omissa in praesens Achaia (causae in
incerto fuere) urbem reuisit, prouincias Orientis, maxime
Aegyptum, secretis imaginationibus agitans. dehinc edicto
testificatus non longam sui absentiam et cuncta in re publica perinde immota ac prospera fore, super ea profectione
2 adiit Capitolium. illic ueneratus deos, cum Vestae quoque
templum inisset, repente cunctos per artus tremens, seu
numine exterrente, seu facinorum recordatione numquam
timore uacuus, deseruit inceptum, cunctas sibi curas amore
3 patriae leuiores dictitans. uidisse maestos ciuium uultus,
audire secretas querimonias, quod tantum itineris aditurus
esset, cuius ne modicos quidem egressus tolerarent, sueti
aduersum fortuita aspectu principis refoueri. ergo ut in
priuatis necessitudinibus proxima pignora praeualerent, ita
populum Romanum uim plurimam habere parendumque
4 retinenti. haec atque talia plebi uolentia fuere, uoluptatum
cupidine et, quae praecipua cura est, rei frumentariae

angustias, si abesset, metuenti. senatus et primores in
incerto erant procul an coram atrocior haberetur: dehinc,
quae natura magnis timoribus, deterius credebant quod
euenerat.

37. Ipse quo fidem adquireret nihil usquam perinde
laetum sibi, publicis locis struere conuiuia totaque urbe
quasi domo uti. et celeberrimae luxu famaque epulae fuere
quas a Tigellino paratas ut exemplum referam, ne saepius
eadem prodigentia narranda sit. igitur in stagno Agrippae 2
fabricatus est ratem cui superpositum conuiuium nauium
aliarum tractu moueretur. naues auro et ebore distinctae,
remigesque exoleti per aetates et scientiam libidinum com-
ponebantur. uolucris et feras diuersis e terris et animalia
maris Oceano abusque petiuerat. crepidinibus stagni lu- 3
panaria adstabant inlustribus feminis completa et contra
scorta uisebantur nudis corporibus. iam gestus motusque
obsceni; et postquam tenebrae incedebant, quantum iuxta
nemoris et circumiecta tecta consonare cantu et luminibus
clarescere. ipse per licita atque inlicita foedatus nihil 4
flagitii reliquerat quo corruptior ageret, nisi paucos post
dies uni ex illo contaminatorum grege (nomen Pythagorae
fuit) in modum sollemnium coniugiorum denupsisset. indi-
tum imperatori flammeum, missi auspices, dos et genialis
torus et faces nuptiales, cuncta denique spectata quae
etiam in femina nox operit.

38. Sequitur clades, forte an dolo principis incertum
(nam utrumque auctores prodidere), sed omnibus quae
huic urbi per uiolentiam ignium acciderunt grauior atque
atrocior. initium in ea parte circi ortum quae Palatino
Caelioque montibus contigua est, ubi per tabernas, quibus
id mercimonium inerat quo flamma alitur, simul coeptus
ignis et statim ualidus ac uento citus longitudinem circi

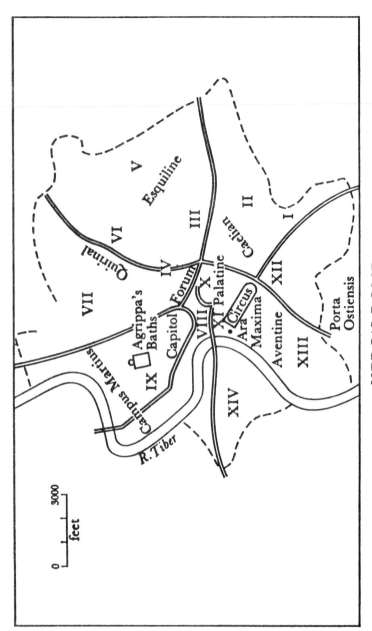

NERO'S ROME

corripuit. neque enim domus munimentis saeptae uel templa muris cincta aut quid aliud morae interiacebat. impetu 3
peruagatum incendium plana primum, deinde in edita ad-
surgens et rursus inferiora populando, antiit remedia
uelocitate mali et obnoxia urbe artis itineribus hucque et
illuc flexis atque enormibus uicis, qualis uetus Roma fuit.
ad hoc lamenta pauentium feminarum, fessa aetate aut 4
rudis pueritiae, quique sibi quique aliis consulebant, dum
trahunt inualidos aut opperiuntur, pars mora, pars fes-
tinans, cuncta impediebant. et saepe dum in tergum re- 5
spectant lateribus aut fronte circumueniebantur, uel si in
proxima euaserant, illis quoque igni correptis, etiam quae
longinqua crediderant in eodem casu reperiebant. postre- 6
mo, quid uitarent quid peterent ambigui, complere uias,
sterni per agros; quidam amissis omnibus fortunis, diurni
quoque uictus, alii caritate suorum, quos eripere nequi-
uerant, quamuis patente effugio interiere. nec quisquam 7
defendere audebat, crebris multorum minis restinguere
prohibentium, et quia alii palam faces iaciebant atque
esse sibi auctorem uociferabantur, siue ut raptus licentius
exercerent seu iussu.

39. Eo in tempore Nero Antii agens non ante in urbem
regressus est quam domui eius, qua Palatium et Maecenatis
hortos continuauerat, ignis propinquaret. neque tamen sisti
potuit quin et Palatium et domus et cuncta circum haurirentur. sed solacium populo exturbato ac profugo campum 2
Martis ac monumenta Agrippae, hortos quin etiam suos
patefecit et subitaria aedificia extruxit quae multitudinem
inopem acciperent; subuectaque utensilia ab Ostia et propinquis municipiis pretiumque frumenti minutum usque ad
ternos nummos. quae quamquam popularia in inritum 3
cadebant, quia peruaserat rumor ipso tempore flagrantis

urbis inisse eum domesticam scaenam et cecinisse Troianum
excidium, praesentia mala uetustis cladibus adsimulantem.

40. Sexto demum die apud imas Esquilias finis incendio
factus, prorutis per immensum aedificiis ut continuae uio-
lentiae campus et uelut uacuum caelum occurreret. necdum positus metus aut redierat plebi spes: rursum grassatus
ignis patulis magis urbis locis; eoque strages hominum
minor, delubra deum et porticus amoenitati dicatae latius
2 procidere./plusque infamiae id incendium habuit quia
praediis Tigellini Aemilianis proruperat uidebaturque Nero
condendae urbis nouae et cognomento suo appellandae
gloriam quaerere. quippe in regiones quattuordecim Roma
diuiditur, quarum quattuor integrae manebant, tres solo
tenus deiectae: septem reliquis pauca tectorum uestigia
supererant, lacera et semusta.

41. Domuum et insularum et templorum quae amissa
sunt numerum inire haud promptum fuerit: sed uetustissima religione, quod Seruius Tullius Lunae et magna ara
fanumque quae praesenti Herculi Arcas Euander sacra-
uerat, aedesque Statoris Iouis uota Romulo Numaeque
regia et delubrum Vestae cum Penatibus populi Romani
exusta; iam opes tot uictoriis quaesitae et Graecarum
artium decora, exim monumenta ingeniorum antiqua et
incorrupta, ut quamuis in tanta resurgentis urbis pulchritu-
dine multa seniores meminerint quae reparari nequibant.
2 fuere qui adnotarent xiiii Kal. Sextilis principium incendii
huius ortum, quo et[1] Senones captam urbem inflammauerint. alii eo usque cura progressi sunt ut totidem annos
mensisque et dies inter utraque incendia numerent.

42. Ceterum Nero usus est patriae ruinis extruxitque

---

[1] O.C.T. et quo.

domum in qua haud proinde gemmae et aurum miraculo
essent, solita pridem et luxu uulgata, quam arua et stagna
et in modum solitudinum hinc siluae inde aperta spatia et
prospectus, magistris et machinatoribus Seuero et Celere,
quibus ingenium et audacia erat etiam quae natura denegauisset per artem temptare et uiribus principis inludere.
namque ab lacu Auerno nauigabilem fossam usque ad ostia 2
Tiberina depressuros promiserant squalenti litore aut per
montis aduersos. neque enim aliud umidum gignendis
aquis occurrit quam Pomptinae paludes: cetera abrupta
aut arentia ac, si perrumpi possent, intolerandus labor nec
satis causae. Nero tamen, ut erat incredibilium cupitor,
effodere proxima Auerno iuga conisus est; manentque
uestigia inritae spei. // *|"

43. Ceterum urbis quae domui supererant non, ut post
Gallica incendia, nulla distinctione nec passim erecta, sed
dimensis uicorum ordinibus et latis uiarum spatiis cohibita-
que aedificiorum altitudine ac patefactis areis additisque.
porticibus quae frontem insularum protegerent. eas porticus 2
Nero sua pecunia extructurum purgatasque areas dominis
traditurum pollicitus est. addidit praemia pro cuiusque
ordine et rei familiaris copiis finiuitque tempus intra quod
effectis domibus aut insulis apiscerentur. ruderi accipiendo 3
Ostiensis paludes destinabat utique naues quae frumentum
Tiberi subuectassent onustae rudere decurrerent; aedificia-
que ipsa certa sui parte sine trabibus saxo Gabino Albanoue
solidarentur, quod is lapis ignibus imperuius est; iam aqua 4
priuatorum licentia intercepta quo largior et pluribus locis
in publicum flueret, custodes; et subsidia reprimendis ignibus in propatulo quisque haberet; nec communione parietum, sed propriis quaeque muris ambirentur. ea ex utilitate 5
accepta decorem quoque nouae urbi attulere. erant tamen

qui crederent ueterem illam formam salubritati magis con-
duxisse, quoniam angustiae itinerum et altitudo tectorum
non perinde solis uapore perrumperentur: at nunc patulam
latitudinem et nulla umbra defensam grauiore aestu
ardescere. .

44. Et haec quidem humanis consiliis prouidebantur.
mox petita dis piacula aditique Sibyllae libri, ex quibus
supplicatum Vulcano et Cereri Proserpinaeque ac pro-
pitiata Iuno per matronas, primum in Capitolio, deinde
apud proximum mare, unde hausta aqua templum et
simulacrum deae perspersum est; et sellisternia ac perui-
2 gilia celebrauere feminae quibus mariti erant. sed non ope
humana, non largitionibus principis aut deum placamentis
decedebat infamia quin iussum incendium crederetur. ergo
abolendo rumori Nero subdidit reos et quaesitissimis poenis
adfecit quos per flagitia inuisos uulgus Christianos appella-
3 bat. auctor nominis eius Christus Tiberio imperitante per
procuratorem Pontium Pilatum supplicio adfectus erat;
repressaque in praesens exitiabilis superstitio rursum erum-
pebat, non modo per Iudaeam, originem eius mali, sed per
urbem etiam quo cuncta undique atrocia aut pudenda
4 confluunt celebranturque. igitur primum correpti qui fatebantur, deinde indicio eorum multitudo ingens haud
proinde in crimine incendii quam odio humani generis
conuicti sunt. et pereuntibus addita ludibria, ut ferarum
tergis contecti laniatu canum interirent, aut crucibus adfixi
aut flammandi, atque ubi defecisset dies in usum nocturni
5 luminis urerentur. hortos suos ei spectaculo Nero obtulerat
et circense ludicrum edebat, habitu aurigae permixtus plebi
uel curriculo insistens. unde quamquam aduersus sontis et
nouissima exempla meritos miseratio oriebatur, tamquam
non utilitate publica sed in saeuitiam unius absumerentur.

✗ 45. Interea conferendis pecuniis peruastata Italia, prouinciae euersae sociique populi et quae ciuitatium liberae
uocantur. inque eam praedam etiam dii cessere, spoliatis
in urbe templis egestoque auro quod triumphis, quod uotis
omnis populi Romani aetas prospere aut in metu sacra-
uerat. enimuero per Asiam atque Achaiam non dona 2
tantum sed simulacra numinum abripiebantur, missis in
eas prouincias Acrato ac Secundo Carrinate. ille libertus
cuicumque flagitio promptus, hic Graeca doctrina ore
tenus exercitus animum bonis artibus non induerat. fere- 3
batur Seneca quo inuidiam sacrilegii a semet auerteret
longinqui ruris secessum orauisse et, postquam non concedebatur, ficta ualetudine quasi aeger neruis cubiculum non
egressus. tradidere quidam uenenum ei per libertum ipsius,
cui nomen Cleonicus, paratum iussu Neronis uitatumque a
Seneca proditione liberti seu propria formidine, dum persimplici uictu et agrestibus pomis ac, si sitis admoneret,
profluente aqua uitam tolerat.

✗ 46. Per idem tempus gladiatores apud oppidum Praeneste temptata eruptione praesidio militis, qui custos adesset, coerciti sunt, iam Spartacum et uetera mala rumoribus
ferente populo, ut est nouarum rerum cupiens pauidusque.
nec multo post clades rei naualis accipitur, non bello 2
(quippe haud alias tam immota pax), sed certum ad diem
in Campaniam redire classem Nero iusserat, non exceptis
maris casibus. ergo gubernatores, quamuis saeuiente pela-
go, a Formiis mouere; et graui Africo, dum promunturium Miseni superare contendunt, Cumanis litoribus
impacti triremium plerasque et minora nauigia passim
amiserunt.

✗ 47. Fine anni uulgantur prodigia imminentium malorum
nuntia: uis fulgurum non alias crebrior et sidus cometes,

sanguine inlustri semper Neroni expiatum; bicipites hominum aliorumue animalium partus abiecti in publicum aut
in sacrificiis, quibus grauidas hostias immolare mos est,
2 reperti. et in agro Placentino uiam propter natus uitulus
cui caput in crure esset; secutaque haruspicum interpretatio, parari rerum humanarum aliud caput, sed non fore
ualidum neque occultum, quia in utero repressum aut iter
iuxta editum sit.

√ 48. Ineunt deinde consulatum Silius Nerua et Atticus
Vestinus, coepta simul et aucta coniuratione in quam certa-
tim nomina dederant senatores eques miles, feminae etiam,
2 cum odio Neronis tum fauore in C. Pisonem. is Calpurnio
genere ortus ac multas insignisque familias paterna nobilitate complexus, claro apud uulgum rumore erat per uir-
3 tutem aut species uirtutibus similis. namque facundiam
tuendis ciuibus exercebat, largitionem aduersum amicos, et
ignotis quoque comi sermone et congressu; aderant etiam
fortuita, corpus procerum, decora facies: sed procul
grauitas morum aut uoluptatum parsimonia; leuitati ac
· magnificentiae et aliquando luxu indulgebat, idque pluribus probabatur qui in tanta uitiorum dulcedine summum
imperium non restrictum nec perseuerum uolunt.

49. Initium coniurationi non a cupidine ipsius fuit: nec
tamen facile memorauerim quis primus auctor, cuius in-
2 stinctu concitum sit quod tam multi sumpserunt. promptis-
simos Subrium Flauum tribunum praetoriae cohortis et
Sulpicium Asprum centurionem extitisse constantia exitus
3 docuit; et Lucanus Annaeus Plautiusque Lateranus uiuida
odia intulere. Lucanum propriae causae accendebant, quod
famam carminum eius premebat Nero prohibueratque ostentare, uanus adsimulatione: Lateranum consulem desig-
4 natum nulla iniuria sed amor rei publicae sociauit. at

Flauius Scaeuinus et Afranius Quintianus, uterque senatorii ordinis, contra famam sui principium tanti facinoris
capessiuere: nam Scaeuino dissoluta luxu mens et proinde
uita somno languida; Quintianus mollitia corporis infamis
et a Nerone probroso carmine diffamatus contumeliam
ultum ibat.

50. Ergo dum scelera principis et finem adesse imperio
deligendumque qui fessis rebus succurreret inter se aut inter
amicos iaciunt, adgregauere Claudium Senecionem, Cerua-
rium Proculum, Vulcacium Araricum, Iulium Augurinum,
Munatium Gratum, Antonium Natalem, Marcium Festum,
equites Romanos; ex quibus Senecio, e praecipua familia- 2
ritate Neronis, speciem amicitiae etiam tum retinens eo
pluribus periculis conflictabatur: Natalis particeps ad omne
secretum Pisoni erat; ceteris spes ex nouis rebus petebatur.
adscitae sunt super Subrium et Sulpicium, de quibus 3
rettuli, militares manus Gauius Siluanus et Statius Proxumus tribuni cohortium praetoriarum, Maximus Scaurus et
Venetus Paulus centuriones. sed summum robur in Faenio
Rufo praefecto uidebatur, quem uita famaque laudatum
per saeuitiam impudicitiamque Tigellinus in animo principis antibat fatigabatque criminationibus ac saepe in metum
adduxerat quasi adulterum Agrippinae et desiderio eius
ultioni intentum. igitur ubi coniuratis praefectum quoque 4
praetorii in partis descendisse crebro ipsius sermone facta
fides, promptius iam de tempore ac loco caedis agitabant.
et cepisse impetum Subrius Flauus ferebatur in scaena
canentem Neronem adgrediendi, aut cum ardente domo.
per noctem huc illuc cursaret incustoditus. hic occasio
solitudinis, ibi ipsa frequentia tanti decoris testis pulcherrima animum extimulauerant, nisi impunitatis cupido
retinuisset, magnis semper conatibus aduersa.

51. Interim cunctantibus prolatantibusque spem ac metum Epicharis quaedam, incertum quonam modo scis-
citata (neque illi ante ulla rerum honestarum cura fuerat),
accendere et arguere coniuratos, ac postremum lentitudinis
eorum pertaesa et in Campania agens primores classiario-
rum Misenensium labefacere et conscientia inligare conisa
2 est tali initio. erat nauarchus in ea classe Volusius Proculus, occidendae matris Neroni inter ministros, non ex
magnitudine sceleris prouectus, ut rebatur. is mulieri olim
cognitus, seu recens orta amicitia, dum merita erga Neronem sua et quam in inritum cecidissent aperit adicitque
questus et destinationem uindictae, si facultas oreretur,
spem dedit posse impelli et pluris conciliare: nec leue
auxilium in classe, crebras occasiones, quia Nero multo
3 apud Puteolos et Misenum maris usu laetabatur. ergo
Epicharis plura; et omnia scelera principis orditur, neque
senatui quidquam manere. sed prouisum quonam modo
poenas euersae rei publicae daret: accingeretur modo
nauare operam et militum acerrimos ducere in partis, ac
digna pretia expectaret; nomina tamen coniuratorum
4 reticuit. unde Proculi indicium inritum fuit, quamuis ea
quae audierat ad Neronem detulisset. accita quippe Epicharis et cum indice composita nullis testibus innisum facile
confutauit. sed ipsa in custodia retenta est, suspectante
Nerone haud falsa esse etiam quae uera non probabantur.

52. Coniuratis tamen metu proditionis permotis placi-
tum maturare caedem apud Baias in uilla Pisonis, cuius
amoenitate captus Caesar crebro uentitabat balneasque et
epulas inibat omissis excubiis et fortunae suae mole. sed
abnuit Piso inuidiam praetendens, si sacra mensae diique
hospitales caede qualiscumque principis cruentarentur:
melius apud urbem in illa inuisa et spoliis ciuium extructa

domo uel in publico patraturos quod pro re publica susce-
pissent. haec in commune, ceterum timore occulto ne L. 2
Silanus eximia nobilitate disciplinaque C. Cassii, apud
quem educatus erat, ad omnem claritudinem sublatus
imperium inuaderet, prompte daturis qui a coniuratione
integri essent quique miserarentur Neronem tamquam per
scelus interfectum. plerique Vestini quoque consulis acre 3
ingenium uitauisse Pisonem crediderunt, ne ad libertatem
oreretur uel delecto imperatore alio sui muneris rem publicam faceret. etenim expers coniurationis erat, quamuis
super eo crimine Nero uetus aduersum insontem odium
expleuerit.

, 53. Tandem statuere circensium ludorum die, qui Cereri
celebratur, exequi destinata, quia Caesar rarus egressu
domoque aut hortis clausus ad ludicra circi uentitabat
promptioresque aditus erant laetitia spectaculi. ′ ordinem 2
insidiis composuerant, ut Lateranus, quasi subsidium rei
familiari oraret, deprecabundus et genibus principis ac-
cidens prosterneret incautum premeretque, animi ualidus
et corpore ingens; tum iacentem et impeditum tribuni et
centuriones et ceterorum, ut quisque audentiae habuisset,
adcurrerent trucidarentque, primas sibi partis expostu-
lante Scaeuino, qui pugionem templo Salutis siue, ut alii
tradidere, Fortunae Ferentino in oppido detraxerat gesta-
batque uelut magno operi sacrum. interim Piso apud 3
aedem Cereris opperiretur, unde eum praefectus Faenius
et ceteri accitum ferrent in castra, comitante Antonia,
Claudii Caesaris filia, ad eliciendum uulgi fauorem, quod
C. Plinius memorat. nobis quoquo modo traditum non 4
occultare in animo fuit, quamuis absurdum uideretur aut
inanem ad spem Antoniam nomen et periculum commodauisse aut Pisonem notum amore uxoris alii matrimonio se

obstrinxisse, nisi si cupido dominandi cunctis adfectibus flagrantior est.

ᐟ 54. Sed mirum quam inter diuersi generis ordinis, aetatis sexus, ditis pauperes taciturnitate omnia cohibita sint, donec proditio coepit e domo Scaeuini; qui pridie insidiarum multo sermone cum Antonio Natale, dein regressus domum testamentum obsignauit, promptum uagina pugionem, de quo supra rettuli, uetustate obtusum increpans asperari saxo et in mucronem ardescere iussit eamque 2 curam liberto Milicho mandauit. simul adfluentius solito conuiuium initum, seruorum carissimi libertate et alii pecunia donati; atque ipse maestus et magnae cogitationis manifestus erat, quamuis laetitiam uagis sermonibus simu- 3 laret. postremo uulneribus ligamenta quibusque sistitur sanguis parare eundem Milichum monet, siue gnarum coniurationis et illuc usque fidum, seu nescium et tunc primum 4 arreptis suspicionibus, ut plerique tradidere. nam cum secum seruilis animus praemia perfidiae reputauit simulque immensa pecunia et potentia obuersabantur, cessit fas et salus patroni et acceptae libertatis memoria. etenim uxoris quoque consilium adsumpserat muliebre ac deterius: quippe ultro metum intentabat, multosque adstitisse libertos ac seruos qui eadem uiderint: nihil profuturum unius silentium, at praemia penes unum fore qui indicio praeuenisset.

ᐟ 55. Igitur coepta luce Milichus in hortos Seruilianos pergit; et cum foribus arceretur, magna et atrocia adferre dictitans deductusque ab ianitoribus ad libertum Neronis Epaphroditum, mox ab eo ad Neronem, urgens periculum, grauis coniuratos et cetera quae audiuerat coniectauerat docet. telum quoque in necem eius paratum ostendit acci- 2 rique reum iussit. is raptus per milites et defensionem orsus, ferrum cuius argueretur olim religione patria cultum

et in cubiculo habitum ac fraude liberti subreptum respondit. tabulas testamenti saepius a se et incustodita
dierum obseruatione signatas. pecunias et libertates seruis
et ante dono datas, sed ideo tunc largius quia tenui iam re
familiari et instantibus creditoribus testamento diffideret.
enimuero liberalis semper epulas struxisse, uitam amoenam 3
et duris iudicibus parum probatam. fomenta uulneribus
nulla iussu suo sed, quia cetera palam uana obiecisset,
adiungere crimen cuius se pariter indicem et testem faceret.
adicit dictis constantiam; incusat ultro intestabilem et con- 4
sceleratum tanta uocis ac uultus securitate ut labaret indicium, nisi Milichum uxor admonuisset Antonium Natalem
multa cum Scaeuino ac secreta conlocutum et esse utrosque
C. Pisonis intimos.

56. Ergo accitur Natalis et diuersi interrogantur quisnam
is sermo, qua de re fuisset. tum exorta suspicio, quia non
congruentia responderant, inditaque uincla. et tormentorum aspectum ac minas non tulere: prior tamen Natalis, 2
totius conspirationis magis gnarus, simul arguendi peritior,
de Pisone primum fatetur, deinde adicit Annaeum Senecam, siue internuntius inter eum Pisonemque fuit, siue ut
Neronis gratiam pararet, qui infensus Senecae omnis ad
eum opprimendum artes conquirebat. tum cognito Natalis 3
indicio Scaeuinus quoque pari imbecillitate, an cuncta
iam patefacta credens nec ullum silentii emolumentum,
edidit ceteros. ex quibus Lucanus Quintianusque et 4
Senecio diu abnuere: post promissa impunitate corrupti,
quo tarditatem excusarent, Lucanus Aciliam matrem suam,
Quintianus Glitium Gallum, Senecio Annium Pollionem,
amicorum praecipuos, nominauere.

• 57. Atque interim Nero recordatus Volusii Proculi indicio Epicharin attineri ratusque muliebre corpus impar

dolori tormentis dilacerari iubet. at illam non uerbera,
non ignes, non ira eo acrius torquentium ne a femina
spernerentur, peruicere quin obiecta denegaret. sic primus
2 quaestionis dies contemptus. [postero cum ad eosdem
cruciatus retraheretur gestamine sellae (nam dissolutis
membris insistere nequibat), uinclo fasciae, quam pectori
detraxerat, in modum laquei ad arcum sellae restricto indi-
dit ceruicem et corporis pondere conisa tenuem iam
spiritum expressit, clariore exemplo libertina mulier in
tanta necessitate alienos ac prope ignotos protegendo, cum
ingenui et uiri et equites Romani senatoresque intacti tor-
3 mentis carissima suorum quisque pignorum proderent. non
enim omittebant Lucanus quoque et Senecio et Quintianus
passim conscios edere, magis magisque pauido Nerone,
quamquam multiplicatis excubiis semet saepsisset.

58. Quin et urbem per manipulos occupatis moenibus,
insesso etiam mari et amne, uelut in custodiam dedit. uoli-
tabantque per fora, per domos, rura quoque et proxima
municipiorum pedites equitesque, permixti Germanis, qui-
2 bus fidebat princeps quasi externis. continua hinc et uincta
agmina trahi ac foribus hortorum adiacere. atque ubi
dicendam ad causam introissent, laetatum erga coniuratos
et fortuitus sermo et subiti occursus, si conuiuium, si
spectaculum simul inissent, pro crimine accipi, cum super
Neronis ac Tigellini saeuas percontationes Faenius quoque
Rufus uiolenter urgeret, nondum ab indicibus nominatus,
3 et quo fidem inscitiae pararet, atrox aduersus socios. idem
Subrio Flauo adsistenti adnuentique an inter ipsam cognitionem destringeret gladium caedemque patraret, rennuit
infregitque impetum iam manum ad capulum referentis.

59. Fuere qui prodita coniuratione, dum auditur Milichus, dum dubitat Scaeuinus, hortarentur Pisonem pergere

in castra aut rostra escendere studiaque militum et populi
temptare. si conatibus eius conscii adgregarentur, secu-
turos etiam integros; magnamque motae rei famam, quae
plurimum in nouis consiliis ualeret. nihil aduersum haec 2
Neroni prouisum. etiam fortis uiros subitis terreri, nedum
ille scaenicus, Tigellino scilicet cum paelicibus suis comitante, arma contra cieret. multa experiendo confieri quae
segnibus ardua uideantur. frustra silentium et fidem in tot 3
consciorum animis et corporibus sperare: cruciatui aut
praemio cuncta peruia esse. uenturos qui ipsum quoque
uincirent, postremo indigna nece adficerent. quanto lauda-
bilius periturum, dum amplecitur rem publicam, dum
auxilia libertati inuocat. miles potius deesset et plebes
desereret, dum ipse maioribus, dum posteris, si uita prae-
riperetur, mortem adprobaret. immotus his et paululum in 4
publico uersatus, post domi secretus, animum aduersum
suprema firmabat, donec manus militum adueniret quos
Nero tirones aut stipendiis recentis delegerat: nam uetus
miles timebatur tamquam fauore imbutus. obiit abruptis 5
brachiorum uenis. testamentum foedis aduersus Neronem
adulationibus amori uxoris dedit, quam degenerem et sola
corporis forma commendatam amici matrimonio abstulerat.
nomen mulieri Satria Galla, priori marito Domitius
Silus: hic patientia, illa impudicitia Pisonis infamiam
propagauere.

60. Proximam necem Plautii Laterani consulis designati
Nero adiungit, adeo propere ut non complecti liberos, non
illud breue mortis arbitrium permitteret. raptus in locum
seruilibus poenis sepositum manu Statii tribuni trucida-
tur, plenus constantis silentii nec tribuno obiciens eandem
conscientiam.

Sequitur caedes Annaei Senecae, laetissima principi, 2

non quia coniurationis manifestum compererat, sed ut ferro
3 grassaretur, quando uenenum non processerat. solus quippe
Natalis et hactenus prompsit missum se ad aegrotum
Senecam uti uiseret conquerereturque cur Pisonem aditu
arceret: melius fore si amicitiam familiari congressu exer-
cuissent; et respondisse Senecam sermones mutuos et crebra
conloquia neutri conducere; ceterum salutem suam inco-
4 lumitate Pisonis inniti. haec ferre Gauius Siluanus tribunus
praetoriae cohortis et an dicta Natalis suaque responsa
nosceret percontari Senecam iubetur. is forte an prudens
ad eum diem ex Campania remeauerat quartumque apud
lapidem suburbano rure substiterat. illo propinqua uespera
tribunus uenit et uillam globis militum saepsit; tum ipsi
cum Pompeia Paulina uxore et amicis duobus epulanti
mandata imperatoris edidit.

61. Seneca missum ad se Natalem conquestumque nomine Pisonis quod a uisendo eo prohiberetur, seque ratio-
nem ualetudinis et amorem quietis excusauisse respondit.
cur salutem priuati hominis incolumitati suae anteferret
causam non habuisse; nec sibi promptum in adulationes
ingenium. idque nulli magis gnarum quam Neroni, qui
saepius libertatem Senecae quam seruitium expertus esset.
2 ubi haec a tribuno relata sunt Poppaea et Tigellino coram,
quod erat saeuienti principi intimum consiliorum, inter-
rogat an Seneca uoluntariam mortem pararet. tum tribunus nulla pauoris signa, nihil triste in uerbis eius aut
uultu deprensum confirmauit. ergo regredi et indicere
3 mortem iubetur. tradit Fabius Rusticus non eo quo uenerat
itinere reditum sed flexisse ad Faenium praefectum, et
expositis Caesaris iussis an obtemperaret interrogauisse,
monitumque ab eo ut exequeretur, fatali omnium ignauia.
4 nam et Siluanus inter coniuratos erat augebatque scelera

in quorum ultionem consenserat. uoci tamen et aspectui pepercit intromisitque ad Senecam unum ex centurionibus qui necessitatem ultimam denuntiaret.

62. Ille interritus poscit testamenti tabulas; ac denegante centurione conuersus ad amicos, quando meritis eorum referre gratiam prohiberetur, quod unum iam et tamen pulcherrimum habeat, imaginem uitae suae relinquere testatur, cuius si memores essent, bonarum artium famam fructum constantis amicitiae laturos. simul lacrimas 2 eorum modo sermone, modo intentior in modum coercentis ad firmitudinem reuocat, rogitans ubi praecepta sapientiae, ubi tot per annos meditata ratio aduersum imminentia? cui enim ignaram fuisse saeuitiam Neronis? neque aliud superesse post matrem fratremque interfectos quam ut educatoris praeceptorisque necem adiceret.

63. Vbi haec atque talia uelut in commune disseruit, complectitur uxorem et paululum aduersus praesentem fortitudinem mollitus rogat oratque temperaret dolori neu aeternum susciperet, sed in contemplatione uitae per uirtutem actae desiderium mariti solaciis honestis toleraret. illa contra sibi quoque destinatam mortem adseuerat manumque percussoris exposcit. tum Seneca gloriae eius non 2 aduersus, simul amore, ne sibi unice dilectam ad iniurias relinqueret, ' uitae ' inquit ' delenimenta monstraueram tibi, tu mortis decus mauis: non inuidebo exemplo. [sit huius tam fortis exitus constantia penes utrosque par, claritudinis plus in tuo fine.'] post quae eodem ictu brachia ferro exoluunt. Seneca, quoniam senile corpus et parco 3 uictu tenuatum lenta effugia sanguini praebebat, crurum quoque et poplitum uenas abrumpit; saeuisque cruciatibus defessus, ne dolore suo animum uxoris infringeret atque ipse uisendo eius tormenta ad impatientiam delaberetur, suadet in aliud cubiculum abscedere. et nouissimo quoque momento suppeditante eloquentia aduocatis scriptoribus pleraque tradidit, quae in uulgus edita eius uerbis inuertere supersedeo.

64. At Nero nullo in Paulinam proprio odio, ac ne glisceret inuidia crudelitatis, iubet inhiberi mortem. hortantibus militibus serui libertique obligant brachia, pre-
2 munt sanguinem, incertum an ignarae. nam ut est uulgus ad deteriora promptum, non defuere qui crederent, donec implacabilem Neronem timuerit, famam sociatae cum marito mortis petiuisse, deinde oblata mitiore spe blandimentis uitae euictam; cui addidit paucos postea annos, laudabili in maritum memoria et ore ac membris in eum pallorem albentibus ut ostentui esset multum uitalis
3 spiritus egestum. Seneca interim, durante tractu et lentitudine mortis, Statium Annaeum, diu sibi amicitiae fide et arte medicinae probatum, orat prouisum pridem uenenum quo damnati publico Atheniensium iudicio extinguerentur promeret; adlatumque hausit frustra, frigidus iam
4 artus et cluso corpore aduersum uim ueneni. postremo stagnum calidae aquae introiit, respergens proximos seruorum addita uoce libare se liquorem illum Ioui liberatori. exim balneo inlatus et uapore eius exanimatus sine ullo funeris sollemni crematur. ita codicillis praescripserat, cum etiam tum praediues et praepotens supremis suis consuleret.

65. Fama fuit Subrium Flauum cum centurionibus occulto consilio neque tamen ignorante Seneca destinauisse ut post occisum opera Pisonis Neronem Piso quoque interficeretur tradereturque imperium Senecae, quasi insontibus claritudine uirtutum ad summum fastigium delecto. quin et uerba Flaui uulgabantur, non referre dedecori si citha-

roedus demoueretur et tragoedus succederet, quia ut Nero
cithara, ita Piso tragico ornatu canebat.

66. Ceterum militaris quoque conspiratio non ultra fe-
fellit, accensis indicibus ad prodendum Faenium Rufum,
quem eundem conscium et inquisitorem non tolerabant.
ergo instanti minitantique renidens Scaeuinus neminem
ait plura scire quam ipsum, hortaturque ultro redderet
tam bono principi uicem. non uox aduersum ea Faenio,
non silentium, sed uerba sua praepediens et pauoris manifestus, ceterisque ac maxime Ceruario Proculo equite
Romano ad conuincendum eum conisis, iussu imperatoris
a Cassio milite, qui ob insigne corporis robur adstabat,
corripitur uinciturque.

67. Mox eorundem indicio Subrius Flauus tribunus
peruertitur, primo dissimilitudinem morum ad defensionem
trahens, neque se armatum cum inermibus et effeminatis
tantum facinus consociaturum; dein, postquam urgebatur, 2
confessionis gloriam amplexus. interrogatusque a Nerone
quibus causis ad obliuionem sacramenti processisset, ' oderam te ' inquit, ' nec quisquam tibi fidelior militum fuit,
dum amari meruisti. odisse coepi, postquam parricida
matris et uxoris, auriga et histrio et incendiarius extitisti.'
ipsa rettuli uerba, quia non, ut Senecae, uulgata erant, nec 3
minus nosci decebat militaris uiri sensus incomptos et
ualidos. nihil in illa coniuratione grauius auribus Neronis
accidisse constitit, qui ut faciendis sceleribus promptus, ita
audiendi quae faceret insolens erat. poena Flaui Veianio 4
Nigro tribuno mandatur. is proximo in agro scrobem effodi
iussit, quam Flauus ut humilem et angustam increpans,
circumstantibus militibus, ' ne hoc quidem ' inquit ' ex
disciplina.' admonitusque fortiter protendere ceruicem,
' utinam ' ait ' tu tam fortiter ferias! ' et ille multum

tremens, cum uix duobus ictibus caput amputauisset, saeuitiam apud Neronem iactauit, sesquiplaga interfectum a se dicendo.

68. Proximum constantiae exemplum Sulpicius Asper centurio praebuit, percontanti Neroni cur in caedem suam conspirauisset breuiter respondens non aliter tot flagitiis eius subueniri potuisse: tum iussam poenam subiit. nec ceteri centuriones in perpetiendis suppliciis degenerauere: at non Faenio Rufo par animus, sed lamentationes suas etiam in testamentum contulit.

2 Opperiebatur Nero ut Vestinus quoque consul in crimen traheretur, uiolentum et infensum ratus: sed ex coniuratis consilia cum Vestino non miscuerant, quidam uetustis in eum simultatibus, plures quia praecipitem et insociabilem 3 credebant. ceterum Neroni odium aduersus Vestinum ex intima sodalitate coeperat, dum hic ignauiam principis penitus cognitam despicit, ille ferociam amici metuit, saepe asperis facetiis inlusus, quae ubi multum ex uero traxere, acrem sui memoriam relinquunt. accesserat repens causa quod Vestinus Statiliam Messalinam matrimonio sibi iunxerat, haud nescius inter adulteros eius et Caesarem esse.

69. Igitur non crimine, non accusatore existente, quia speciem iudicis induere non poterat, ad uim dominationis conuersus Gerellanum tribunum cum cohorte militum immittit iubetque praeuenire conatus consulis, occupare uelut arcem eius, opprimere delectam iuuentutem, quia Vestinus imminentis foro aedis decoraque seruitia et pari 2 aetate habebat. cuncta eo die munia consulis impleuerat conuiuiumque celebrabat, nihil metuens an dissimulando metu, cum ingressi milites uocari eum a tribuno dixere. ille nihil demoratus exsurgit et omnia simul properantur:

clauditur cubiculo, praesto est medicus, abscinduntur
uenae, uigens adhuc balneo infertur, calida aqua mersatur,
nulla edita uoce qua semet miseraretur. circumdati in- 3
terim custodia qui simul discubuerant, nec nisi prouecta
nocte ómissi sunt, postquam pauorem eorum, ex mensa
exitium opperientium, et imaginatus et inridens Nero
satis supplicii luisse ait pro epulis consularibus.

70. Exim Annaei Lucani caedem imperat. is profluente
sanguine ubi frigescere pedes manusque et paulatim ab
extremis cedere spiritum feruido adhuc et compote mentis
pectore intellegit, recordatus carmen a se compositum quo
uulneratum militem per eius modi mortis imaginem obisse
tradiderat, uersus ipsos rettulit eaque illi suprema uox fuit.
Senecio posthac et Quintianus et Scaeuinus non ex priore 2
uitae mollitia, mox reliqui coniuratorum periere, nullo
facto dictoue memorando.

71. Sed compleri interim urbs funeribus, Capitolium
uictimis; alius filio, fratre alius aut propinquo aut amico
interfectis, agere grates deis, ornare lauru domum, genua
ipsius aduolui et dextram osculis fatigare. atque ille gaudium id credens Antonii Natalis et Ceruarii Proculi festinata indicia impunitate remuneratur. Milichus praemiis
ditatus conseruatoris sibi nomen, Graeco eius rei uocabulo,
adsumpsit. e tribunis Gauius Siluanus quamuis absolutus 2
sua manu cecidit; Statius Proxumus ueniam quam ab
imperatore acceperat uanitate exitus corrupit. exuti dehinc
tribunatu * * Pompeius, Cornelius Martialis, Flauius Nepos,
Statius Domitius, quasi principem non quidem odissent sed
tamen existimarentur. Nouio Prisco per amicitiam Senecae 3
et Glitio Gallo atque Annio Pollioni infamatis magis quam
conuictis data exilia. Priscum Artoria Flaccilla coniunx
comitata est, Gallum Egnatia Maximilla, magnis primum

et integris opibus, post ademptis; quae utraque gloriam
4 eius auxere. pellitur et Rufrius Crispinus occasione coniurationis, sed Neroni inuisus quod Poppaeam quondam
matrimonio tenuerat. Verginium Flauum et Musonium
Rufum claritudo nominis expulit: nam Verginius studia
iuuenum eloquentia, Musonius praeceptis sapientiae foue-
bat. Cluuidieno Quieto, Iulio Agrippae, Blitio Catulino,
Petronio Prisco, Iulio Altino uelut in agmen et numerum,
Aegaei maris insulae permittuntur. at Caedicia uxor
Scaeuini et Caesennius Maximus Italia prohibentur, reos
fuisse se tantum poena experti. Acilia mater Annaei
Lucani sine absolutione, sine supplicio dissimulata.

72. Quibus perpetratis Nero et contione militum habita
bina nummum milia uiritim manipularibus diuisit addiditque sine pretio frumentum, quo ante ex modo annonae ute-
bantur. tum quasi gesta bello expositurus uocat senatum
et triumphale decus Petronio Turpiliano consulari, Cocceio
Neruae praetori designato, Tigellino praefecto praetorii
tribuit, Tigellinum et Neruam ita extollens ut super trium-
phalis in foro imagines apud Palatium quoque effigies
2 eorum sisteret. consularia insignia Nymphidio * * * quia
nunc primum oblatus est, pauca repetam: nam et ipse pars
Romanarum cladium erit. igitur matre libertina ortus quae
corpus decorum inter seruos libertosque principum uulga-
uerat, ex G. Caesare se genitum ferebat, quoniam forte
quadam habitu procerus et toruo uultu erat, siue G. Caesar,
scortorum quoque cupiens, etiam matri eius inlusit * * *

73. Sed Nero uocato senatu, oratione inter patres habita,
edictum apud populum et conlata in libros indicia confes-
sionesque damnatorum adiunxit. etenim crebro uulgi rumore lacerabatur, tamquam uiros claros et insontis ob
2 inuidiam aut metum extinxisset. ceterum coeptam adul-

tamque et reuictam coniurationem neque tunc dubitauere
quibus uerum noscendi cura erat, et fatentur qui post interitum Neronis in urbem regressi sunt. at in senatu cunc- 3
tis, ut cuique plurimum maeroris, in adulationem demissis,
Iunium Gallionem, Senecae fratris morte pauidum et pro
sua incolumitate supplicem, increpuit Salienus Clemens,
hostem et parricidam uocans, donec consensu patrum
deterritus est, ne publicis malis abuti ad occasionem
priuati odii uideretur, neu composita aut oblitterata man-
suetudine principis nouam ad saeuitiam retraheret.

74. Tum dona et grates deis decernuntur, propriusque
honos Soli, cui est uetus aedes apud circum in quo facinus
parabatur, qui occulta coniurationis numine retexisset;
utque circensium Cerealium ludicrum pluribus equorum
cursibus celebraretur mensisque Aprilis Neronis cognomentum acciperet; templum Saluti extrueretur eo loci * * *
ex quo Scaeuinus ferrum prompserat. ipse eum pugionem 2
apud Capitolium sacrauit inscripsitque Ioui Vindici: in
praesens haud animaduersum; post arma Iulii Vindicis ad
auspicium et praesagium futurae ultionis trahebatur. re- 3
perio in commentariis senatus Cerialem Anicium consulem
designatum pro sententia dixisse ut templum diuo Neroni
quam maturrime publica pecunia poneretur. quod quidem
ille decernebat tamquam mortale fastigium egresso et
uenerationem hominum merito, sed ipse prohibuit, ne
interpretatione quorundam ad omen malum sui exitus
uerteretur: nam deum honor principi non ante habetur
quam agere inter homines desierit.

Abbreviations used in the Notes

AJP   *American Journal of Philology*
CIL   *Corpus Inscriptionum Latinarum*
CQ   *Classical Quarterly*
CR   *Classical Review*
Dorey   *Tacitus* (ed. T. A. Dorey: London, Routledge & Kegan Paul, 1969)
Goodyear   *Tacitus* (by F. R. D. Goodyear: Greece & Rome, New Surveys in the Classics, no. 4, Oxford, 1970)
ILS   *Inscriptiones Latinae Selectae* (ed. Dessau: Berlin, 1892)
JRS   *Journal of Roman Studies*
Mattingly   H. Mattingly, *Coins of the Roman Empire in the British Museum* (London, 1965)
Mendell   C. W. Mendell, *Tacitus, The Man and his Work* (Yale/Oxford, 1957)
RG   *Res Gestae diui Augusti* (ed. Brunt & Moore, Oxford, 1967)
RIC   *Roman Imperial Coinage* (ed. Mattingly & Sydenham, London, 1923)
Smallwood   E. M. Smallwood, *Documents illustrating the Principates of Gaius, Claudius and Nero* (Cambridge, 1967)
SRF   *Scaenicae Romanorum Poesis Fragmenta* (ed. Ribbeck, Leipzig, 1871)
Starr   C. G. Starr, *The Roman Imperial Navy* (Cambridge, 1960)
Syme   R. Syme, *Tacitus* (Oxford, 1958)
TAPA   *Transactions & Proceedings of the American Philological Association*

Webster   G. Webster, *The Roman Imperial Army* (London, Black, 1969)

References to the works of Tacitus are made (without the author's name) as follows: *D.*, *Ag.*, *G.*, *H.*, *A.* References to the text of *A.* 15 give only the chapter and section numbers, e.g. 25,2.

Notes

Chapters 1–3   The Parthians decide on action in Armenia, and Corbulo takes counter-measures.

Chapter 1

1. **interea**: into his record of the year A.D. 62 (dated by its consuls at *A*. 14,48: the account of 63 starts at *A*. 15,23) Tacitus has inserted a block of narrative about Armenia and Parthia (see Introd. 4). In *A*. 13–15, he records the Armenian campaigns not annually, but in groups – at *A*. 13,34–41 (A.D. 58): *A*. 14,23–6 (A.D. 60): *A*. 15,1–17 (A.D. 62): and *A*. 15,24–31 (A.D. 63). This causes chronological confusion, and Tacitus has been reasonably blamed for imprecision and lack of detail. But there is another side to the problem. He is writing, not a history of the Parthian Wars, but a history of the Roman Empire, and he is selecting and arranging his material in accordance with his judgement of its importance. Every reader of *A*. 13–15 is aware of the prominence of Parthia : but the prominence is presented through the crises and the highlights, not by the cumulative detail of repetitive and inconclusive campaigns. The final settlement with Parthia is important, and Tacitus presents it in detail : it, and the events leading up to it, dominate the first half of *A*. 15. The manoeuvring, both military and diplomatic, is complex, and so, inevitably, is its record : but the narrative is basically coherent and comprehensible, as well as dramatic. For further discussion of Tacitus as a military historian, see K. Wellesley in Dorey, pp. 63–97: Syme, 390–6: Mendell, 166–88.

Vologeses: king of Parthia from A.D. 51 (*A*. 12,14) until his death in 78/9.

Corbulonis rebus: Corbulo's activities of the previous year, the chief ones being those mentioned in the next two phrases. He was now in Syria (*A*. 14,26).

Cn. Domitius Corbulo was almost certainly the son of the Domitius Corbulo mentioned in *A*. 3,31 and of Vistilia (Pliny, *N.H.* 7,39). He was consul certainly before 46/7, legate of Lower Germany in 47 (*A*. 11,18–20), and possibly proconsul of Asia about 51/2. After his appointment by Nero in 54/5 (*A*. 13,8) to a command with special responsibility for Armenia, he spent some thirteen years in the Near East, until summoned

by Nero to meet him in Greece, and there forced to commit suicide
(Dio 63,17,5–6). Tacitus may have exaggerated Corbulo's importance
in the history of the period, but he was undoubtedly a professional soldier
of considerable competence.

regemque f.: *esse* is, as often in Tacitus, omitted: and the acc.
and inf. clause depends on the general idea of knowledge implicit in
cognitis.

alienigenam: Tigranes seems in fact to have had some connection
with the royal house of Parthia and Armenia (*RG* 27,2): but the
connection was a remote one, and his years in Rome (see below) made
him suspect.

Tigranen: the use of the Greek acc. ending on Greek or Eastern
names was a device of the poets (cf. Virg. *Georg.* 4,547 *Eurydicen*) and like
many poetic mannerisms, it came into prose in the Silver Latin period.
Cf. *Tiridaten* 2,1.

Tigranes V was a great-grandson of both Archelaus of Cappadocia
and of Herod the Great: he had spent years in Rome as a hostage, and
is presented as a pawn in the Parthian chess game. Cf. *A.* 14,26.

Tiridate: he was the Parthian nominee for the throne of Armenia,
placed there about A.D. 53 (*A.* 12,50), and dislodged by the arrival of
Tigranes (*A.* 14,26).

spretum . . . fastigium: the emphasis lies on the participle, and the
meaning of the participle with noun is equivalent to an abstract noun
phrase (' the scorning of . . . ', ' the insult to '). Cf. 62,2 *post matrem
fratremque interfectos.*

continui: the treaty of friendship dating from 20 B.C. (*RG* 29,2) had
never been formally broken. It had actually several times been renewed
(*A.* 2,58: Dio 59,27,3), and Rome and Parthia were never technically at
war. Neither, presumably, wanted full-scale warfare, and Tacitus'
assessment of Vologeses' motive may be quite right.

cunctator ingenio: the *-tor* suffix often implies the professional (cf.
machinatoribus 42,1: *cupitor* 42,2). Vologeses was ' constitutionally
cautious '.

Hyrcanorum: the Hyrcani lived at the SE corner of the Caspian Sea,
and had been in revolt since at least A.D. 58 (*A.* 13,37).

multisque ex eo bellis: the campaigns of the years from 58 on.
ex eo is an adverbial phrase meaning ' consequently '. For its position see
4,3 n. on *comminus*.

2. **nouus insuper**: *nouus* emphasises the effect of the last straw, and
insuper emphasises *nouus*.

extimulat: the ' historic ' present tense in Latin presents an incident
as an eye-witness report, vivid and immediate: it is followed by normal
historic sequence (see 14,3 *pepigissent*). In English, this tense is colloquial

and poetical, and should normally be avoided in translating historical narrative.

Adiabenos: they lived in the land east of the Tigris, around Nineveh.

primores gentium: the leaders of the various nations which made up the Parthian Empire.

eo contemptionis descensum: ' they had become so contemptible, they said, that . . . ' *esse* is to be supplied, and the sentence is in indirect speech, expressing their feelings vividly, but not interrupting the flow of the narrative. Cf. §§3–4.

temeritate obsidis: it is the *obses*, and not his *temeritas*, who is leading the invasion. But the quasi-personification of the quality makes it more striking than an adjective agreeing with *obses* would be. Cf. 6,4 *umbra regis*.

3. **Monobazus:** hereditary king of Adiabene, he took part, according to Dio 62,20,2, with Monaeses, in the siege of Tigranocerta (4,2): he officially witnessed the capitulation of Paetus (14,3) and gave hostages to Corbulo after the agreement with Tiridates (Dio 62,23,4). He was obviously a ruler of some importance.

quem penes: like most prepositions, *penes* normally precedes its noun, as it does, e.g., in 14,2. But already in Plautus, the relative pronoun sometimes precedes it (cf. *Poen.* 1188 *quem penes*). This displacing (anastrophe) of the preposition is further developed by the poets, who found it metrically convenient and striking: cf. Virg. *Aen.* 12,59. Tacitus uses it freely: cf. 17,3 *ultra*: 18,2 *in*: 23,3 *infra*: 24,2 & 61,2 *coram*: 37,2 *e* and *abusque*: 47,2 *propter* and *iuxta*.

quod . . . rogitans: *peteret* is the verb of both clauses, and is indirect deliberative subjunctive. *rogitans*, the frequentative verb, implies both persistence and insistence.

proxima trahi: ' the borderlands were in process of being seized '.

nisi defendant . . . esse: the sentence is elliptical – ' (he said that) if the Parthians did not defend them (they would surrender, for) Rome's yoke was easier on the submissive than on the captive '. The tense of *defendant* preserves the vividness of direct speech, while the subjunctive mood is correctly indirect. This device, known as *repraesentatio*, allows an historian to introduce variety and vividness into indirect speech, and also to indicate subtleties of tense usage which normal secondary sequence would obscure. See *CR* 1951, 142–6.

4. **regni profugus:** *profugus* is normally and naturally used with an abl. of separation, cf. *A.* 3,62 *patris ira profugus*. But the genitive case defines the sphere of reference of the word it accompanies, and can produce much the same meaning: he is a refugee ' in respect of his kingdom ' and therefore from it. Cf. the very similar *patriae . . . exsul* in Hor. *Od.* 2,16,19.

per silentium aut . . . querendo: Tacitus combines two ways of expressing means/cause, to give variety instead of exact balance. Cf. 6,2 *per otium . . . bello.*

grauior: ' more impressive'.

non enim f.: Tiridates' point is made in short but telling sentences. ' It was not inactivity that preserved great empires: they needed men and arms to fight for them: for those with supreme power might was right: preservation of property was a matter for pride for a private family, but a king won glory by claiming the property of others.'

sua: *suus* can always be used to indicate an emphatic ' one's own ', even where it does not refer to the subject of the clause. Here it refers to the logical, even if not the grammatical, subject of the sentence. Cf. Cic. *Diu.* 1,63 *eos . . . peccatorum suorum . . . paenitet.*

Chapter 2

1. **igitur:** Cicero rarely starts a sentence with *igitur*, but in the historians and post-Augustan writers this position is common, and in Tacitus it is almost invariable. When he does put it second, it is usually to ensure euphony, or to emphasise the word which precedes it.

concilium: the composition and functions of this council are not clear, but it was probably composed of leading nobles (*megistanes* cf. 27,3), and perhaps also of wise men and magi (Strabo 11,9,3). It was a feudal body, not an assembly of citizens.

ita orditur: there is no reason to suppose that Tacitus found anywhere a record of Vologeses' words. The use of dramatic speech was a convention which enabled the ancient historian to present, in vivid and striking form, facts or ideas which he wished to emphasise. Here, necessary background information, certain aspects of Vologeses' character, and the reasons for an action which is to have important consequences, are presented more memorably, because more personally, than by straightforward narrative. For Tacitus' use of such dramatic speech, see *AJP* 1964, 279–96.

eodem mecum patre: Vologeses' mother (*A.* 12,44) was a Greek concubine, but for inheritance it was paternity that counted. *cum* after *idem* is a rare construction, and may be intended to emphasise the close connection between the brothers, as does the interwoven order of the phrase.

cum . . . concessisset: the ' King of Kings ' (*summum nomen*) had to be an Arsacid, but (in spite of *per aetatem*) not necessarily the eldest son. Vologeses was appointed (*A.* 12,44) *concessu fratrum* i.e. they acquiesced in the appointment and relinquished their own claims to the title. *per aetatem* therefore represents Vologeses as conciliatory and diplomatic.

qui: the relative pronoun, which refers to Armenia, is by a common Latin idiom attracted to the gender of the predicate. Cf. 61,2 and Caes. *B.G.* 7,68,1 *Alesiam, quod est oppidum Mandubiorum.*

Pacorus: here mentioned for the first time – presumably because he is only marginally important in the clash between Rome and Parthia. He ruled Media Atropatene, which lay south of Armenia, near the Caspian Sea.

uetera . . . odia: it was not unknown even in Rome for a potential rival claimant to the throne to be removed (cf. *A.* 1,6: 13,1). But the vague system of inheritance and the loose structure of the Parthian Empire created more rivals and made them more dangerous than at Rome. Family struggles, plots and assassinations were common. See *A.* 11,9f.

penatis: the family gods are used to symbolise family affairs.

2. **ipsis**: the dative case expresses a person's interest in the action of the clause. Sometimes, as here, that person is also the agent by whom the action is accomplished.

in exitium suum abrumpunt: the variation of construction and the final harsh metaphor combine to emphasise the statement.

3. **non ibo infitias**: the phrase (whose acc. expresses goal) is archaic and so adds a certain solemnity to Vologeses' statement. It appears only here in Tacitus, and is immediately followed by another word rare in Tacitus, *aequitas*. It is perhaps with intentional irony that Vologeses is represented as being prevented by Romans from exercising a virtue which Roman emperors were fond of claiming as their own. Cf. the coins of Galba and Vitellius, *RIC*, I, pp. 213,136: 227,17.

malueram: ' I should have preferred.' With words expressing a standard, Latin tended, quite logically, to use the indicative to express the standard, and to allow any contingency involved to be deduced from the context. Thus *idoneum est* = ' it would be suitable ' and *satis erat* = ' it would have been more satisfactory '. Then, as the imperf. subjunctive came regularly to express potentiality unfulfilled in present time, and the pluperf. subjunctive potentiality unfulfilled in past time, the corresponding tenses of the indicative began to be used with the expressions of standard and propriety: e.g. *melius erat* = ' it would be better ' and *melius fuerat* = ' it would have been better '. And the construction was extended by analogy to verbs of similar meaning, e.g. *malo*. Cf. Cic. *Att.* 2,19,3 *malueram . . . silentio transiri.*

uestra: the word, like the speech, is addressed to the Parthian nobles. The use of plural for singular is in Latin not a ' royal ' plural, but a sign of modesty. It is therefore used only in the first person, never in the second or third.

in integro: ' in an untouched state ' i.e. ' untarnished '. Such adverbial phrases, expressing aim, manner or attendant circumstances, are found as early as Plautus, but the analogy of similar Greek constructions helped their growth in and after the Augustan age. Cf., e.g., 15,1 *per diuersum*: 30,1 *in maius*: 13,3 *ex aequo*: 16,3 *in obscuro*.

4. **diademate . . . euinxit**: *diadema* is foreign and exotic, *euincio is* archaic, poetical and ritualistic (cf. Virg. *Aen.* 5,269): they add solemnity to the action narrated.

Monaesi: he besieged, with these forces, Tigranocerta (4–5) and later acted as go-between for Vologeses and Corbulo.

minitans: the frequentative verb implies a persistent threat to Syria and Cappadocia, and its final position increases its force.

Chapter 3

1. **legiones duas**: see 6,3 n.

Verulano Seuero: a legate of Corbulo's (*A.* 14,26), who was consul *suffectus* towards the end of Nero's reign (*CIL* VI, 10055).

Vettio Bolano: consul *suffectus* in A.D. 66 (*CIL* VI, 2044), governor of Britain 69–71 (*Ag.* 8,1 & 16,5), and proconsul of Asia about 78–80 (Stat. *Sil.* 5,2,57).

subsidium: instead of the predicative dat. which is more usual with verbs of sending (cf. *H.* 4,27 *misitque subsidio cohortem*), Tacitus here employs an acc. in apposition. Cf. Livy 2,22,6 *coronam auream Ioui donum in Capitolium mittunt.*

compositius . . . agerent: this clause contains the only example in the *Annals* of the normal classical ' double comparative ' construction: the adverb *composite* makes here its solitary appearance in Tacitus: the omission of *ut* makes the instruction more vivid and immediate (' with the secret instruction, let them . . . '): and the final position of the phrase is emphatic. Tacitus is using stylistic means to point his interpretation.

quippe . . . malebat: the phrase could (just) mean that Corbulo wanted to avoid open warfare with Parthia: but in view of the stylistic points just mentioned, and the remarks about Corbulo in 6,2 & 4; 10,4; and 28,2, it seems likely that Tacitus is presenting Corbulo as ambitious. If he completed the campaign or suffered defeat (both possible in *bellum gerere*), he might be recalled: to keep the war simmering (*habere*) would ensure that he was needed to supervise it. Whether this view of Corbulo is based on evidence, or on Tacitus' opinion of human nature, is impossible to decide.

Syriam: an important province (see Introd. 4) which it was Corbulo's first duty to safeguard. He had been appointed its governor in A.D. 60 (*A.* 14,26).

ingruente: used of people, this verb is poetical and vivid. Cf. Virg. *Aen.* 11,899.

2. **reliquas**: probably three in number. See 6,3 n.

pro: ' along the bank.' Cf. 5,3 *pro Syria*, ' on the Syrian frontier '.

.locat ... armat ... intercipit: the series of short principal clauses, in historic present (see 1,2 n.), and without connectives, suggests the swift series of actions.

ingressus: ' entry points ', rather than ' invasions '. Corbulo is taking precautionary measures, not fighting off an attack. He blocked the Euphrates crossings by strong points.

egena aquarum: *egenus* is an archaic and poetic word, used with gen. or abl. (see 12,1 n.), as *egeo* is. After the swift action of the previous sentence, it makes the description more picturesque.

est: not an historic present, but a statement of permanent fact. Corbulo made things difficult for an invading army by cutting off all possible water supplies in a desert area.

Chapters 4 and 5   Siege of Tigranocerta, and withdrawal of the Parthians.

Chapter 4

1. **tuendae Syriae**: dat. of purpose. The interest of a thing, as distinct from a person, expressed by the dat., lies in the fulfilment of the action. Tacitus uses the gerundive dat. of purpose, as here, a great deal. Cf., e.g., 6,3: 10,2: 14,2.

ut famam sui praeiret: he wanted to get there before the news did. *sui* for *suam* is a Silver Latin variation on the normal construction. Cf. 36, 1 *sui absentiam*.

2. **occupauerat**: the subject is Tigranes, the person emphasised by the clause which ends the previous sentence.

Tigranocertam: here and in 5,2 fem. sing., in 6,2 and 8,1 it is neut. pl. Such names were in Latin simply an approximation of the foreign sound, and their form could be adjusted to produce clarity, euphony or variety.

The exact location of the city, which was founded by Tigranes I early in the first century B.C., remains uncertain. Our sources of information (Strabo 12,539 & 16,747: Pliny *N.H.* 6,26-7 & 129: Plutarch, *Lucullus* 24: *A.* 15,4,2 & 5,2) are contradictory, and until the archaeologists find Tigranocerta for us, it is impossible to be sure who (or whose source, or text) is mistaken. Scholars at the moment tend to place the city north rather than south of Mt Masius and the Tigris: see p. xxii and Syme, 396.

copia . . . commeatus: Tacitus varies his account of the city's defences, to avoid a catalogue.

haud spernenda latitudine: with *amnis*, an abl. of quality: ' a river of respectable width '.

milites: the Roman forces given by Corbulo to Tigranes, as escort, when he arrived to claim his kingdom (*A.* 14,26): and perhaps also the two legions mentioned 3,1.

subuectu: ' in the collecting of which ', abl. expressing attendant circumstances. The word appears only here in classical literature.

repentinis: its use of people is not common, but cf. Livy 39,1,6 *hostis . . . repentinus*.

accenderant: it is not the men, but the fact of their being surrounded, which is the logical subject of the verb. See 1,1 n. on *spretum*. Strictly speaking, *accendo* can apply only to *ira*, but by the figure of Zeugma ('joining '), a general sense of ' inspired ' can be extracted from it for *metu*. Cf. 34,1 : 53,4.

3. **Partho:** the collective singular is especially common in military contexts (cf. 6,3 *priorque Syriae miles*) and with national names (cf. Cic. *Att.* 5,16,4 *de Partho silentium est*). It adds variety and individuality to the narrative. The dative here indicates possession.

nulla comminus audacia: ' no hand-to-hand courage '. The adjectival use of an adverb is easy for Greek (' the now men ' i.e. ' men of today '), because it possesses a definite article and can enclose the adverb so that its precise application is clear. Latin imitates the usage early (cf. Ennius, *Varia* 113 *ceteros tunc homines*) but cautiously, either enclosing it by an adjective (as here) or using it with a verbal noun (cf. Cic. *Caec.* 43 *ictu comminus*) or so arranging the sentence that syntactically the adverb may be taken with the verb (cf. Cic. *Ep. Brut.* 1,15,10 *intellexi ex tuis saepe litteris*). The poets are freer in their use of the device, and prose writers from Livy on follow them. Cf. 7,2 *nulla palam causa*: 10,3 *uana rursus fiducia*: 27,2 *quantum intus discordiarum*: 29,2 *magna utrimque specie*. The Parthians, being primarily mounted archers, were better at guerilla tactics than at the close, more static work of a siege.

machinamenta: siege engines, such as battering rams and catapults. For a description of such devices, see 9,1 n., and Webster, 231 f.

Chapter 5

1. **quamuis . . . suis:** the abl. absolute can express (among other things) condition, concession or cause, and it is sometimes introduced by a relevant adverb or conjunction, to indicate its precise meaning. The usage began in classical Latin, but is much commoner in Silver writers. Cf., e.g., 8,2 with *quasi*: 25,1 with *tamquam*.

uim prouinciae: the province must be Syria. But it had not been invaded, only (3,1) threatened. Corbulo is probably indicating that an

attack on Armenia is an attack on Rome's interests, and will be resisted.
Cohortis: a cohort (480 men) was one-tenth of a legion.

omitteret . . . aut . . . positurum: the indirect form of *omitte . . .
aut . . . ponam*. The complaint is presented vividly and forcefully as a
report of Corbulo's own words.

2. **Casperius**: he had been on a similar mission before (*A*. 12,45-6).

Nisibin: situated south of Mt Masius and the Tigris, on the river
Mygdonius, it occupied an important strategic position.

a Tigranocerta: prepositions are used with names of towns when
distance, and not movement from a source, is being expressed.

adit . . . edidit: the present tense gives a vivid picture of the scene,
and the change to the perfect makes specific and emphatic the main point
of the sentence.

3. **Vologesi f.**: for a discussion of the structure of this sentence, see
Introd. 2.

uitandi: other examples of this odd genitive of the gerund are to be
found at 21,2 (*ostentandi*) and *A*. 13,26 (*retinendi*). All three seem to lack a
noun on which the gen. could depend: but it is extremely unlikely that
in all three instances the same odd construction has been caused by the
same accident of textual transmission. It is more probably an example of
Tacitean experimentation with language. Some Latin phrases may be
used with either the infinitive or the genitive of the gerund (cf., e.g.,
Cic. *Att*. 5,5,1 *ibi enim Pomptinum . . . exspectare consilium est* and Cic. *Fam*.
5,20,4 *Volusii liberandi meum consilium fuit*), and there is some evidence
(see Löfstedt in *Dragma*, Lund 1939, 297f.) to suggest that this produced
a certain blurring of the lines between the two constructions. The infinitive would be unexceptional here: but the meaning of the three passages
has never been in doubt, and the unusual syntax has certainly attracted
readers' attention to them.

manu et copiis: ' soldiers and supplies '. Cf. 4,2.

ambederat: an emendation, but a convincing one. M's text *exorta ui
locustarum aberat*, ' a plague of locusts had occurred and there was an
absence of anything grassy or leafy ', gives the required sense, but not the
required emphasis. Tacitus nowhere else uses *uis* = ' crowd ' in any case
other than nom. or acc.: the ' absence ' of greenery is less striking than
the characteristic activity of locusts in ' devouring ' it: and a rare word is
especially liable to misunderstanding and alteration by a copyist.
ambedo is rare, but appears twice in Virgil (*Aen*. 3,257: 5,752), and
Tacitus is fond of Virgilian vocabulary.

4. **super**: in this meaning (= *de*) it is rare in classical prose, but common in Tacitus and other Silver writers. Cf. 24,1: 36,1. Vologeses was
now prepared to consider getting *de facto* control of Armenia by acknow-
ledging Rome's nominal suzerainty over that country. See Introd. 4.

Chapter 6   Arrival of Paetus, and division of forces.

Chapter 6

1. **alii f.**: the second suggested explanation is weighted by position, length and the indirect speech which follows it. It is not necessary to suppose that Corbulo's memoirs (16,1 n.) would have resolved the problem here presented: or that Tacitus would have believed them if they had.

pepigisse: the subject is Corbulo, whose conduct is the point under debate.

2. **cur . . . deductum**: supply *esse*. Rhetorical questions, a forceful method of making a statement, become acc. and inf. in indirect speech: *cur . . . deductus esset* would expect an answer. Cf. 62,2.

a Tigranocertis: see 4,2 n. *a* is normal with names of towns when departure from the neighbourhood is also implied. Cf. 46,2.

defenderant: the indicative may be retained in a subordinate clause in indirect speech, when the clause is a pure periphrasis (here = ' his war-gains '), and so in a sense presents the author's explanation rather than the speaker's words. Cf. Cic. *Arch.* 20 *putabat ea quae gesserat* (i.e. ' his exploits ') *posse celebrari*: 49,1 : 61,3.

an: marks an indignant or ironical question. The information about the withdrawal of Tigranes and his Roman escort, and the passage of time to the following spring, is given only in this oblique way. Tacitus wants the emotional effect of dramatic speech, and wishes to avoid unnecessary repetition.

in extrema Cappadocia: they had withdrawn from Armenia, and wintered in the mountains of what is now central Turkey.

tuguriis: ' *tugurium . . . turpe* ' says Afranius (*SRF* II, p. 215). Tacitus uses it only here, thus emphasising their complaint.

cum alio: this is a predictable charge, in the circumstances: there may even be some truth in it. But Corbulo had (3,1 n.) perfectly proper reasons for deferring conflict.

non: the negative stands within a final clause, but belongs only to *ultra*. Cf. Cic. *Cael.* 42 *non omnia uoluptatibus denegentur*.

3. **ut rettuli**: in 3,1.

Caesennius Paetus: he had been consul in A.D. 61 (*A.* 14,29). In spite of his catastrophic campaign in Armenia, narrated in the following chapters, he served as legate of Syria under Vespasian in 70-72 (Jos. *B.I.* 7,59 and 219 f.).

legiones: the standing army of Syria was four legions (*A.* 4,5). These were III *Gallica*, VI *Ferrata*, X *Fretensis* and XII *Fulminata* (*A.* 13,8,38,40: Jos. *B.I.* 7,17: for their *cognomina* see below). To them had been added

(*A.* 13,35) IV *Scythica* (probably: not IV *Germanica* as Tacitus implies), and now V *Macedonica*. If III, VI and X were ' remaining ' with Corbulo, then IV and XII must have been the legions sent to help Tigranes (3,1).

Legions were numbered in order of formation. During the civil wars of the first century B.C., various generals were forming legions, and duplication of numbers naturally followed. When Augustus reorganised the army, he recognised that the *ethos* of a regiment can be mysteriously linked to its name, and so many of the duplications remained. Confusion was avoided by the use of *cognomina*, honorific titles or nick-names, awarded for a variety of reasons. Thus, III *Gallica* was formed from the veterans of Julius Caesar's Gallic legions, VI *Ferrata* boasted men of iron, X *Fretensis* fought in the Sicilian Straits in the war between Octavian and Sextus Pompeius, XII *Fulminata* went into action like a thunderbolt, V *Macedonica* fought with distinction in that area, and XV *Apollinaris* (25,3) was founded by Augustus and named after his protecting deity. Inscriptions (tombstones, dedications etc.) give us valuable information about the names and movements of legions, and help to supplement or correct the information provided by the literary historians. See Webster, 109f.

auxilia: light infantry or cavalry, used to support the heavy infantry of the legions. They were not normally composed of Roman citizens.

prior ... miles: also auxiliaries.

cetera: ' everything else ' would be any remaining auxiliary or local forces.

4. **aemuli patiens:** the participle with gen. describes a permanent characteristic, not an isolated incident. Cf. 46,1 *rerum cupiens*: 72,2.

satis ... erat: for the indicative, see 2,3 n. Here it also helps to suggest a Tacitean comment on Paetus' ability.

despiciebat: ' constantly expressed scorn for '. The imperfect tense expresses not only action, but attitude, here reinforced by the frequentative *dictitans*.

nomine tenus: ' in name only '. Cf. 45,2.

se: very emphatic, by its position and the indirect speech.

tributa ... leges ... ius: he proposed to make Armenia a regular province. Tacitus presents Paetus as a vain fool: neither the campaign which follows, nor any other source, suggests that he is wrong in his estimate.

pro umbra regis: ' in place of a shadow consisting of a king ' i.e. ' instead of a phantom king '. For the usage, see 1,2 n.

Chapters 7-12   The Parthians and Paetus: fighting in Armenia: Paetus asks Corbulo for assistance.

Chapter 7

1. **sub idem tempus:** in the spring of A.D. 62.

memoraui: see 5,4.

inriti: its use of persons is almost entirely poetical and post-Augustan. Cf. 25,3.

duabus legionibus: abl. expressing accompaniment.

Funisulanus . . . Calauius: Calavius is otherwise unknown, but Funisulanus is shown by inscriptions (e.g., *ILS* 1005) to have had a distinguished military and political career under Domitian.

eo in tempore: unlike *in tempore* ('at the right time') or *tali in tempore* ('in such circumstances of crisis'), this phrase is purely temporal and so normally used without *in*. Tacitus employs it on three other occasions (*A.* 11,29: 13,47: 15,39), and it appears spasmodically in writers before and after him. It may be a colloquialism.

tristi omine: the position of the phrase (and of its adjective) emphasises the content. The singular noun, followed by three omens, either indicates an abl. of attendant circumstances ('inauspiciously'), or refers primarily to the first omen, which marked the entry proper.

Omens and their record were part of the ancient way of life. Tacitus, like most historians, sometimes includes them (cf. 34,1: 36,2: 47: 74,2): but he is obviously selective, and occasionally caustic, and fairly clearly employs them as a literary device, to create foreboding and tension. Paetus' *débâcle* is being presented with all the trimmings.

2. **nulla palam causa:** see 4,3 n.

consularia insignia: probably the *fasces*, his badge of office (the phrase has a different meaning in 72,2). Omens occurring at the start of an enterprise were considered especially significant: and a similar catastrophe had occurred at Crassus' crossing of the same river (Plut. *Crass.* 19).

hostia: anything involving a sacrifice was also significant. The animal was being kept (*adsistens*, ' standing by ') to be sacrificed when the winter quarters were complete – a sort of ' topping out ' ceremony.

semifacta: the word is rare, occurs only here in Tacitus, and precedes its noun, thus helping to stress the omen.

pila . . . arsere: the omen indicated that these were the weapons they would have to use: and the Roman legionary preferred to use his short sword.

Chapter 8

1. **spretis . . . necdum . . . nullo**: Paetus' behaviour is presented as negative and reprehensible. Tacitus' account may be coloured by Corbulo's (16,1 n.), but it is difficult to make a real case for Paetus. Note how the abl. phrases build up to the climax of Paetus' action.

prouisu: this word is used only by Tacitus, and only in the abl.

rapit: for this meaning of ‘ rapidly led ’, cf. Virg. *Aen.* 10,308–9 *rapit . . . aciem.*

reciperandis . . . Tigranocertis: it had been abandoned (6,2). Paetus probably crossed the Euphrates at Melitene, and approached Tigranocerta from the north, over Taurus.

omisisset: the subjunctive shows that this is part of Paetus' statement.

2. **partum, si . . . habuisset**: *erat* is to be supplied, not *esset.* The real apodosis is suppressed, being emphatically replaced by a related fact. ‘ He had obtained (and could have kept) . . . if only . . . ’ The construction is much commoner with an imperfect tense in the apodosis (cf. 55,4), but the pluperfect is found – cf. 37,4 : 50,4.

percursando: this abl. of the gerund, in meaning indistinguishable from a present participle agreeing with the subject (which, in modern Italian, it has become) is used by the poets and post-Augustan writers to express attendant circumstances. Cf. 38,3 : 57,2 : 67,4 : 69,2.

qui captus erat: the implication is that Paetus had not brought or organised proper provisions for his army.

quasi confecto: see 5,1 n.

uerbis . . . uacuas: the position and variation of the phrases add emphasis.

Chapter 9

1. **ponti iniciendo**: the crossing (at Zeugma) had no permanent bridge, but the materials to construct a pontoon bridge were always ready. Cf. *A.* 6,37 *ponte nauibus effecto.*

subiectis campis: ‘ lying near ’ (the river), and so ‘ low-lying ’. The abl. is local, and Tacitus, like the poets, uses it freely without *in.* Cf. 60,4 *suburbano rure.*

nauis . . . auctas: the floating battery is impressively presented. The ships' size is first emphasised, and the further description arranged as a chiasmus (where the balance is not in parallel, but crossed ✕ in the form of the Greek letter ‘ chi ’).

catapultisque et ballistis: the catapults were machines rather like cross-bows, which hurled bolts (*hastae*): the *ballistae* were enormous slings, using rocks (*saxa*) as ammunition. See Webster, 232-6.

longius: the mechanically-propelled missiles had a longer range than the arrows of the Parthian cavalry.

2. aduersi: on the opposite side of the river.

imminentium nescius: ' in ignorance of what was threatening '.

reliquas: legions IV and XII. Cf. 6,3.

promiscis ... commeatibus: ' by indiscriminate grants of leave '.

infirmauerat: this verb occurs in Tacitus only here and at 17,1. Both passages describe Paetus' folly, and may conceivably be founded on Corbulo's memoirs (16,1 n.).

Chapter 10

1. accitur: see §3 n. on *castello*.

et unde f.: ' and his lack of numbers was revealed (by the source) from which he had hoped for an impression of increased forces '. When the legion arrived, it was demonstrably under strength.

poterat: for the indicative, see 2,3 n. It here also emphasises the fact that success was still possible – had Paetus been different. The verb agrees with its nearer subject.

tractu belli: ' by the drawing out of the war '. Cf. 37,2 n.

uerum ubi f.: Tacitus paints a vivid picture of the ineffectual leader, torn between a need for support and a desire to prove his own adequacy. His hesitancy is resolved, as often, in action which is decisive, deliberately contrary, and disastrous.

uiris militaribus: military advisers or experts.

2. clamitans: this belongs (cf. *duxit, remeauit*) to an incident and not to a series of actions, so the frequentative verb indicates intensity.

quasi ... certaturus: ' with the air of one about to decide the issue by battle '. The use of *quasi* with the participle is like that already noted (5,1 n.) with the abl. abs., but here the influence of Greek is very clear.

3. rursus: used adjectivally. See 4,3 n.

quo f.: probably an example of final *quo* used without a comparative. Cf. Sall. *Cat.* 58,3 *ego uos, quo pauca monerem, aduocaui, simul uti causam ... aperirem.*

castello: the exact position of this fort, as of the entire operation, is not immediately clear (though it can be deduced) from Tacitus' narrative. Paetus had crossed Taurus (8,1) and returned (8,2) but was still in its vicinity (10,3): Vologeses had retreated from Euphrates into southern Armenia (9,2): Paetus' HQ were the winter quarters of the IV legion (10,1 & 2 – XII had to be summoned), and that stood on the River Arsanias (15,1), some forty to sixty miles from Melitene and the border of Cappadocia (16,1 & 3): and the *castellum* must have been nearby, because the Parthians could switch their attack from one to the other (13,1). Dio (62,21,1) says that the camp was at Rhandeia, on the River Arsanias, and this fits well enough with the area about fifty miles east of Melitene. The whole section is an interesting example of one aspect of Tacitus' narrative technique, and its effect on the historical content.

Arsamosata: this cannot be the city mentioned by Polybius (8,23,1) and Pliny (*N.H.* 6,26). It is obviously a small fort.

in uno habitus: the participial phrase serves, as often in Greek, as the protasis of a conditional sentence.

4. ferunt: Dio (62,21,3) says that Paetus had repeatedly sent for Corbulo. There are signs in Tacitus' account of a source other than the main one used by himself and Dio, and this information may come from there. It certainly fits with the picture of Paetus which he has been presenting.

instantem: *hostem esse* is to be supplied.

nec a Corbulone: the omission of the verb makes it uncertain whether this statement is the source's (supply *esse*) or Tacitus' (supply *est*). In either case, it is presented by Tacitus as part of his picture of Corbulo's character.

gliscentibus: *gliscere* ' to grow ', is an old and poetic word, much used by Tacitus, largely of undesirable qualities (cf. *inuidia* 64,1). It is also used of number (*multitudo*, e.g., *A.* 3,25) and occasionally of good qualities (*gloria* 23,4: but *pericula* is also in the context).

The structure is pointed, *gliscentibus* and *augeretur* bracketing the clause, but in different constructions: the emotive word emphasises the first half, the variation and the longer phrase the second.

tribus legionibus: III, VI and X (6,3 n.). These legionary detachments were supported by auxiliary (6,3 n.) troops, both cavalry (*alarios*) and infantry (*cohortibus*, cf. 9,2).

Chapter 11

1. at: marking a change of scene and of emphasis. Cf. 18,1 : 26,1.

nihil: adverbial acc., = ' not at all '.

sed: instead of using a balancing abl. abs., Tacitus presents Vologeses' action in finite verbs and asyndeton construction, and continues the sentence with two linked abl. abs. The effect is to make Vologeses' action central, and to end with the impression of a confused struggle by the Roman soldiers.

Tarquitio: Tacitus may have found his name in Corbulo's account of the action.

donec ... circumueniretur: here, as often in Latin from Livy on, the subjunctive indicates only subordination and time, not intention. Cf. 59,4.

2. **longinqua et auia**: this depends on *petiuere*, supplied from *repetiuere*.

facili credulitate: the abl. expresses attendant circumstances.

3. **obniti**: historic infinitive. This is used in rapid narrative, often in series (cf. 12,3) to provide the essential verbal meaning, without trimmings of person or tense: its subject stays in the nominative. Cf. 13,1: 16,4: 27,3 etc.

precibus, ueniret: the omission of *ut* makes the request more direct and immediate. Cf. 17,3: 63,1: 66,1.

signa et aquilas et nomen: these are emotive words. The *signa* (29,2 n.) were subsidiary standards, but the legion's own: the eagle was the symbol of the legion's identity, its rallying point and its display of battle honours – loss of the eagle usually meant disbandment of the legion, obliteration of reputation and name. They are particularly emotive words in a context involving Parthians (Introd. 4).

Chapter 12

1. **ille**: the initial pronoun marks the change of subject to Corbulo.

et: grammatically unnecessary, but sometimes used by Tacitus to point a carefully disjointed pair of expressions.

munimenta: cf. 9,1. Corbulo was taking precautions, in case the attack on Paetus was a feint, to draw him away and leave Syria open.

qua proximum et . . . egenum: ' by which (route it was) nearest and provisioned ' lit. *qua* is normally so used without *uia*: the verb ' to be ' is easily supplied: and *petere* (from *petiuit*) is to be understood as the subject of the clause.

egenus (see 3,2 n.) seems to be used with the abl. only by Tacitus (here, and at *A.* 12,46 *commeatu*) and a few later writers. The rare construction, the poetic word and the compressed expression make the clause pointed, an effect continued by the different ways of describing the districts in the main clause.

Commagenam: a small country lying between Syria and Cappadocia, which was important to Rome because it contained one of the Euphrates crossings (Samosata). It was sometimes governed by a client king (*A.* 12,55), sometimes incorporated in the province of Syria (*A.* 2,56). Vespasian finally and permanently so incorporated it in A.D. 73 (Suet. *Vesp.* 8).

Armenios: Corbulo met Paetus (16,4: 17,1) before reaching Armenia.

onusta frumenti: like *egenus*, *onustus* may with linguistic logic be used with either gen. or abl. But the gen. is the rarer construction and the more strained usage. It is archaistic (Plaut. *Aul.* 611) and perhaps colloquial (*Bell. Afr.* 63,3). Tacitus uses it only here, in a chapter full of pointed style.

depelleret: the subject is Corbulo and not *uis*. The camel train has been allowed prominence in the sentence, for its exotic and picturesque effect, but the main agent is Corbulo, and he is the subject of the next two main verbs.

2. **primum f.**: the first contact between Corbulo and Paetus' men is marked by alliteration.

primi pili: a centurion of the first rank, the senior centurion of a legion. After the reforms of Marius (at the end of the second century B.C.), a Roman legion consisted of ten cohorts containing six centuries (and centurions) each. In cohorts II–X, the senior centurion was called *secundus* (*tertius* etc.) *pilus prior*, but in cohort I he was simply *primus pilus*, and he carried considerable responsibility for the whole legion, ranking next to the military tribune. The implication is clear, that a man of this rank should not have been *leading* a retreat.

redire ... experiri: *moneo* and its compounds are occasionally found with the infin., even in classical prose (e.g., Cic. *Verr.* 2,1,63 *ut eum suae libidines facere monebant*). But it is commoner in the poets and historians. Cf. 54,3: 67,4.

Corbulo's ' correct ' behaviour, the detailed information and the emotional tone, suggest that the chapter may be based on his memoirs (16,1 n.).

3. **adire, hortari ... admonere ... ostendere**: historic infinitives. See 11,3 n.

si singulis f.: ' if any private soldier could win from the Emperor's hand the special crown for saving a citizen ... ' The *ciuica corona*, a crown of oak leaves, was the highest award for bravery in the field. It was open to all ranks, and awarded only for saving a Roman citizen's life at risk of one's own. Julius Caesar held it, and *A.* 12,31 records its award to M. Ostorius in A.D. 50, the last known conferment of the honour. It carried with it certain privileges, see Pliny *N.H.* 16,13.

ubi par ... numerus: this is illogical, because the numbers are just as equal when they are one to one, and the glory arguably as great. But emotion, not logic, is the keynote, and what Corbulo is really saying is ' it is a splendid thing to save an army '.

4. **in commune**: ' as a whole '. See 2,3 n.

incenderent: ' generic ' subjunctive, used to characterise rather than to define an antecedent, which in this construction is usually either negative or indefinite. In other words, *ille erat qui diceret* means ' he was the sort of man to say ' while *ille erat qui dixit* means ' he was the speaker '.

Cf. the significant change of mood in Hor. *Ep.* 2,2,182 *sunt qui non habeant, est qui non curat habere.* Cf. 42,1.

diu noctuque: a variation on the normal phrase, involving an archaism (*diu* cf. Quint. 1,4,29) and the rarer locative *noctu* for *nocte*.

iter properabant: the transitive use of *propero* is mainly poetical. Tacitus uses it quite frequently, cf. 69,2. With these two distinctive phrases, Tacitus ends a very carefully wrought chapter, where the style is clearly designed to emphasise certain aspects of his subject matter.

Chapters 13–17　　Paetus is besieged, and surrenders to the Parthians: meeting of Paetus and Corbulo : Armenia left neutral.

Chapter 13

1. **eoque**: ' and for that reason '. Cf. 28,1 : 40,1.

castellum: see 10,3 and n.

propius . . . quam mos: see 4,3 n.

si . . . eliceret: ' in the hope that he might entice . . . ' This use of *si* and the subjunctive is very common after verbs of waiting and trying. It is also found when (as here) the main clause expresses a general sense of expectation or effort. Cf. Livy 1,7,6 *pergit ad proximam speluncam, si forte eo uestigia ferrent.*

2. **extracti**: supply *sunt. contuberniis* may be abl. (with *ex-*) or dat. (of disadvantage).

nec aliud quam: the ellipse of a verb such as *faciebant* turns this phrase into something resembling an adverb, meaning ' merely ' or ' only '. Cf. *H.* 2,91 *non tamen ultra quam tribunos plebis in auxilium . . . aduocauit.*

pacis: the text of M (*exemplis caudi nenum antineque eandem*) obviously contains a reference to the notorious disasters at Caudium and Numantia, and can easily be reassembled and corrected to *exemplis Caudin(a)e Numantin(a)eque (neque) eandem.* It still then lacks a noun for ' surrender ': *pacis* (cf. Livy 9,7,4 *Caudinaeque pacis*) provides the right sense, and might easily have been lost after the *-plis* of *exemplis.*

In 321 B.C., a Roman army was trapped by the Samnites in the narrow pass of the Caudine Forks, and forced to surrender and to pass beneath the yoke (Livy 9,1–6: see 15,2 n.): at Numantia in NE Spain in 137 B.C., the consul Hostilius Mancinus in panic surrendered his army (Appian, *Hisp.* 80). The soldiers here argue (in indirect speech starting *neque eandem*) that Roman armies have surrendered before, and with less justification. Their argument about the Samnites is not entirely logical, because the Rome who surrendered to the Samnites was not a world power either. But men in such a position are not logicians.

The reluctance of the soldiers to move is mirrored in the long, slow syllables of the start of the sentence: the subdivisions (*pars . . . alii*) and their reasons, are out of balance, with the weight on the second half: the abl. absolute (*prouisis f.*) provides a reason for their behaviour and an introduction to their arguments, which are dramatically presented. The structure is not organic, but it is emphatic and effective.

antiquitatem: abstract for concrete: ' the heroes of old '.

3. **quod f.**: the ' quotation ' of Paetus' words helps to present him as desperate and bombastic.

Romanae dicionis: 'within the jurisdiction of Rome '. The gen. describes the sphere of reference.

orbem terrarum: a Roman naturally equates the Empire with the known world. Cf. *A.* 11,24 *specie deductarum per orbem terrae legionum*.

Chapter 14

1. **nihil pro causa**: ' nothing to do with the case ', ' evasively '. **fratres**: cf. 2,1.

consilio destinatum quid f.: ' had been chosen for deliberation (about) what they should decide '. The clause depends on *consilio* as if on a verb of discussion. Cf. 16,2 *litterae an . . .*

cernerent: for *decernerent*. The use of the simple verb in the meaning of one of its compounds is a conceit of Tacitean style, which he has borrowed from the poets. Brevity and novelty appealed to both. Cf. 44,4 *flammare* for *inflammare*: 63,3 *tenuare* for *extenuare*. This is an especially striking example, because *cerno* = *decerno* is archaic (cf. Sen. *Ep.* 58,3) and is used so only here in Tacitus.

dignum Arsacidarum: ' a thing worthy of the Arsacidae '. The neuter adjective is used as a noun. Cf. 34,1 *triste . . . prouidum*. The gen. (of reference) with *dignus* is rare in Latin, archaic (Plaut. *Trin.* 1153) and poetical (Virg. *Aen.* 12,649), and used only here by Tacitus.

ut: the clause explains *dignum*, ' namely that they should . . . '

2. **Lucullos Pompeios**: generalising plurals, for rhetorical effect. They sound impressive but do not commit the speaker to stating who the ' men like Lucullus and Pompey ' (Introd. 4) might be.

et si qua: ' and anything which '. The *si* clause of indefinite frequency is often so used to sum up a series. *qua* is an old form of the neuter plural of the pronoun, which persists in certain phrases. For the activities of the various emperors, see Introd. 4.

imaginem: Tacitus is fond of contrasting essential power with its phantom. Cf. *A.* 3,60 *Tiberius, uim principatus sibi firmans, imaginem antiquitatis senatui praebebat*: 15,1.

3. **multum . . . disceptato**: 'after a good deal of discussion'. *multum* is adverbial acc., and *disceptato* an impersonal abl. abs.

Monobazus: see 1,3 n.

pepigissent: 'to witness such things as they had (by then) agreed'. The subjunctive is generic (12,4 n.), and part of his purpose.

perpetratis: an impressive verb, used again in 72,1 to sum up the treatment of the Pisonian conspirators. It ironically points the 'privilege' accorded to Vologeses.

fieret: expresses an indirect command, one of the provisions of the agreement.

Chapter 15

1. **flumini Arsaniae**: from the geographical details available (see 10,3 n.), this is probably the River Murat, a major branch of the northern Euphrates.

praefluebat: 'flowed past' =*praeterfluebat*. The poets and post-Augustan writers tended thus to substitute the shorter form. Cf. Hor. *Od.* 4,14,26: Livy 44,31,3.

imposuit: the subject is Paetus, as is clear from the rest of the sentence.

specie . . . sed: appearance and reality again (cf. 14,2 n.). The main clause further emphasises the reality.

illud iter: the retreat just agreed on (14,3).

quasi: here, as often in Tacitus, it gives the real and not a supposed reason. Cf. 33,2: 50,3: 58,1: 65: 71,2.

per diuersum: 'differently' i.e. 'by a different route'. See 2,3 n.

It is possible to deduce (from §3 and from 9,2) that the Parthians advanced from the south, and that the camp therefore stood on the north bank of the river. This is confirmed by Dio's account (62,21,4). If the Romans did not use the bridge, they must have retreated westwards along the north bank of the river.

2. **rumor**: that such a report existed is confirmed by Suetonius (*Nero* 39), who reports it as fact. Dio does not mention it, and Tacitus clearly does not credit it, but uses it to intensify the disgrace to Roman arms.

sub iugum missas: the 'yoke' was (Livy 3,28,11) an arrangement of spears to form an archway, under which defeated and disarmed troops were sometimes forced to stoop, in formal display of submission.

alia f.: 'other things resulting from disgrace, of which a semblance was employed by the Armenians'. The Armenians, i.e., subjected the defeated troops to something like the indignities sometimes formally inflicted on defeated armies. *simulacrum =simile aliquid* is odd, but cf.

Plaut. *Most.* 89 *hominem quoius rei . . . similem esse arbitrarer simulacrumque habere.*

captiua: = *capta*, ' previously captured ' (by the Romans). The usage is poetical in origin.

3. **caesorum**: those killed in the original siege, presumably (11,1).

fugientium: its inappropriateness to *legionum* is emphasised by its position.

fama f.: a cynical comment, pointed by the structure, with variation of tense, case and main/subordinate clause. The pluperfect with *postquam* implies not only temporal precedence, but a logical relationship – it was necessary for his pride to be satisfied before he could start thinking about moderation. Cf. 20,2.

proximus quisque regem: ' the king's staff '. The use of the acc. with *proximus* (on the analogy of *prope*) seems to be an archaism (cf. Plaut. *Poen.* 1120) which is employed mainly by the historians. Cf. Caesar *B.G.* 1,54,1 : Sallust *Jug.* 49,6: Livy 28,15,9.

ualidum et fidum: this seems to show a pride in Roman workmanship and honour, even in such circumstances.

Chapter 16

1. **constitit**: on Tacitus' use of sources, see Introd. 1.

prodiderit: the subjunctive appears to be a kind of virtual oblique, produced by a confused association with *constitit.* Cf. 46,1 n. on *adesset.*

Tacitus is clearly using, directly or indirectly, Corbulo's own account of the Armenian campaign (cf. Pliny *N.H.* 2,180: 5,83: 6,23). His attitude to the memoirs (§3) suggests direct acquaintance with them. Cf. Introd. 1.

pabulo: in view of *attrito* (' rubbed away '), *pabulum* here probably means ' foraging ground ' rather than ' forage '. Cf. *A.* 6,34 *infensare pabula.*

relicturos: *fuisse*, which is to be supplied, is not, for reasons of clarity, often omitted. Here, the following *afuisse* resolves ambiguity and makes omission possible.

2. **cautum**: supply *esse.* ' Security was given '.

apud signa: the ' chapel ' housing the legion's standards was the most sacred place in any camp. Cf. 24,2: *A.* 1,39.

testificando: dat. of purpose (4,1 n.). The gerund is much rarer than the gerundive construction, but cf. Cic. *Fam.* 15,6,2 *scribendo adfuisti.*

neminem Romanum: Dio (62,21,2) says that Paetus also swore that Nero would give Armenia to Tiridates. It seems a rash undertaking, even for Paetus, and Tacitus' version is more likely to be correct.

an: from its use with expressions of doubt (*haud scio an* etc.), it is extended to other expressions of similar meaning. Cf. 20,1 *in sua potestate sita an* . . .

adnueret: the verb ('to nod assent to' and so 'to agree to') is used mainly by the poets and historians, and has a certain solemn quality, because of its frequent use of the gods. Cf. Livy 31,5,7 *precationi adnuisse deos*.

3. **ut** . . . **sic**: a comparison comes close to a contrast, and these adverbs often carry a meaning something like 'though . . . yet' or 'granted . . . but'. Tacitus sees the possibility of bias in his source, but also its value.

quadraginta milium: that is, double the normal marching rate (Veg. 1,9).

4. **apud ripam**: probably near Melitene.

insignium: the *insignia* were the awards (like our medals) given to soldiers and officers for individual acts of bravery or at the close of a campaign. They consisted of, e.g., crowns, necklets, armlets and silver spear-shafts (cf. *ILS* 2648: Pliny *N.H.* 7,102). They were (like medals) normally worn on dress parades and special occasions. A meeting of legions would normally be such an occasion, but not in these circumstances.

consalutatio: the mutual formal greeting. Cf. *H.* 4,72 *nulla inter coeuntes . . . consalutatio*.

Tacitus' presentation of the dramatic meeting is interesting. Corbulo is correct, but negative: the soldiers' sadness is reflected by alliterative, moaning m's: pathos is produced by a general reflection: and the sting in the tail is characteristically Tacitean.

Chapter 17

1. **hoc**: Corbulo. He has been most recently mentioned, and is the focus of interest at this point of the narrative.

laborem: his campaign of the previous year, which had 'subdued' Armenia.

integra . . . cuncta: 'all was whole' i.e. 'nothing was yet lost'.

2. **non** . . . **Corbulo**: the negative, and the man pronouncing it, bracket the sentence, with his authority enclosed between them. The verb (of saying) is to be supplied from the context: see 51,3 n.

periculo . . . egressum: only the danger to Roman legions had drawn him from the province which it was his first duty to defend. The statement is rhetorical, but demonstrates the basic judgement which Paetus so clearly lacked.

in incerto: see 2,3 n. and 12,1 n.

pedes: his own forces, who had marched day and night (12,4) to rescue Paetus.

3. **detraheret:** vivid indirect command (11,3n.).

castella: the *munimenta Euphrati imposita* (9,1 and 12,1).

concessit rex: Vologeses clearly realised that Corbulo was a very different proposition from Paetus, and that compromise would be necessary.

ultra: for the word order, see 1,3n.

sine arbitro: ' without a controller ' and so ' without interference '.

Chapters 18–22   Senatorial business in Rome: speech of Thrasea about Votes of Thanks to provincial governors.

Chapter 18

1. **at Romae:** this marks the transition from one block of narrative to another. The strong adversative, indicating contrast, is immediately followed by a word identifying the new topic. Cf. 26,1 *at Corbulo.*

tropaea: the word is Greek, and so is the custom of setting up a pile of captured arms as a mark of victory. Such a trophy was usually erected on the spot (cf. *A.* 2,18), and was never so popular among the Romans as other forms of memorial, such as the triumphal arch next mentioned.

arcus: this particular arch has vanished, but many examples remain, in Rome and elsewhere, of this peculiarly Roman type of monument. The Arch of Titus, e.g., commemorating the victory of A.D. 70 in the Jewish War, still spans the Via Sacra at the other end of the Forum: and at least three can be seen at Pompeii.

neque tum omissa f.: is this unreasonable criticism? Did the Romans know what was happening, before the spring of 63 (24,1: 25,1)? What is the meaning of *tum*? They were acting on the insufficient evidence of Paetus' despatch: but they had at this point no positively contradictory information.

2. **dissimulandis . . . curis:** motive is confidently attributed to Nero: is there any real connection with Armenia?

frumentum plebis: Rome's basic food was corn, and most of it had to be imported. It was therefore expensive, and its arrival was also likely to be impeded by storm, pirates or war. A regular dole of cheap or free corn was allotted to the urban populace, and all emperors concerned themselves with its supply.

securitatem . . . sustentaret: his aim was to ' maintain a feeling of security with reference to the corn supply ': his action indicated that there were sufficient stocks to stand the loss.

pretio: the corn in question was therefore subsidised, and not free.

portu in ipso: in Ostia, where Claudius had recently established a great new harbour.

3. **L. Pisonem f.**: Piso had been consul with Nero in A.D. 57 (*A.* 13, 31): the year of Geminus' consulship is unknown: Paulinus was probably the brother of Seneca's wife (60,4), and legate of Upper Germany in A.D. 56 (*A.* 13,53). A commission of this kind, to investigate public expenditure, had been established by Augustus (Dio 55,25,6) in A.D. 6, and another was set up by Vespasian in 70 (*H.* 4,40).

uectigalibus publicis: *uectigalia* are, strictly speaking, the indirect taxes – harbour dues, death duties etc. But the context suggests strongly that it here means all income from taxation which supplied the funds of the state treasury. This *aerarium publicum* originally received all public revenues: but with the growth of the Empire, there developed another treasury, the *fiscus*, which probably dealt with the emperor's public as well as private income and expenditure. The *tributum* (land and property tax) from the senatorial provinces still went to the *aerarium*, and seems to be included in the income mentioned here.

antissent: they had spent more than they could reasonably expect to get in. The subjunct. is virtual oblique, representing Nero's charge, which is a standard one to make against one's predecessors.

sexcenties sestertium: *sestertius* is one sesterce: large sums were expressed in units of 100,000 – *centena milia sestertium* (gen. pl.) – multiplied by the relevant adverb e.g. *sexcenties*. Because the phrase was so standard, *centena milia* was often omitted, and *sestertium* then declined as a neuter singular noun, meaning 100,000 sesterces. So the whole phrase, adverb with *sestertium*, can stand as the object of a verb (cf. *A.* 1,75 *decies sestertium largitus est*), and even have (as here) an adjective agreeing with it. The sum is 60,000,000: its size may be judged from the fact that Cicero thought (*Att.* 16,1) 80,000 sesterces a generous annual allowance for his student son in Athens, and that (Juv. 9,140) 20,000 sesterces could be considered a barely possible annual ' retirement pension '.

se . . . largiri: Nero's precise meaning is not clear. It could mean either that he gave money to support the Treasury from his privy purse, as Augustus claims to have done on four occasions (*RG* 17): but this would hardly be an annual grant. Or it could mean that he paid from the *fiscus* (see above) expenses which would normally be borne by the *aerarium*.

Chapter 19

1. **propinquis comitiis**: ' as the elections approached, or the lot-drawing for the provinces '. The governorships of the senatorial provinces were allocated by lot to the ex-praetors and ex-consuls who each year became eligible for such offices.

orbi: childless men. The century of civil war and disorder which preceded the Principate had destroyed many potential fathers of families,

and discouraged others from having children: while many wealthy childless men enjoyed the attentions of those who hoped for legacies, and had
no .wish to discourage such attentions by producing legal heirs. These
factors combined to produce a rapid decline in the birthrate of Roman
citizens, and the position was aggravated by the ' dilution ' of society by
numbers of manumitted slaves. Augustus tried to deal with the problem
by a series of laws, which culminated in the *Lex Papia Poppaea* of A.D. 9.
These measures encouraged marriage and the production of children
by offering privileges – e.g., a man could stand for office as many years
before the legal age as he had children, and, if votes for two candidates
were equal, preference was given to the father of the larger family: they
also imposed sanctions on the unmarried and childless – e.g., by prevent-
ing them from receiving legacies except from blood relations, and sometimes permitting only a proportion of these.

Such enactments were still in force, and the *orbi* are here represented
as trying to have it both ways. To avoid the expense and trouble of rear-
ing children, to keep their following of flattering legacy hunters, and at
the same time to have a good chance of election to office, they evolved
the scheme of legal but temporary adoption.

fictis: they were a legal fiction. They would be disavowed after
election day.

praeturas . . . sortiti: the praetors were elected to office, but the
particular offices held during the year (*praetor urbanus, praetor peregrinus*
etc.) were allocated by lot. Even in the drawing of lots, fathers of families
had a privileged position (Dio 53,13,2).

The praetorship is mentioned, not only for its alliterative value with
prouincias, but because it was the highest office for which there was still
real competition. The consulship was now, for all practical purposes, in
the gift of the emperor.

inter patres: ' as (genuine) fathers of families '.

emitterent manu: a variation on the usual phrase (*manu mittere*),
and an archaism. Cf. Plaut. *Asin.* 411. It appears occasionally in the
historians from Livy on.

2. **magna cum inuidia:** ' with great indignation '. The people
expressing it are clearly the genuine fathers, but there is something
missing from the text.

fraudem et artes: ' fraudulent artifice ', contrasted with *ius naturae.*
The phrase is a hendiadys, which co-ordinates aspects of a statement,
instead of subordinating one to another (cf. *ui et armis* for *ui armorum*).

satis pretii esse: their complaint continues in indirect speech and
works to a climax.

honores: it can hardly in the context mean ' office ', but rather
' marks of respect ' cf. *A.* 1,14 *feminarum honores.*

quando quis: *quis*, the indefinite pronoun, is used not only ' after *si*, *nisi*, *ne* and *num* ', but also in certain relative and temporal expressions, where a conditional meaning is also present. Cf. *A.* 1,2 *quanto quis seruitio promptior*: and see 38,2 n.

sine sollicitudine . . . sine luctu: he became a parent by one set of legal proceedings, and ' lost ' his son by another.

3. **simulata**: genuine adoption obviously (and reasonably) did count. It did not increase the birth rate, but it provided for the up-bringing and education of future citizens, and it involved the expenses and responsibilities of parenthood.

Chapter 20

1. **exim**: this kind of arrangement, where one piece of senatorial business follows immediately on another, is one of the reasons why Tacitus is thought to have used the senatorial archives. See 74,3 n. and Introd. 1.

reus agitur: he was probably arraigned before the Senate, because Crete (with Cyrene) was a senatorial province (*A.* 3,38).

ceteris criminibus: the charges were the usual ones involving extortion, but this man had also insulted the Senate.

penetrauerat: ' had gone so far as to . . . '

dictitasset: subjunct. of the charge, virtual oblique. Tacitus some-times (10,2 n.) uses the frequentative verb as an emphatic form, but here it is probably literal: ' because, it was alleged, he had frequently stated . . .

an: see 16,2 n.

grates: a formal ' token of esteem and regard ', it was voted by the local assembly and spoken by a delegate, in the Senate (22,1): such statements on record could be useful to an ex-governor having to account for his term of office. It is a practice obviously open to abuse, from both sides: but it was a practice of long standing (cf. Cic. *Verr.* 2,2,13), and, in spite of Nero's action (22,1), it was still going on in the time of Trajan (Pliny *Paneg.* 70,8) and even later.

2. **Paetus Thrasea**: P. Clodius Thrasea Paetus was a notable Stoic and a notable Roman, in the tradition of Cato and Brutus. He was a native of Padua (*A.* 16,21), had a distinguished public career, being consul in A.D. 56, and his personal integrity and his regard for the dignity of the Senate brought him into conflict with Nero, by whom he was eventually condemned and forced to suicide. The story of his end forms the closing chapters of the extant portion of the *Annals* (*A.* 16,34–5). Tacitus obviously admires his character and his opinions, though he sometimes criticises his opposition as useless.

Reversal of names is sometimes found in Cicero, usually when (as here) the *praenomen* is omitted. But Tacitus often uses it, apparently arbitrarily and for variety of style.

censuerat: for the tense, see 15,3 n. He had to record his verdict first.

3. **haec addidit**: this is the longest direct speech in *A.* 15, and the only one of any length in it. It may or may not be based on a speech actually delivered, but it is certainly part of the pattern of history which Tacitus is presenting. The sentiments are those of a ' noble Roman ', the language has overtones of Cato and Sallust (see Martin in Dorey, 140) and both sentiments and speaker are meant to be noticed.

Cinciam rogationem: the *Lex Cincia de donis et muneribus* of 204 B.C. forbade payment to legal advocates, probably from a desire to stop sharp practice by men whose fees might depend on their winning a case.

Iulias leges: the *Leges Iuliae de ambitu*, of 18 B.C. and 8 B.C., excluded from office for five years any man convicted of bribery (of juries or electors), and required a candidate for office to deposit money as surety against corrupt practice.

Calpurnia scita: the *Lex Calpurnia* of 149 B.C. first established a permanent court to try cases of extortion.

All these measures were laws passed in the same way, and the variation in description is for stylistic variety and emphasis. Cf. the various words for temple in 41,1.

4. **fide constantiaque**: *fides* is what causes them to look after the provincials' welfare (*quo . . . derogetur*), *constantia* is their own self-respect which requires them to reject the idea (*nobis . . . decedat*) that anyone's opinion of their actions is of value, except a Roman's. So simplified, the statement sounds crude, and it is indeed the sentiment of a ruling nation. But it has a certain dignity, and it is aimed, not at the Cretan assembly, but at men like Claudius Timarchus who manipulated it for their own ends.

Chapter 21

1. **priuati**: a reference to the practice of *libera legatio*, whereby a senator visiting a province on private business was given the status of *legatus*, and would in return report on anything of interest to the government. Cf. Cic. *Fam.* 12,21 *negotiorum suorum causa legatus est in Africam legatione libera.*

Thrasea is exaggerating: such men were not officially ' sent ', and the practice was open to abuse (Cic. *Leg.* 3,18).

accusatio: charges (usually of extortion) could be brought by provincials against a Roman governor. Such charges were not in fact so frequent or so necessary as they had been under the Republic.

2. **ostentandi**: see 5,3 n.

3. **plura f.**: 'more harm is often done by obliging than in giving offence'.

immo: its unusual position in second place draws attention to the context.

4. **inde**: 'this means that . . .'

arceantur . . . regentur: the indicative emphasises the certainty of the main clause happening if the hypothesis stands. 'If such abuses could be checked . . . then (inevitably) provincial government will improve.'

aequabilius atque constantius: an echo of Sall. *Cat.* 2,3, which helps to invoke the 'old order'.

repetundarum: the phrase is so standard that *quaestionis* can be omitted. What restrains greed is not fear of extortion, but fear of prosecution for extortion.

Chapter 22

1. **abnuentibus . . . relatum**: the question before the House was (20,1) whether Claudius Timarchus was guilty or not. It was possible for a speaker *egredi relationem* (*A.* 2,38) and alter the question: but before an amendment could become a substantive motion, it had to be put by the consuls, and it would be a rash move for them to do so before discovering the Emperor's views: it would be particularly rash when the proposer of the amendment was Thrasea.

auctore principe: the Emperor in fact approved, and sponsored the motion himself, thus ensuring its safe passage.

concilium sociorum: in each province, the altar to Rome and Augustus provided an official cult centre, and its service provided an occasion for assembly. The *concilium* met, usually, once each year, and after the rites discussed any business that concerned the province. Any formal expressions of thanks would be voted here, and conveyed by a delegation to the Senate. See 20,1 n.

pro praetoribus proue consulibus: this covers all provincial governors. The imperial provinces were governed by *legati Augusti pro praetore*, and all governors of senatorial provinces were normally styled proconsuls, although only these holding Africa and Asia were of consular rank.

2. **isdem consulibus**: Tacitus often ends his account of a year's history with such a collection of oddments (cf. 32: 46–7). They comprise events worth mentioning, but not to the extent of interrupting a connected narrative. It is possible that some official record (? the *acta senatus*) did the same, and that Tacitus takes his material from there.

gymnasium: this was built and dedicated by Nero in A.D. 61

(*A.* 14,47) for the Neronian Games, and as part of his campaign to encourage Greek institutions. Its short existence, and the fate of the statue, are recorded without comment: but the record serves much the same purpose as a list of portents (7,1 n.).

motu terrae . . . Pompei: a forerunner of the great eruption of A.D. 79. Seneca (*Quaest. Nat.* 6,1,2) places this earlier eruption not in 62 but in 63, specifically *nonis Februariis . . . Regulo et Verginio consulibus* (see 23,1). Scholars are still disputing whether the professional historian or the contemporary writer should be believed, and whether the date in Seneca is an interpolation.

uirgo Vestalis: the Vestals were six in number, and replacements were made only when one retired after the statutory thirty years' service, or (as here) died. They were therefore sufficiently infrequent to warrant mention.

capta est: the candidates for a vacancy, girls between the ages of six and twelve, were offered by their families and selected by the Pontifex Maximus with the formula *te, Amata, capio.*

Chapter 23   A daughter is born to Poppaea and Nero, but dies. Various signs of the feelings of people, senate and emperor.

Chapter 23

1. **Memmio Regulo et Verginio Rufo consulibus:** the year is A.D. 63. Memmius Regulus was the son of a more famous father (*A.* 14, 47); Verginius Rufus, as legate of Germany, crushed the rising of Vindex (74,2 n.), but refused to be hailed emperor in Nero's place. He served both Galba and Otho in 69, held the consulship again in 97 and died soon afterwards. Pliny (*Ep.* 2,1) describes his state funeral, where the oration was pronounced *a consule Cornelio Tacito.*

Poppaea: Poppaea Sabina, Nero's second wife (he was her third husband), whose character and personality are described by Tacitus at *A.* 13,45 (*huic mulieri cuncta alia fuere praeter honestum animum*), seems to have been in many ways a fit mate for him, and it appears that, although Nero was responsible for her death (*A.* 16,6), there was genuine affection between them. To what extent she really influenced Nero's actions, remains doubtful.

ultra mortale gaudium: Nero's ' emotional threshold ' seems at all times to have been remarkably low.

Augustam: her name was Claudia Augusta (Smallwood 24). The title was first formally conferred, on Livia, by Augustus' will (*A.* 1,8): it was first given to the wife of a living emperor, by Claudius to Agrippina (*A.* 12,26): now for the first time it is granted to an imperial infant.

Antium: the modern Anzio, on the coast of Latium, about twenty miles south of Ostia.

2. **senatus . . . commendauerat**: parts of the relevant Act of the Arval Brethren are still extant (Smallwood 24).

supplicationes: a *supplicatio* was a general adoration of the gods' statues, either in thanksgiving or intercession – a kind of national day of prayer. Cf. Livy 26,21,3.

Actiacae religionis: to celebrate his victory at Actium, Augustus founded Nicopolis (Victoryville) near by, and there instituted quinquennial games (Suet. *Aug.* 18). Augustus kept the Greek games in a Greek setting, but Nero is anxious to encourage Greek practices in Italy.

utque: the change of construction adds variety and emphasis.

Fortunarum effigies: there were various cults of Fortune, but only at Antium were plural deities worshipped. Cf. Suet. *Gaius* 57 *Fortunae Antiatinae*.

Capitolini Iouis: Jupiter Optimus Maximus Capitolinus was the great god of the Roman state, so the association is significant.

circense: chariot racing in the circus was a form of entertainment popular among Romans. For an amusing account of attendance at the Races, see Ovid, *Amores* 3,2.

apud Bouillas: a town on the Appian Way, near the Alban Lake. It was founded from Alba Longa, itself traditionally founded by Iulus, son of Aeneas and legendary founder of the *gens Iulia*, to which Julius Caesar and Augustus belonged. For *apud* see 51,2 n.

Claudiae Domitiaeque: both were old Roman *gentes*, and both appeared in Nero's ancestry. See the genealogical table, p. xviii.

3. **quae fluxa fuere**: the preceding accumulation of extravagant honours helps to emphasise the anti-climax, and to characterise Nero.

diuae: formal deification was usually awarded only to dead emperors, and not always to them. See 74,3 n.

puluinar: ' a couch '. This meant that her image would be produced at a *lectisternium* (see 44,1 n.), when a banquet was spread before the gods' images.

laetitiae . . . maeroris: the genitive indicates the sphere of reference of the adjective.

4. **Antium . . . effuso**: it had become customary for the Senate so to indicate respect.

ferunt: whatever Tacitus' source, it is clear that he quotes the story to illustrate economically the personalities of three of his chief characters, and to underline a point about the possible dangers of speaking freely.

Senecam: L. Annaeus Seneca, younger of that name, the great exponent of Roman Stoicism, was recalled from exile by Agrippina to be the young Nero's tutor (*A.* 12,8), and had been his chief minister during the early years of his reign. He was currently in semi-retirement (*A.* 14,56), and his association here with Thrasea is ominous.

Chapters 24–7   Parthian envoys reach Rome, and reveal the true situation in Armenia: Corbulo is appointed to a special command, and invades Armenia.

Chapter 24

1. **legati Parthorum**: see 14,3 and 16,2.

in eandem formam: ' on the same lines ', an adverbial phrase (cf. *in hunc modum*), formed on the same principle as those discussed in 2,3 n.

omittere: it is sound rhetorical policy, as Cicero frequently demonstrates (e.g. *Flacc.* 79), to list the topics that one is not going to discuss. This gives an impression of restraint, neatly reminds the listener or reader of the relevant points, and avoids argument about their validity.

potentium populorum ... possessionem Parthis: the alliteration adds force to the unwelcome news. Note that Vologeses does not say that the Parthians have withdrawn (17,3).

ignominia Romana: an echo of a phrase in Livy's account (9,15,10) of the Caudine Forks disaster, already (13,2) linked with this one.

2. **nuper f.**: the events are very summarily reported here, because they have already been fully described in the narrative.

recusaturum: the omission of *esse* or *fuisse* leaves the statement more open.

sacerdotii religione: he was (Pliny *N.H.* 30,16-17) a Magian, who considered that the sea was polluted by human *effluuia*, and would not contribute to the pollution by travelling on the water. When he did eventually come to Rome, he crossed the sea only at the Hellespont, and travelled from there by the long land route: but he appears to have returned by Brundisium–Dyrrhachium (Dio 63,7,1). His religious scruples could clearly be overcome, which suggests that Vologeses is here trying to see how far he can go.

signa et effigies principis: with the standards was kept the *imago* of the Emperor (*Veg.* 2,7), and all were kept in the ' regimental chapel ' (16,2 n.). Such token homage would probably have satisfied Nero, but not the populace.

Chapter 25

1. **scribebat**: ' was still writing ', implying more dispatches than the ones mentioned in 8,2.

2. **barbarum**: this is the old form of the gen. plural (cf. 72,1 *nummum*).

inrisu: the Romans did not like being laughed at, but they had the wit to see an opening for diplomacy, and their treatment of the *legati* (§3) shows that they used it.

peterent: causal relative, ' since they were asking . . . '

inter primores ciuitatis: from the time of Augustus on, a number of leading men in Rome formed the semi-official body known as the *amici principis*, from which the Emperor could draw a *consilium* of advisers, or a retinue for court or travel. The body had no constitutional standing, but had its own formality: its members belonged to the *prima* or *secunda admissio* (to the morning reception), and used *amicus principis* and *ex prima admissione* as titles on inscriptions. See J. Crook, *Consilium Principis*, ch. III.

3. **executio**: ' executive authority ' over Syria: he took over the civil administration of the province, to free its governor Corbulo for military operations.

C. Cestio: an emendation, but a fairly certain one. The MSS *Citio* is not a known Roman name, and lacks the *praenomen* or *cognomen* which usually identifies a character on first appearance. C. Cestius Gallus was legate of Syria two years later (Josephus, *B.I.* 1,20).

quinta decima legio: XV Apollinaris (see 6,3 n.), was one of the standing legions of Pannonia (*A.* 1,23). Its legate Marius Celsus later played an important part in the civil wars of A.D. 69 (*H.* 1 & 2), and may have written about his eastern service.

scribitur tetrarchis f.: the instructions were sent to all governors and rulers, of every rank, of all countries bordering on Armenia. They are presented in rising order of importance, to emphasise the extent of Corbulo's command. *tetrarchus*, originally a ruler of one fourth of a country, now generally describes the ruler of a small eastern state: the kings are client kings: *praefecti* probably indicates the military commanders of small provinces or districts: procurators govern small provinces, often those with temporary provincial status, see 44,3: praetors govern larger and more important provinces.

obsequi: *scribitur* = ' written instructions were sent ' and is therefore followed by the construction of a verb of ordering. Cf. *A.* 12,29 *scripsit . . . componere*. Cicero uses it with *ut* and the subjunct., cf. *Att.* 13,45,1.

in tantum ferme modum: his authority was, technically, greater than Pompey's. What the Lex Gabinia of 67 B.C. conferred on Pompey was *imperium aequum . . . cum proconsulibus* (Vell. 2,31,1), what Corbulo had was clearly *imperium maius*. But although Pompey later had a kind of *imperium maius* (Cic. *Att.* 4,1,7), it was his original and unprecedented commission to clear the sea of pirates which in its range and location provides a parallel with Corbulo's appointment here.

4. **his ferme uerbis**: Nero's deflationary rebuke to Paetus is given extra point by the structure (which reserves the barb to the end), by the

alliterative description of Paetus, and by the final verb *aegresco*, which is poetic in origin (cf. Lucr. 3,521 : Virg. *Aen.* 12,46) and appears only here in Tacitus.

Chapter 26

1. **quarta et duodecima**: two of Paetus' legions (6,3), with which he had invaded Armenia (7,1) and been blockaded (10,1).

parum habiles proelio: ' unfit for active service '. *parum* (lit. ' too little ') is often employed by Tacitus and others as a strong negative: cf. 55,3.

sextam ... ac tertiam: see 6,3 n.

in Armeniam: ' towards Armenia '. Invasion proper starts with the crossing of Euphrates.

2. **quintam**: see 6,3 and 9,3.

quintadecimanos: cf. 25,3. This brought the total of legions to seven (see 6,3 n.): as X is not mentioned, we may assume that it was left in Syria as a defensive force.

uexilla: the *uexillum*, a banner-like standard, was usually the standard of a unit smaller than a legion (e.g. cavalry *H.* 3,17: veterans *A.* 1,17). Here, as in *A.* 1,38, it indicates a section detailed for special service.

Illyrico: the district corresponds roughly to Jugoslavia and Hungary.

quodque: supply *erat*: ' and what there was of auxiliary cavalry and infantry ' lit. i.e. ' all the auxiliary forces that he had '.

auxilia regum: local forces of the client kings, as distinct from the *alae* and *cohortes*, who are part of the regular Roman army.

Notice the skill with which Tacitus avoids a catalogue of forces, by varying cases, constructions and vocabulary. The necessary information is presented in an acceptable literary form.

Melitenen: Melitene was one of the major crossings of the Euphrates (see Introd. 4), and almost certainly the place where Paetus crossed in the previous year (7,2).

3. **lustratum**: purificatory sacrifice was normal at the start of a campaign. Cf. *A.* 6,37.

magnifica: Corbulo has already been described (*A.* 13,8) as a man *uerbis magnificis*.

auspiciis imperatoris: all imperial armies fought under the Emperor's auspices.

aduersa ... declinans: ' imputing reverses to . . . ' The phrase is apparently borrowed from Sallust (*Hist.* 2,30D), and the echo adds authority and tradition to the passage.

auctoritate ... pro facundia: most generals were not trained orators, and so not technically *facundi* – cf. *H.* 4,73. But a natural gift for eloquence is possible, and Tacitus recognises it in Corbulo. His remarks sound like the comments of one who has actually read the speech: it is possible that Corbulo incorporated it in his memoirs (16,1 n.).

Chapter 27

1. **L. Lucullo**: this refers to his campaign of 69 B.C. (Introd. 4).

apertis: technically, *eis* is supplied from the relative clause which follows: in practical terms, the clause replaces the noun of the ablative absolute, ' opening what the passage of time had blocked '. Lucullus would have done a certain amount of road-making *en route*, but the roads had not been maintained.

pergit: all the narrative in this chapter is presented in vivid historic present (1,2 n.) or rapid historic infinitive (11,3 n.).

nec enim f.: the indirect speech, set at the heart of a vigorous narrative, presents the reasoned case for negotiation, and does so with greater force because the presentation is made in the form of a message from one important character to another.

2. **documento**: ' to serve as a warning ', predicative dat. Such a comment on the content of a clause is more often provided by an acc. in apposition to it, which expresses the goal of the action stated by the clause (cf. 39,2 *solacium*). For the dat., cf. *A.* 12,14 *uiuere iubet, ostentui clementiae suae et in nos dehonestamento*.

scire: the subject is Corbulo. He is the speaker, and the argument is that *he* knows the weakness of the Parthian position.

intus: for its adjectival use, see 4,3 n.

3. **adicere**: historic infin. With *simul* we return to narrative.

megistanas: an exotic word, coming from Persian *mehestàn* through Hellenistic Greek (cf. S. Mark 6,21) to Latin. Tacitus uses it only here, and it is part of his pattern of powerful narrative, which is working towards the climax of ch. 29. As the sentence progresses, the tempo increases: connections are dropped, clauses are shorter, and the double polar expression (37,4 n.) vividly conveys the idea of ' everyone everywhere ': the rhythm and meaning of the final words reinforce the terror which Corbulo inspired.

Chapters 28–31   A settlement is finally reached between Rome and Parthia: after ceremonies and celebrations, Romans and Parthians go their separate ways.

Chapter 28

1. **fidum**: its use of things is poetical and post-Augustan. Cf. *A.* 1,52 *fida oratione*.

praefecturis: Armenia was (Pliny *N.H.* 6,27) divided into one hundred and twenty such districts. Vologeses' concern is for those Corbulo has been ravaging (27,3).

2. **locus:** the place chosen was Rhandeia (10,3 n.).

ut . . . augeret: Dio (62,23,2) says that Corbulo wanted to wipe out the disgrace of a Roman defeat there. Tacitus' explanation chimes with his other remarks about Corbulo (3,1 and 10,4). The development of the theme in the next sentence suggests careful consideration of evidence.

ducere . . . operire: the poets had always (since Terence, e.g. *And.* 842) shown examples of the shorter infinitive construction with *impero*, and Sallust and the post-Augustan writers follow their practice. Cf. *A.* 2,25 *ire . . . imperat.*

3. **Tiberius Alexander:** this man was later to play a considerable part in Roman imperial history. He was an Alexandrian Jew, who under Claudius was procurator of Judaea (Jos. *Ant.* 20,100). From A.D. 67 to 70 he was Prefect of Egypt, which was the top job for an *eques* in public administration. He renounced Judaism, helped Vespasian to become emperor, and assisted Titus in the Jewish War. He may have been, finally, Praetorian Prefect in Rome. See E. G. Turner in *JRS* 1954, 54–64.

minister bello datus: ' who had been seconded as a military administrator '. He was not a soldier, but attached to deal with e.g. supplies and finance: a Q post, in effect.

Vinicianus Annius: he probably held his appointment at an early age precisely because he was Corbulo's son-in-law. His father (Dio 60,15), brother (56,4) and he himself (Suet. *Nero* 36,1) were all concerned in conspiracies against emperors, which may have helped to make Nero suspicious of Corbulo (1,1 n.).

senatoria aetate: he was not yet twenty-five, the minimum legal age at which a man could hold the quaestorship, and so enter the Senate.

pro legato: he could not officially, as a non-senator, command a legion.

tali pignore: the presence of two such obviously important men was a guarantee of Corbulo's good faith.

rex: Tiridates, as is clear from §1 and 29,1.

dexteras miscuere: the novel verb (in place of the normal *iunxere*) draws attention to the handshake, not (Jos. *Ant.* 18,328) to people like the Parthians simply a polite gesture, but an important mark of accord.

Chapter 29

1. **iturum quippe Romam:** we do not, unfortunately, have Tacitus' account of this visit in A.D. 66. It is referred to as imminent in

A. 16,23–4, but the last extant chapters of the book deal with the death of Thrasea. See Dio 63, 1–7.

non aduersis . . . supplicem: normally, Arsacids were seen in Rome only when in exile from their own kingdoms.

insigne regium: his *diadema* (2,4 and §3 below).

2. **magna utrimque specie**: for the use of *utrimque* as an adjective, see 4,3 n. On such an occasion each side would try to outdo the other: and each displayed its particular strength and glory – Parthian cavalry and Roman legions.

fulgentibus: the eagles of this period were of gold or silver-gilt (Dio 40,18), and the *signa* (11,3 n.) were silver. They consisted of, e.g., zodiac signs (of founder or commander), suitable deities (e.g. Mars) or discs indicating identity or battle honours. See Webster, 137–9. Note the greater detail devoted to the Roman standards.

sedem curulem: the *sella curulis*, an ivory folding stool, was the official mark of high office at Rome.

3. **diadema**: this central and symbolic word is bracketed by the two halves of Tiridates' action, arranged in a kind of chiasmus, with the emphasis on the second half.

magnis . . . motibus: the prospect of a peaceful settlement after such prolonged warfare produced an atmosphere charged with emotion.

insita . . . oculis: what they had seen of the camp was in effect implanted in their eyes and in their mind.

exercituum: probably the plural = legions. Cf. *A.* 1,52 *apud Pannonicos exercitus*.

uersos: supply *esse*. This represents the thoughts of the legions.

ostentui: ' for an exhibition ' i.e. ' and so demonstrate to the world ... '

quanto minus quam: we should say ' how little short of '.

Chapter 30

1. **rogitante . . . adfecit**: we might have expected *rogitantem*. This loose style of composition is (in spite of the grammar books) quite familiar at all periods of Latin literature, and is found even in a careful writer like Caesar (e.g., *B.G.* 7,4,1 *conuocatis suis clientibus facile incendit*). It can be simply a change of construction, but its effect is often to make the abl. phrase more emphatic by detaching it, and this effect is not necessarily accidental. Cf. 51,1.

ut: ' as, for example ... '

initia uigiliarum: the night was divided into four watches, the leading centurion was responsible for their organisation (Polyb. 6,35,12), and each change was marked by the *bucina* (Livy 7,35,1) and (apparently) by a report to the commanding officer.

conuiuium bucina dimitti: Polybius (14,3,6) states that the start of the meal was so marked: presumably so also was its end.

ante augurale aram . . . accendi: the alliteration, the elaboration and the position mark a climax. It probably therefore does indicate the consumption of the altar as well as of the offerings. It was obviously specially erected (*structum*), and may have had some connection with the official banquet and its offerings.

The *augurale* was where, in former days, the commanding general took the auguries, and so means his headquarters.

in maius: for the adverbial phrase, see 2,3 n. Corbulo was naturally grandiloquent (26,3), and probably also wanted to impress Tiridates with the antiquity of Roman tradition.

2. **fratres:** Dio (62,23,4) says that Vologeses also came to Corbulo, but it may have been on a later occasion. Tacitus is quite specific in his information, and there is no other evidence to suggest that he is wrong.

Chapter 31

Ecbatanis: almost certainly the modern Hamadan, some two hundred miles SW of Teheran.

propriis: ' his own ', as distinct from the joint embassy of 27,1.

imaginem: an outward sign, such as those next mentioned. Vologeses wanted his brother to be a state visitor, not a supplicant.

ferrum traderet: it was not (for obvious reasons) customary to enter the emperor's presence armed. But foreign visitors might feel the need of arms for display or reassurance: Parthians in particular remembered the surrender of a Parthian sword to Pompey (Plut. *Pomp.* 33). Tiridates in the event solved the problem by nailing his sword to its scabbard. (Dio 63,2,4).

complexu: the formal embrace (as between Corbulo and Tiridates 29,1) was used only between important officials or those close to the emperor. Originally an Eastern custom, it seems to have become part of Roman life in the time of Augustus.

foribusue . . . adsisteret: to attempt to demonstrate one's importance by keeping a caller waiting, is clearly a practice with a long history.

scilicet f.: this scathing dismissal of the trappings of power as opposed to its reality is very Tacitean: but to one in Tiridates' position, such outward signs can be important: and real power can co-exist with trappings.

Chapter 32 Various activities in Rome, as the year ends.

Chapter 32

eodem anno: for a similar collection of heterogeneous information, see 22,2 and n.

Alpium maritimarum: this small province was formed by Augustus in 14 B.C. (Dio 54,24,3), and contained the land behind Nice. Tacitus had family connections with this district, through his father-in-law, Agricola, which may be why he has included the item.

ius Latii: the ' Latin right ' dates from the fourth century B.C., when Rome conquered Latium. Its chief effect was to confer Roman citizen-ship on anyone who held a magistracy in a Latin town. When in 89 B.C. all Latins became Roman citizens, the principle, with the name, was extended to other peoples beginning to qualify for limited citizenship, the Transpadane Gauls, and later to parts of Gaul and Spain. It benefited both sides, because it opened the possibility of the coveted citizenship to provincials, and ensured a supply of citizens for the service of Rome.

equitum . . . locos: Tacitus' statement here, that Nero allocated special seats in the circus to the *equites*, is supported by Pliny (*N.H.* 8,21) and Suetonius (*Nero* 11): but according to Livy (1,35,8), when the circus was first built in the time of the Kings, *loca diuisa patribus equitibusque, ubi spectacula quisque facerent, fori appellati*, and Dio (55,22,4) implies that in the time of Augustas the *equites* sat apart. Livy's statement can apply only loosely to the *ordines* and arrangements of the Republic and Empire: and while *equites* (and senators) may long have sat in groups, it seems clear that blocks of seats were not formally reserved for them in the circus until the time of Claudius (for senators, cf. Suet. *Claud.* 21,3) and Nero.

indiscreti: they were ' indistinguishable ', because they had no officially separate block of seats.

lex Roscia: this law, of 67 B.C. (Livy Epit. 99) gave *equites* attending the theatre the exclusive right to the fourteen rows immediately behind the seats reserved (in the orchestra) for senators. But it said nothing about seats in the circus.

feminarum . . . senatorumque: Tacitus has so far (*A.* 14,14-15) mentioned only *equites* in the arena, and women and senators on the stage: but *plures* here implies earlier instances. Dio (61,17,3) and Suetonius (*Nero* 12) mention women and senators at games in A.D. 59.

It was, for Romans, a disgrace to make a public spectacle of oneself: any senator or knight so appearing was *déclassé* (Suet. *Tib.* 35,2), and such an appearance was sometimes actually inflicted as a punishment (Dio 59,10,4). The Greeks, on the other hand, held actors and athletes in high regard, and Nero was probably trying to encourage a Greek custom, rather than deliberately debauching and insulting Romans. But the Romans remained unconvinced.

Chapters 33–7   Activities of Nero: appearance on the stage, removal of a rival, projected tour of the Orient, and an orgy.

Chapter 33

1. **C. Laecanio M. Licinio consulibus**: the year is A.D. 64. Laecanius lived until the time of Vespasian (Pliny *N.H.* 26,5), Licinius was apparently accused and condemned before the end of Nero's reign (*H.* 4,42).

acriore . . . cupidine: Tacitus here begins a careful presentation of the profligate Nero, successively in the context of theatrical performance (33), worthless companions (34,2), the murder of a rival (35), a notorious banquet (37), the great Fire (38f.) and the carnage following a conspiracy (48f.). The cumulative effect is considerable. The factual content is confirmed from other sources, but the presentation is Tacitus' own.

The sentence is economical and effective. The sharpening of desire is expressed by the position of *acriore* and the addition of *in dies*: the compulsive quality of *cupidine* is underlined by *adigebatur*: Nero is placed between the compulsive verb and the emphatic adjective *promiscas*: and the final verb suggests that his desire was for *constant* publicity.

Iuuenalibus ludis: the ceremony of the first shaving of a young Roman's beard was a family festival (Dio 48,34,2): Nero enlarged his ' family ', and celebrated the occasion by founding these games (*A.* 14,15), which were repeated on several anniversaries. They were clearly not entirely public, and Nero now desired a larger audience.

parum . . . angustos: Nero's motive is clearly defined, and his standard of performance ironically implied. Both are supported by other sources (e.g. Suet. *Nero* 20 and Dio 61,20,2): but they could possibly be wrong. Nero's thirst for constant applause seems indubitable, but a musical gift can be exercised only in performance, and Roman disapproval of such performance might affect the verdict on its standard.

2. **Neapolim quasi Graecam urbem**: Naples *was* a Greek city (founded from Chalcis *via* Cumae about 600 B.C., see Livy 8,22,5): *quasi* therefore = ' as being ', see 15,1 n.

Although it had long been part of Roman Italy, Naples always retained much of its Greek cultural inheritance, and its theatrical performances and games were on Greek not Roman lines. It therefore provided a more sympathetic setting for Nero's début.

fore: the motive is vividly presented in the form of Nero's thoughts.

Achaiam: mainland Greece.

coronas: the wreaths traditionally awarded as prizes in Greek contests, athletic and cultural. Nero could, clearly, be sure of winning if he competed.

ciuium: the citizens of Rome, as contrasted with the *oppidani* §3, who are Neapolitans.

3. **coloniis et municipiis:** the towns of Italy. The distinction between the original *coloniae* (settlements of Roman citizens) and *municipia* (self-governing Italian towns in alliance with Rome) had by now largely disappeared, because *coloniae* had a large measure of independence, and *municipia* had Roman citizenship. See *CQ* 1914, 132 & 1915, 57.

militum: probably mainly Praetorians (see 49,2 n.).

Chapter 34

1. **triste ... prouidum:** the neuter adjective is used for the noun.

conlapsum est: Suetonius (*Nero* 20) says that there was an earthquake, which shook the theatre when Nero was performing. Both may be right, simply viewing a series of incidents from different standpoints.

compositos: i.e., they were not extempore.

celebrans: it belongs, strictly, to *fortunam*, but by a zeugma (4,2 n.) is used with *grates* also.

petiturus: ' on his way to ... ' The collocation of present and future participles is striking.

Hadriae traiectus: he was on his way to Brundisium, to take ship for Greece. Beneventum was on the Appian Way, where Nero would join it from Naples.

The striking participles, the poetic use of the noun *Hadria* (cf. Hor. *Od.* 1,3,15) in apposition, instead of an adjective, the use of *traiectus* (found only here in Tacitus), combine to work towards the mention of Vatinius, and the sketch of him which then follows. For *apud* see 51,2 n.

2. **Vatinius:** he was a native of Beneventum (Juv. 5,46) and a new type of court character – the licensed buffoon. But such men, in Roman as in medieval times, could be powerful and dangerous. Tacitus recognises his importance, and his colour-value in the narrative.

ostenta: ' things shown ' i.e. portents, prodigies. Variation of construction, and vivid vocabulary (*sutrinus* and *scurrilis* appear only here in Tacitus) tellingly arranged, combine to make an impressive portrait of a man and a type. Vatinius is (in savage circumlocution) a nursling of a cobbler's shop, a cripple and a bitter wit.

facetiis scurrilibus: Dio 63,15,1 quotes one of these, and vouches for its accuracy. ' I hate you, Nero, because you are of senatorial rank.' This pleased Nero, because he hated the Senate.

criminatione: he became an informer. Successful cases brought by informers were rewarded, often with the victim's confiscated goods. Thus Vatinius won for himself influence (with Nero, and with those trying to appease the informer), wealth, and the power to hurt others (which perhaps gratified him in his deformity). His attributes are emphasised by being placed in asyndeton (i.e., juxtaposed, without connection), and by their association with the final cutting phrase (even in that collection of crooks, Vatinius was remarkable) and the Sallustian verb (*praemineret*) which it contains.

Chapter 35

1. **Torquatus Silanus:** D. Junius Silanus Torquatus, consul in A.D. 53 (*A.* 12,58), stood in the same relationship to Augustus as did Nero (see Genealogical Table, p. xviii). He is therefore a potential rival, and is removed.

Iuniae familiae: it included such families as the Bruti.

ferebat: ' carried ' i.e. ' boasted '. Cf. *A.* 2,43 *auunculum Augustum ferens.*

2. **prodigum largitionibus:** the two words accuse him of being (*a*) poor, and so dangerous, as seeing in revolution his only hope of recouping his fortunes, (*b*) responsible for his poverty, because of extravagance, and (*c*) over-generous, with overtones of bribery. Great wealth could be dangerous, and Dio (62,27,2) suggests that Torquatus may have squandered his deliberately.

ab epistulis f.: these titles (Private Secretary, Appeals Secretary and Accountant) had become so associated with the Emperor's Household (cf. Suet. *Claud.* 28) that a private citizen using them could be accused of claiming for himself the machinery of Empire. The abl. in the phrase expresses direction, point of view and therefore function. Cf. Cic. *Att.* 8,5,1 *seruum a pedibus meis.*

nomina . . . meditamenta: ' titles involving the highest concern, and preparations (for it) ', i.e. ' titles suggesting preparation for Imperial duties '. *meditamentum* appears to be a Tacitean invention, and he uses it only twice in the extant works (cf. *H.* 4,26).

3. **interscidit:** the word is rare, and is found only here in Tacitus (*abscindo* is so used at 69,2 and *A.* 16,11). It is used to emphasise Torquatus as a victim.

Suicide was employed (*A.* 6,29) to anticipate condemnation, and to ensure an easier death, proper burial and the validity of the accused's will.

ex more: cf. *A.* 2,31, where Tiberius makes a similar statement. *oratio* implies a formal, public statement, presumably in the Senate.

iudicis: Nero himself: the trial would have taken place *intra cubiculum* (*A.* 11,2). Tacitus' whole presentation of the statement is sardonic: probably not without cause.

Chapter 36

1. **in praesens**: he went to Greece in A.D. 66 (Dio 63,8,2).

in incerto: he may conceivably have had some warning of conspiracy.

sui: see 4,1 n. It here adds emphasis.

Capitolium: the temple of Jupiter, with whom were associated Juno and Minerva, was the focus of Rome's official religion.

2. **Vestae**: the temple of Vesta, in the Forum below the Capitol, was the ' hearth ' of the Roman family.

seu . . . seu: the presentation is typical of Tacitus – alternative explanations, constructions carefully out of balance, and the stylistic emphasis on the second half.

dictitans: probably (10,2 n.) the emphatic use of the frequentative verb: ' asserting ', probably by means of another edict: the language sounds official.

3. Nero's statement is reported in indirect speech, which makes it sound official, and also adds a sardonic tone – Tacitus is so obviously reporting ' without comment '.

uidisse . . . audire: the change of tense is significant: their protests (though private) were ringing in his ears.

tantum itineris aditurus: the phrase echoes Tiridates' words in 30,2. Another prince is contemplating a journey, and there is implicit comparison and comment.

ergo ut f.: the alliterative *p*'s mark the balance (*priuatis . . . populum*), emphasise the point of comparison (*praeualerent . . . plurimam*), and point the decision (*parendum*).

4. **haec atque talia**: a standard phrase, but it sounds contemptuous in this context.

uolentia: not ' willing ' but ' welcome '. This middle/passive use of the present participle is found occasionally from Sallust on (cf. *Hist.* 4,31 D *uolentia plebi*). It is probably a Graecism.

cupidine . . . metuenti: the change of construction, the longer phrase and the final position emphasise *metuenti*: bread was more important than circuses. See 18,2 n.

si abesset: the subjunctive is virtually indirect, expressing their fear. The apodosis of the condition is contained in *angustias*. Cf. 51,2 *destinationem*: 52,1.

in incerto f.: the phrase echoes one of Sallust's (*Jug.* 46,8 *ut, absens an praesens . . . perniciosior esset, in incerto haberetur*). This, with the preceding *plebi uolentia*, and the emphasis on *uoluptates* and power politics, gives a Sallustian flavour to the passage.

deterius f.: an acid, but shrewd comment, given emphasis by its position.

Chapter 37

1. This chapter marks the climax of Nero's Rake's Progress, and it is presented with poetical vocabulary and constructions, rare and emotive words, and careful structure.

quo: see 10,3 n. ' To acquire the reputation that nothing anywhere (was) as pleasant for him (as Rome) '. The suggested motive and the implication that it is a discreditable one are initial and emphatic.

struere . . . uti: the historic infinitives mark a swift and vivid narrative. *struere* is used of ' providing ' a banquet again in 55,3: it is perhaps significant that it is also used of ' contriving ' a plot or crime, cf. *A.* 1,13.

Tigellino: Ofonius Tigellinus, Nero's Praetorian Prefect, is presented as his evil genius (cf. *A.* 14,51 & 57). He was a freedman, wealthy, powerful and unscrupulous – the kind of man Tacitus especially dislikes: but there seems good reason for his dislike of Tigellinus. He outlived Nero, and was forced to suicide by Otho in 69. Tacitus describes his end and his character in *H.* 1,72.

ut exemplum referam: a reasonable proceeding. Tacitus picks his example with care, and presents it with artistry, to demonstrate the moral degeneracy of Nero and his friends. But the banquet is attested from other sources too – Dio 62,15 is even more lavish in detail.

prodigentia: this vigorous and allusive word (' monstrous behaviour ') is used by Tacitus on two other occasions only (*A.* 6,14 & *A.* 13,1) and is found nowhere else in extant Latin literature.

2. **igitur**: this returns, as often, to the main theme which has been interrupted by a parenthesis. Cf. 44,4: 69,1: 72,2.

in stagno Agrippae: references in Ovid (*Pont.* 1,8,38) and Frontinus (*Aqued.* 2,84) make it fairly clear that this was a reservoir storing water for Agrippa's Baths, and that it stood near them (and near the Pantheon) in the Campus Martius.

superpositum: the word occurs in Tacitus only here.

tractu: Tacitus uses this word only four times, three of them in this book (cf. 10,1 & 64,3: the other example is in the description of the storm in *A.* 2,23). It is noteworthy that all four contexts are highly wrought and emotive. The word has poetic (cf. Virg. *Georg.* 3,183) and Sallustian (*Jug.* 78,3) associations.

diuersis e terris: the anastrophe of the preposition (1,3 n.) and the extended meaning of *diuersus* (=' distant ' cf. Virg. *Aen.* 11,261) are poetical and striking.

Oceano abusque: anastrophe again, this time of a rare and poetic preposition (cf. Virg. *Aen.* 7,289): the effect is to make the ' sea-beasts ' very rare and exotic indeed.

3. **crepidinibus**: another Tacitean ' solitary '. The word was in current literary use (cf. Cic. *Verr.* 5,97: Virg. *Aen.* 10,653), though not very common: it is more impressive, in sound, length and rarity, than e.g. *ripis*, and it is further emphasised by its position. The case is probably dative, cf. *A.* 14,8 *cui (cubiculo) adstabant.*

iam . . . obsceni: supply *sunt/erant.* So presented, the gestures have almost independent existence. This emphasis is increased by the final adjective, which Tacitus uses only here.

postquam . . . incedebant: *postquam* with the imperfect indicative describes an action which continues up to the time of the main verb. Because of this, it often conveys a causal connection too, ' now that '. The construction is especially characteristic of Livy and Tacitus, though not confined to them. Cf. 45,3: 67,2. *incedo* for the advance of night is rare.

consonare . . . clarescere: the clause as a whole displays variation, alliteration, chiasmus and assonance, which combine to convey the colour and sound of the proceedings.

4. **ipse**: the scene, presented so far kaleidoscopically and impressionistically, is now focused sharply on Nero's activities. After a general introduction, one scandalous incident is described in detail, with the technical vocabulary of the formal marriage ceremony adding to the outrage of this perversion of it.

W. Allen Jr. (*Numen* 1962, 99f.) has made the ingenious suggestion that this mock-marriage might be connected with a religious rite – a festival of Flora, or something like a Mithraic ceremony – and so be a ' mystic ' marriage. It is not impossible, given Nero's temperament and interests: but it is strange that neither Tacitus nor Suetonius (*Nero* 28–9) makes such a connection: following a strange ritual would have made another charge. What is clear, is Roman outrage at the distortion of ancient ceremony.

per licita atque inlicita: ' polar ' expression, using the two extremes to cover the whole range of activity which they embrace.

reliquerat . . . nisi . . . denupsisset: see 8,2 n.

contaminatorum grege: a reminiscence of Horace (*Od.* 1,37,9), which provides not only a vivid phrase, but a pointed comparison with Cleopatra's associates.

Pythagorae: this could be dative (Latin says either *nomen est mihi Marcus* or *nomen est mihi Marco*). But Tacitus seems to use the dat.

construction only when the name is an adjective (cf. *A.* 1,31 *exercitus* . . . *cui nomen superiori*). It may therefore be genitive (of definition), which he does use elsewhere, cf. *H.* 4,18 *castra, quibus Veterum nomen est.*

imperatori: in pointed prominence, and in juxtaposition to the Roman objects which he was mis-using. The *flammeum* was the bridal veil, *auspices* were necessary for the ceremony (Cic. *Diu.* 1,28), the dowry was officially transferred, the marriage bed was prominently displayed, and the procession was accompanied by torch-bearers. Cf. *Cat.* 61.

missi: the *auspices* delivered their reading of the omens to the bride (*A.* 11.27: Juv. 10,336), and *denupsisset* shows that this was Nero's rôle in the ceremony.

genialis: the Genius of the family is naturally associated with efforts to promote its survival.

Chapters 38–41   The great Fire at Rome: its origin, course and consequences.

Chapter 38

1. **sequitur clades**: the fire began (41,2) on 19 July A.D. 64

forte an dolo: the structure points the insinuation. But it is interesting that no other extant source admits of any doubt at all – Dio (62,16), Suetonius (*Nero* 38) and Pliny (*N.H.* 17,5: see *Hermes* 1960, 111 f.) all attribute the fire to Nero. There obviously was a divided tradition, but without Tacitus we should never have known it.

auctores: on Tacitus' sources, see Introd. 1.

omnibus: from the sack of Rome by the Gauls in 390 B.C. (Livy 5,41–2), the city had been subject to many fires, deliberate and accidental (cf. *A.* 4,64 & 6,45). The form, site and structure of the old city made it peculiarly vulnerable to fire.

2. **initium** . . . **ortum**: the apparent tautology is for emphasis. Cf. *A.* 1,31.

in ea parte circi: at the SE corner of the Circus Maximus. See p. 20.

mercimonium: Tacitus uses the word only here, and it is an archaism, and rare.

coeptus . . . **citus** . . . **circi corripuit**: the alliteration points the progress of the fire.

domus . . . **templa**: self-contained houses, and temples, would have had walled grounds which might have stopped the flames: instead, there were only *insulae* (41,1), blocks of flats crowding narrow streets, which caught and spread the fire.

aut quid: see 19,2n. Here *quid*, in a negative phrase, does duty for *quidquam*.

3. **impetu**: the abl. of manner normally requires *cum* or an adjective, except for those forms stereotyped as adverbs (e.g. *iure, iniuria*). Tacitus extends the usage.

populando: for the abl., see 8,2 n.

enormibus: 'irregular'. There were no tidy boundaries within which the fire could be contained. Livy (5,55,4), describing the re-building of Rome after the fire of 390 B.C., says *festinatio curam exemit uicos dirigendi*.

uetus Roma: the Rome which Tacitus knew was largely of Nero's rebuilding.

4. **fessa aetate**: the general sense is clear – that weeping women, the old and infirm, and helpless children contributed to the confusion. But the text (*fessa aetate aut rudis pueritiae aetas* M, where either *aetate* or *aetas* must go: *fessa senum aut rudis pueritiae aetas* L, which is an obvious emendation) and the syntax, present difficulties. The best solution still seems to be to read M's text without *aetas*. Tacitus nowhere else separates *fessa . . . aetas*: the bold use of ablative and genitive of quality alone is not very different from other verbal short cuts (e.g. *inter diuersi generis ordinis* f. 54,1: and cf. Livy 39,8,6 *mixti feminis mares, aetatis tenerae maioribus*): the context shows variety and boldness being deliberately contrived: and the very boldness of expression is probably the cause of the textual corruption.

5. **in proxima**: to a neighbouring district.

6. **quid . . . quid**: the anaphora (repetition of a word at the begin-ning of successive phrases or clauses, so making a conjunction unneces-sary) here emphasises their bewilderment.

diurni . . . uictus: the genitive depends on the general idea of ' provision ' contained in *fortunis*.

interiere: a solemn and rhythmical climax.

7. **crebris f.**: the interwoven order emphasises the numbers and the threats, and the change of construction to *quia* marks the more positive action.

siue ut . . . seu iussu: the variation and the order again insinuate Nero's responsibility. But Tacitus does see and record another possible explanation.

The description of the fire moves rapidly and economically from date and disastrous nature §1, *via* location and contributory causes §2, to the force and extent §3, and the people affected by it §§4–6: arson is sug-gested at the beginning and the end: the chapter shows striking vocabu-lary, striking constructions, variety and compression – the variability and confusion of the action, e.g., is suggested by the variety and accumu-lation of constructions in §§3–6. The technique is impressionistic, but such factual details as are provided seem accurate (and others are added in 39–41). It is a splendid study of the chaos produced by calamity, and of the human suffering involved.

Chapter 39

1. **Nero Antii agens:** Nero's absence from Rome, and his attitude, support the view that he was not responsible for the outbreak of the fire.

qua ... continuauerat: Augustus had established a residence on the Palatine, and later emperors continued to live there: Maecenas, Augustus' friend, had gardens on the Esquiline (Suet. *Tib.* 15), which he left to Augustus and Augustus to his successors: Nero had a house of his own in the valley between the two (where the Colosseum now stands).

haurirentur: 'were devastated'. Cf. *A.* 3,72 *Pompei theatrum igne fortuito haustum.*

2. **solacium:** acc. in apposition to the phrase. See 27,2 n.

campum Martis: the use of the genitive in place of the more usual adjective *Martius*, focuses attention on the phrase. Cf. 44,1 *Sibyllae libri.*

monumenta Agrippae: these buildings stood on the *campus Martius*, and included the Baths (37,2) and the Pantheon.

quin etiam: anastrophe of conjunctions, as of prepositions (1,3 n.) starts naturally in the poets, and then comes into post-Augustan prose. Except in the *Dialogus*, Tacitus never uses this phrase in the initial position. It marks a climax, and its position here gives greater emphasis to *suos*. The gardens were at the foot of the Vatican hill (*A.* 14,14).

utensilia: 'necessaries'.

ab Ostia: the preposition is used to ensure clarity. *Ostia* may be either fem. sing. or neut. pl., and it is essential here that the direction should be clear. The preposition is also required for *municipiis*, and stands more naturally and conveniently at the beginning of the whole phrase.

pretium frumenti: the average price of corn in Nero's time can be deduced from Pliny *N.H.* 18,90 as five sesterces.

3. **rumor:** see 15,2 n. Tacitus is using the story to create atmosphere, without committing himself about its truth. Both Suetonius (*Nero* 38) and Dio (62,18,1) state it as fact, and place the performance on the Tower of Maecenas and the roof of the Palace respectively.

domesticam scaenam: see 33,1 and n.

Troianum excidium: i.e., he sang the *Halosis Ilii*, almost certainly his own composition (Dio 62,18,1: Juv. 8,221). Nero *may* have been moved by the fire to artistic expression: but it is perhaps more likely that disapproval of such performances by the Emperor combined with his unpopularity after the fire, to produce the story.

Chapter 40

1. **sexto . . . die:** Suetonius (*Nero* 38) gives six days and seven nights as the duration of the fire: Dio (62,17,1) ' several ' days and nights. An inscription (*CIL* VI, 1,826) mentions nine days, which suggests that the second outbreak lasted for three days.

prorutis: a ' scorched earth ' policy was the only way of stopping the fire.

per immensum: see 2,3 n. Buildings were demolished on a vast scale, so that the ground resembled a flat plain, and the skyline was empty.

necdum . . . spes: the text is an emendation, and far from certain. But the general sense is clear: before people had time to recover from the first outbreak, there was a second.

eoque: the open ground allowed people to escape, but left buildings unprotected.

porticus: the colonnades where people walked and talked. Cf. Hor. *Sat.* 1,4,134.

2. **praediis . . . Aemilianis.** the exact location is uncertain, but it probably lay between the *campus Martius* and the Capitol (see Map. p. 20). Cf. Varro *R.R.* 3,2,6: Suet. *Claud.* 18. The ablative indicates origin.

uidebatur: it is not impossible that Nero or Tigellinus was responsible for the second fire, wishing to clear the ground for proper reconstruction of the damaged city. But it is equally possible that smouldering embers came somewhere to life again, and that human nature's instinctive desire to blame *someone* for disaster, has combined with the Nero legend to allot the blame to him.

quippe . . . diuiditur: this looks (Hartman, *Analecta Tacitea*, 203) very like a gloss on the text. Tacitus' readers knew this: and he has already referred (*A.* 14,12) simply to *quattuordecim urbis regiones.*

quattuor integrae: these would be the districts farthest from the centre of the city and the fire, and would certainly include XIV (*Trans-tiberina*): as the fire stopped *apud imas Esquilias* §1, V (*Esquiliae*) may have been another: the other possibilities are I (*Porta Capena*), VI (*Alta Semita*) and VII (*Via Lata*).

tres . . . deiectae: XI (*Circus Maximus*) certainly, probably with X (*Palatium*) and IV (*Subura*).

pauca . . . uestigia: although the damage to the city was clearly great, this must be exaggeration. The Capitol (44,1) and Forum (*A.* 16, 27) were apparently largely unaffected: Tiberius' house on the Palatine still stood five years later (*H.* 1,27): and even the Circus was in use again in the following year (53,1).

lacera et semusta: the closing adjectives, poetic and pathetic, point the picture.

Chapter 41

1. **fuerit**: the potential subjunctive expresses mild assertion, and the perfect is so used from the time of Cicero. Cf. 49,1 *memorauerim*, and the common *dixerit aliquis*.

uetustissima religione: a loosely attached abl. of attendant circumstances or quality.

Seruius Tullius Lunae: Servius Tullius was traditionally (Livy 1,41,3) the sixth of the kings of Rome. The temple of Luna was on the Aventine (Livy 40,2,2), and Servius is nowhere else mentioned in connection with it: but he did found the temple of Diana, also on the Aventine (Livy 1,45,1), and this may be either an associated shrine, or another way of referring to the same temple (Diana/Artemis was after all the Moon goddess). *Lucinae* L presents even greater difficulties: no such temple is known, and *Graecarum artium decora* suggests that Luna is the right goddess, because Vitruvius (5,5,8) says that Corinthian bronzes were kept in her temple.

magna ara: the Ara Maxima, situated near the NW end of the Circus (and so right in the path of the first flames) was traditionally founded by Evander after Hercules had killed Cacus, the stealer of his cattle. The story is told by Livy (1,7,4f.) and Virgil (*Aen.* 8,185f.) among others. Various versions of the story and of the significance of the worship are found, but Tacitus is here obviously emphasising the legendary nature of the foundation, in order to emphasise the antiquity of the shrine destroyed.

fanumque: probably not a ' shrine ' in the sense of a building, but a ' holy place '.

Statoris Iouis: the temple (Livy 1,12,4f.) vowed by Romulus to Jupiter if he would ' stay ' the flight of the Romans before the Sabines. It stood in the Forum, near the Arch of Titus.

Numaeque regia: traditionally the palace of Numa Pompilius, second king of Rome (Livy 1,18,5), it was later used as the official residence of the Pontifex Maximus. It stood in the Forum, near the temple of Vesta, and was given to the Vestals by Augustus. Some of its foundations are still visible.

Penatibus populi Romani: these were probably sacred objects said to have been brought by Aeneas from Troy (Virg. *Aen.* 3,148) and kept in the *penetralia Vestae*.

The different words for ' temple ' in this sentence add variety and emphasis. See 20,3 n.

opes: rich spoils of all kinds. *decora* means specifically ' works of art ': cf. *H.* 3,71 *statuas, decora maiorum.*

monumenta ingeniorum: 'old and authentic records of men of genius '. Definitive texts of literary works are meant. The reference is probably not to losses from, e.g., the great Palatine Library, which survived the fire, but to texts in family archives.

2. **XIIII Kal. Sextilis**: 19 July. The formula for expressing dates is so stereotyped that the *ante diem* can be omitted. Cf. the treatment of the money formula 18,3 n.

quo et: *et quo* M puts the point of comparison in the wrong place, *eo quo* L lacks an essential element of the comparison. This seems the easiest and best correction.

The Gauls burned Rome on this day in 390 B.C. (Livy 5,39 & 6,1,11).

inflammauerint: subjunct. of virtual oblique – ' on which day the Senones too (they pointed out) fired the city they had captured '.

totidem annos f.: from 390 B.C. to A.D. 64 is (on Roman inclusive reckoning) 454 years: this can be expressed as 418 years, 418 months (34 years, 10 months) and 418 days (14 months). The calculation has about as much real significance as have attempts to express the names of, e.g., Napoleon or Hitler in terms of the number of the Beast in *Revelation* 13,18, and Tacitus' comment indicates his opinion of such activities.

Chapters 42-3   The rebuilding of Rome : Nero's new Palace.

Chapter 42

1. **ceterum**: transitional, not adversative. ' Meanwhile, Nero . . . ' Cf. 43,1.

domum: Nero's Golden House, which from all accounts was a lavish and luxurious estate, covering the Palatine and the Esquiline and most of the ground between, combined the grounds of a country house with the treasures of a museum and the mechanical contrivances which delighted Nero's heart. It was never completed, and never popular, being too opulent, too oriental and too aesthetic for the Roman senators. See M. P. Charlesworth in *JRS* 1950, 69f.: J. B. Ward-Perkins in *Antiquity* 1956, 209f.: M. P. O. Morford in *Eranos* 1968, 158f.

essent: the subjunctive expresses Nero's purpose.

luxu uulgata: ' (things) long commonplace as regards luxury '.

arua et stagna f.: part of the wonder of the estate was the introduction of features usually reserved for country properties into the centre of Rome. It is interesting to compare Tacitus' account of the place with Suetonius' catalogue of its splendours (*Nero* 31): Tacitus mentions only enough to indicate the sort of place it was, and passes on (*via* its architects) to further follies of Nero's engineering.

magistris et machinatoribus: 'architects and contractors'. Nothing more is known of them. For the noun in -*tor* cf. §2 and see 1,1 n.

denegauisset: generic subjunct., see 12,4 n. 'Who had the ability and the audacity to attempt artificially even such things as Nature had declined.' *denego* appears in the *Annals* only in this book – here, and at 57,1 and 62,1, all important contexts.

uiribus principis inludere: 'to fool away the resources of an emperor'.

2. **ab lacu Auerno:** by joining this inland lake, *via* Lake Lucrinus, to the Bay of Naples, Agrippa had in 37 b.c. created a safe harbour (cf. Virg. *Georg.* 2,161 f.). An inland waterway from there to Rome would have allowed corn ships and naval vessels to avoid a dangerous stretch of coastline (46,2), and also helped to drain some undesirable marshland (see below). It was a scheme which, like that to cut a Corinth canal (Suet. *Nero* 19) showed vision, but little grasp of the practical difficulties involved.

squalenti litore: 'along a barren shore or through a mountain barrier'. The difficulties are emphasised by their position, by the variety of construction, and by the vocabulary: *squaleo* is poetic (e.g. Virg. *Georg.* 1,507) and is used by Tacitus only here.

Pomptinae paludes: these lay behind Cape Circeo. They were malarial marshes, and many attempts were made to drain them, unsuccessfully, until about 1930.

nec satis causae: probably, in terms of the labour involved, a sound judgement.

cupitor: Nero's hankering after the impossible is represented as almost professional (see 1,1 n.). The noun appears first in Tacitus, and rarely elsewhere, and may have been coined by him. It is a neat description of one side of Nero's character, and connects him with Sallust's description of Catiline (*Cat.* 5,5) *animus . . . incredibilia . . . semper cupiebat.*

Chapter 43

1. **urbis quae domui supererat:** a caustic observation on Nero's palace. Cf. Suet. *Nero* 39,2 *Roma domus fiet: Veios migrate, Quirites, / Si non et Veios occupat ista domus.*

non . . . sed: Nero tried to turn the disaster to good purpose by proper town planning.

Gallica incendia: see 41,2 n.

cohibita . . . altitudine: emperors from Augustus to Trajan tried to limit the height of buildings in Rome, obviously with no great success.

areis: either inside or around the blocks of flats.

protegerent: the porticoes would provide shade, protection from passing traffic, and a flat roof from which to fight any future fires.

3. **Ostiensis paludes:** formed by the alluvial deposits at the mouth of the Tiber.

utique: *destinabat* controls the structure of §§3–4: the variation between accusative and noun clause helps to articulate the provisions without cataloguing them.

subuectassent: the verb (only here in Tacitus) is mainly poetical. Cf. Virg. *Aen.* 6,303.

sine trabibus: they had (probably on the ground floor) to be stone vaulted.

saxo Gabino Albanoue: from Gabii, on the road to Praeneste, and from Marino, by the Alban Lake, came much of the stone from which Imperial Rome was built. (The quarries at Gabii are still visible.) The Tabularium (Record Office) on the Capitol is faced with Gabine stone, the mouth of the Cloaca Maxima (Main Drain) with Alban.

quod . . . imperuius est: both stones are of volcanic origin, and so have already been tried in the fire. But they are also rough and not very decorative: hence the regulation to ensure their use.

4. **aqua:** subject of *flueret*, but given prominence by the structure. The diversion of public water for private (often ornamental) purposes was a perennial problem of Rome's *curatores aquarum.* Cf. Frontinus, *Aqued.* 2,74–6.

communione parietum: private houses had to be detached, and blocks of flats separated from one another. The abstract noun and the variation of construction emphasise the point.

5. **erant tamen f.:** there always are such people: and they sometimes (as here) have a point.

angustiae itinerum: the narrow streets of Rome were notorious in the ancient world. Cf. Cic. *Leg. Agr.* 2,96.

solis uapore: high buildings and narrow streets provide more shade in a Mediterranean summer.

perrumperentur: subjunct. of virtual oblique: this is part of their case.

ardescere: used here metaphorically of the heat of the sun, but in the circumstances a very appropriate metaphor.

Chapter 44   The Christians accused and punished.

Chapter 44

1. **petita dis piacula:** ' next, they looked for means of appeasing the gods '. *dis* is dat.

Sibyllae libri: for the gen. see 39,2 n. The original books, said to have been bought from a Sibyl by Tarquinius Priscus, were destroyed when the Capitol was burned in 83 B.C. Unofficial versions of the contents were then current, until Augustus had a new and official collection made and deposited in the Palatine Library (*A.* 6,12).

supplicatum: Tacitus emphasises the ritual, and implies its pointlessness, by rare and ritual vocabulary. *supplico, matrona, perspergo* and *sellisternium* occur only here in his works, *propitio* only again at *D.* 9. *propitio* is archaic (cf. Plaut. *Poen.* 378), *perspergo* rare (cf. Cato *R.R.* 130: Cic. *De Or.* 1,159) and *sellisternium* almost unique – apart from its appearance in an inscription of the first century B.C. (*CIL* VI, 32323), it occurs only here and in Festus, a grammarian writing about A.D. 150.

Vulcano f.: the god of fire is, in the context, an obvious deity to appease: the temple of Ceres and Proserpina was near the Circus where the fire started: and Juno is the great state goddess of Rome.

apud proximum mare: at Ostia. The ritual cleansing of cult statues in sea water was both Greek (Eur. *I.T.* 1199) and Roman (Ovid, *Fast.* 4,136) religious practice.

sellisternia: the propitiation of the gods by formal banquets set before their images was introduced to Rome about 400 B.C. (Livy 5,13). The male gods, like the Roman men, reclined at table (*lectisternium*): the goddesses, like Roman women, sat on chairs (Val. Max. 2,1,1–2). *lectisternium* is often used (as in Livy) to describe the ceremony involving both, but here, where only women and female deities are concerned, Tacitus uses the rarer but more specific word.

2. **quin:** *non . . . decedebat infamia* is equivalent to a negative expression of hindering, and so takes an equivalent construction. Cf. 57,1.

Nero . . . Christianos: on this topic, and the interpretation of the rest of the chapter, see Introd. 5.

appellabat: perhaps ' was beginning to call '. The name originated (*Acts* 11,26) in Antioch, some twenty years before this date.

3. **procuratorem:** see 25,3 n. The name of his province is here omitted, because it is to be used two lines below: a typical Tacitean economy. Its omission also emphasises the alliteration of the initial *p*.

Pontium Pilatum: one of the few non-Christian references to him. See also Philo, *Leg. ad Gaium* 299f.: Josephus, *B.I.* 2,169f.

exitiabilis superstitio: to a Roman, all foreign religions (except

Greek) were *superstitiones*: but the stories about Christianity made it seem a particularly deadly one. Cf. Suet. *Nero* 16 *superstitionis nouae et maleficae*: Pliny *Ep.* 10,96 *superstitionem prauam*.

quo cuncta . . . confluunt celebranturque: the alliteration points the bitter generalisation, which is not necessarily confined to religious rites.

4. igitur: see 37,2 n.

multitudo ingens: the term is rhetorically, but not grossly, exaggerated. Such terms (cf. *immensa strages A.* 6,19) are relative to the context: our news media would describe the loss of one hundred men from an army in the field as ' light casualties ', but if an aeroplane crashed with similar losses, that would be a ' major disaster '. Both here and at *A.* 6,19 Tacitus is describing executions, and in such circumstances quite moderate numbers can give the impression of a holocaust.

odio humani generis: both Jews (cf. *H.* 5,5) and Christians were accused of hating their fellow men. Their ' separateness ', their refusal to sacrifice to the community gods or to attend any public occasion connected with such sacrifice, their different moral standards, combined to give the Romans this impression of them. What therefore caused their condemnation was a feeling, not that they were guilty of arson, but that they deserved death in any case.

addita ludibria: they suffered not only death, but a shameful death.

laniatu canum: *laniatus* is rare and emotive, *canis* (though a common word) appears only here in Tacitus. Together they underline that human beings are suffering inhuman indignity.

crucibus adfixi f.: this text, though not entirely satisfactory, gives reasonable sense and syntax. They were to be savaged by dogs, or crucified, or used as human street lamps. These last would be dressed in the *tunica molesta*, a shirt made of inflammable material and lined with pitch. Cf. Juv. 8,235.

defecisset: the subjunct. may indicate repeated action (45,3 n.), or a subordinate clause in indirect speech.

nocturni luminis: the horror is heightened by the use of a Virgilian echo: cf. *Aen.* 7,13.

5. hortos: see 39,2 n.

spectaculo: it was a ' show ' for the populace – like the hangings, drawings and quarterings of Tudor England.

unde: ' from which fact ', i.e. because of Nero's callousness.

quamquam aduersus f.: ' although in face of men guilty and deserving exemplary punishment, pity arose . . . '

tamquam: this expresses, as often in Tacitus, not an unreal comparison, but the grounds of an oblique charge or reason. ' Because (they felt) they were being sacrificed . . . ' Cf. 52,2: 73,1: 74,3.

non utilitate . . . sed in: the change of construction again emphasises the second half.

Chapter 45 Money-raising for building.

Chapter 45

1. **conferendis pecuniis:** ' to raise money ', for public and Neronian buildings..

euersae: ' ruined ', financially.

sociique populi et quae f.: probably a sub-division of *prouinciae*, with *-que* . . . *et* = ' both . . . and ': the *socii populi* are ordinary provincial subjects of Rome, the *ciuitates liberae* (e.g. Athens) the more privileged communities, who did not normally pay tax, but were also financially affected on this occasion. For a similar sub-division, cf. Virg. *Aen.* 2,5–6 and 4,484–5.

in . . . cessere: ' fell to ' i.e. ' formed part of '. Cf. Livy 6,14,12 *aurum . . . in paucorum praedam cessisse*. The gods are put in place of their treasures, to add emotion.

2. **abripiebantur:** Nero's vast plunderings for his Golden House are described by Pliny *N.H.* 34,84. Many of the statues were later given to temples, but *Ag.* 6,5 makes it clear that they were not restored to their original sources.

Acrato: he is mentioned also at *A.* 16,23, but little else is known of him.

Carrinate: probably the son of the rhetorician exiled by Gaius (Dio 59,20,6).

Graeca doctrina: philosophy. But he only talked it, did not practise it.

bonis artibus: *ars* in this phrase, and its opposite *malae artes*, means something like ' motive ', ' character ', ' morals '. Cf. 62,1.

3. **ferebatur . . . tradidere:** Tacitus probably found the stories in his sources, but is not convinced of their truth. But they are too valuable a contribution to his portrait of Nero, to be left out.

Seneca had been refused retirement two years earlier, but had withdrawn as far as possible from city and public life (*A.* 14,56).

postquam . . . concedebatur: see 37,3 n.

ficta ualetudine: *ualetudo* can be good or bad health, according to the context.

aeger neruis: ' suffering from a muscular disease ' – like rheumatism: it would be difficult, especially in those days, to prove that he was *not* suffering from such a disease.

cubiculum non egressus: supply *esse*. The acc. with *egredior* is developed by analogy, either of opposites (*ingredior*), or of verbs of similar meaning (e.g. *relinquo*). Cf. 74,3.

cui nomen: the detail adds verisimilitude, and suggests a source-reference.

seu: this adds a second possible explanation, almost as an afterthought. Cf. 51,2.

persimplici uictu et agrestibus pomis: *persimplex* appears only here in Tacitus and, apparently, nowhere else: *agrestibus pomis* (cf. Sen. *Ep.* 83,6 & 108,16) echoes Virg. *Aen.* 7,111: together they add colour and emphasis to the climax of the story.

si ... admoneret: 'if ever ...' From Livy on, repeated action is as often expressed by the subjunctive as by the classically correct indicative. Examples with *si* and *cum* are found even in Caesar and Cicero, and the construction is probably a development of the generic use of the subjunctive (12,4 n.), perhaps under the influence of Greek. Cf. 58,2.

Chapters 46–7   Minor events of the year.

Chapter 46

1. **per idem tempus**: for the miscellaneous information contained in this chapter and the next, see 22,2 n.

gladiatores apud oppidum Praeneste: gladiators, usually prisoners of war or slaves, but occasionally free men in search of money or adventure, were trained in 'schools': some schools were state- or town-owned, some private. This one, at Palestrina, some twenty miles SE of Rome, was presumably (with its official guard) one of the Imperial schools: such are known to have existed from the time of Gaius (Pliny *N.H.* 11,144).

temptata eruptione: the discipline of the schools was strict, and periodic revolts occurred.

qui custos adesset: the subjunctive is difficult. *aderat* L is its usual essay in the obvious, and does not explain how the reading *adesset* ever arose: *adest* (Nipperdey) makes that explanation easier but implies both the continued existence of the school, and a confusion between the garrison 'then' and 'now'. It seems better to keep *adesset* M, and explain the subjunct. as a compressed or conflated construction, intended to express not only the garrison's presence, but its character and purpose. Cf. 16,1 n. on *prodiderit*.

Spartacum: he started the Slave War of 73–71 B.C. by organising a break-out of gladiators from the school at Capua. The Romans never forgot the bitterness of that war, and were (probably with good reason) terrified by any suggestion of an uprising involving slaves.

ut est f.: the idea of revolution has a fearful fascination. For the gen., see 6,4 n.

2. **immota pax**: the war with Parthia was over, and the temple of Janus soon to be closed. A coin bearing the legend *Ianum clusit pace PR terra mariq. parta* can be dated to this year (Mattingly, I, clxxiv & 209,64).

sed f.: the lack of balance with *non bello* emphasises by length, change and detail of construction, the cause of the disaster.

in Campaniam: to its base at Misenum. This fleet controlled Rome's western approaches, and was important: the Adriatic fleet was stationed at Ravenna. Cf. *A.* 4,5.

maris casibus: these hazards were considerable, and were one of the reasons for Nero's projected canal (42,2 n.). The phrase makes Nero sound unreasonable and irresponsible, but probably exaggerates a perfectly normal order to return to base without fail by a certain date before the start of winter. The fault may well have been the commanders', lingering too long in a pleasanter summer base.

a Formiis: for the preposition, see 6,2 n.

mouere: the intransitive use of this verb is rare in Latin, and appears only here in Tacitus. *naues* could be supplied from the context, but other isolated examples suggest that this is not necessary. Cf. Livy 35,40,7 *terra dies duodequadraginta mouit.*

Africo: the WSW wind, usually stormy (cf. Virg. *Aen.* 1,86) and blowing onshore to Campania.

Miseni: the gen. of definition, instead of the more usual noun in apposition (e.g. *A.* 14,4 *promunturium Misenum*).

Chapter 47

1. **prodigia**: see 7,1 n. Tacitus is here preparing dramatically for the account of the Pisonian Conspiracy, which occupies the rest of the book.

sidus cometes: the noun is used adjectivally. Cf. 34,1 *maris Hadriae.*

semper Neroni expiatum: Tacitus mentions only one other comet in Nero's reign, in A.D. 60 (*A.* 14,22), where it is followed by the exile of Rubellius Plautus. But other writers mention comets at this time (e.g. Suet. *Nero* 36: Pliny *N.H.* 2,92): and R. S. Rogers (*TAPA* 1953, 237f.) says that Chinese records show seven comets visible for long periods of the years 54, 55, 56, 60, 61, 64, 65, 66: various ' illustrious ' deaths certainly belong to the same years. This is the kind of information which Pliny's *History* (53,3 n.) may well have recorded, and Tacitus may be basing his statement upon such information, even though he selects only two comets for special mention.

quibus: ' (to the gods) to whom it was customary . . . ' These would be deities connected with fertility, e.g. Tellus, to whom a cow in calf was regularly offered: cf. Ovid, *Fast.* 4,634.

2. **in agro Placentino**: Placentia (Piacenza) was an old Roman colony, in the plain of Lombardy, SW of Milan.

propter: for its position, see 1,3 n.

esset: subjunct. of virtual oblique. Tacitus does not vouch for the truth of the story.

haruspicum: these were Etruscan in origin, and never regarded by the Romans with the respect accorded to the native augurs. Augurs set out to discover the will of the gods by looking for omens, *haruspices* offered interpretations of portents already manifest. They dealt with *fulgura*, *monstra* and *exta* – on which they overlapped with the augurs. Cf. *A.* 11,15.

interpretatio: the oddity is the significant thing in a portent, and from ' head out of place ', they suggested an abortive attempt at supreme power: as the birth was public, so would the attempt become.

iuxta: see 1,3 n.

Chapters 48–53   A conspiracy against Nero: the conspirators and their plans.

Chapter 48

1. **Silius Nerua et Atticus Vestinus**: consuls for A.D. 65. The former came of a consular family (*A.* 4,68), the latter was probably the son of Claudius' friend L. Vestinus (*Tab. Lugd.* II,11).

coniuratione: the conspiracy (which had clearly already started, see 55,4 n.) ' grew as soon as it was formed '.

senatores f.: the lack of connection emphasises the mixed membership, and the interchange between plural and collective singular adds point. The date, the extent, the membership and the motivation of the conspiracy are effectively presented in one economical sentence.

2. **is**: Piso's exact descent is not clear, but his relationship to the noble *gens Calpurnia* is indubitable. He was exiled by Gaius (Dio 59,8,7), but restored by Claudius and held the consulship during his reign. The contemporary panegyric on him (*Laus Pisonis*) and other references (e.g. Juv. 5,109: *Mart.* 4,40,1) support Tacitus' picture of an amiable nonentity, whose virtues were negative rather than positive.

species: ' appearances like virtues ' i.e. ' or what passed for virtues '.

3. **namque f.**: Tacitus avoids a catalogue effect, and achieves separate emphasis for each quality by varying some part of the construction of each phrase or clause.

et ignotis: ' and he was of courteous conversation and address even to strangers' i.e. ' he was courteous and affable . . . '

procul grauitas morum: Piso had, according to Tacitus, no depth of character.

luxu: the archaic dative form in *-u* (cf. *A.* 3,30) emphasises the climax of Piso's self-indulgence.

perseuerum: the word seems to occur only here in extant Latin literature. Its rarity and position add force to Tacitus' observation about human nature.

Chapter 49

1. **memorauerim**: see 41,1 n.

quis . . . auctor: supply *fuerit*. Tacitus omits subjunctive verbs only when the construction is clear, and often when (as here) another subjunct. follows in a connected construction. Cf. 62,2.

sumpserunt: see 6,2 n.

2. Tacitus begins here his list of the different characters and their differing motives in joining the conspiracy. Few of the motives are presented as creditable.

praetoriae cohortis: this was originally the bodyguard of Republican generals. Augustus formed a permanent body of nine cohorts, to attend the Imperial family and preserve law and order in Italy. Their conditions of service were superior to those of the legions, and their concentration just outside Rome gave them political importance. The association of two of their officers with the conspiracy was important, because without Praetorian support, the conspiracy would have no chance at all of success.

3. **Lucanus Annaeus**: nephew of Seneca, and author of the epic poem *De Bello Ciuili*. He was just twenty-six when (70,1) he was forced to die. For the reversal of his names, see 20,2 n.

Plautiusque Lateranus: he had been involved with Messalina (*A.* 11,30) and expelled from the Senate, but was restored by Nero (*A.* 13,11). On the site of his family house in Rome, St John Lateran now stands.

propriae: 'personal'. Lucan had been one of Nero's close circle (Suet. *Luc.*), and this no doubt made the quarrel more bitter. The opening of his poem still contains the statutory eulogy of the Emperor.

ostentare: 'to make a show' i.e. he was forbidden to recite or to publish his poetry.

uanus adsimulatione: 'vain in his rivalry'. The phrase gains force from its position, and from the rare word (*adsimulatio*) which it contains.

4. **Flauius . . . Afranius**: they are known only from *A.* 15.

senatorii ordinis: gen. of quality, without the generic noun (*uir* etc.) which is normal classical usage. Cf. Livy 30,26,7 *Fabius Maximus moritur exactae aetatis*.

Chapter 50

1. **finem adesse**: Nero's *scelera* threatened the Empire's existence, and suggested that the only hope of saving it was to find another emperor.

qui fessis rebus succurreret: the words echo Virg. *Aen.* 11,335, and the epic association adds dignity to the conspirators, and also suggests that, like Latinus, who uses the words in Virgil, the conspirators may be doomed to failure.

Claudium Senecionem f.: apart from Senecio (*A.* 13,12), the *equites* are known to us mainly from Tacitus' account of the conspiracy.

2. **e praecipua familiaritate**: 'one of Nero's close friends'. The phrase is almost a formal title, like *ex prima admissione* (25,2 n.), and shows the same use of the abstract noun for the people concerned. Cf. *A.* 2,27 *ex intima Libonis amicitia*.

particeps ad: Natalis was in Piso's confidence, and so naturally involved in the conspiracy. The construction with *ad* seems to be unparalleled (*particeps* is normally followed by the partitive genitive), and is perhaps intended to draw attention to the phrase.

3. **rettuli**: see 49,2.

militares manus: 'military hands' lit. The metonymy suggests their readiness for action.

Gauius Siluanus: an inscription from Turin (Smallwood 282) records his military career and distinctions.

Faenio Rufo: he had been in A.D. 62 (*A.* 14,51) appointed joint Prefect of Praetorians with Tigellinus (37,1 n.).

in metum: fear brought Faenius into the conspiracy, and caused him to behave badly once it was discovered (58,3).

quasi: 'charging him with . . . ' See 15,1 n. For Agrippina see Intr. xix.

4. **descendisse**: 'come over'. Cf. *H.* 3,3 *descendisse in causam uidebatur*.

huc illuc f.: there is no indication of such behaviour by Nero during the Fire (39f.): but if his palace were to be fired now, such panic just might result.

occasio solitudinis: this might offer a better chance, the other greater glory. Neither, in fact, was really practicable.

pulcherrima: this agrees with *occasio* and *frequentia*. ' The attraction of the chance offered by solitude . . . and by the crowd to witness such a glorious deed.'

extimulauerant: the real apodosis of the condition is suppressed: see 8,2 n.

Chapter 51

1. **cunctantibus f.**: for the abl. abs., see 30,1 n. The length of the sentence, its structure (which emphasises key words), and its vocabulary, mark the beginning of the action proper.

Epicharis: a freedwoman (57,2): her activities and sufferings are used by Tacitus to contrast pointedly with the behaviour of the ' noble ' Romans.

quonam: the suffix *-nam* adds emphasis. Cf. §3. Epicharis probably became involved through her association with one of the conspirators.

accendere et arguere: probably historic infins. (11,3 n.), and not dependent on *conisa est.*

primores: the officers. For the fleet based on Misenum, see 46,2 n.

2. **nauarchus:** the commander of a unit. See Starr, 38 f. Proculus is not mentioned in the account of Agrippina's murder (*A.* 14,3-8): but it was organised by the commanding officer of the Misenine fleet, who clearly had assistants within it.

merita ... et quam: the variation of noun and noun clause helps to emphasise the second phrase.

in inritum: see 2,3 n.

destinationem uindictae: ' his intention of vengeance '. For the condition, see 36,4 n.

occasiones ... laetabatur: the first half expresses in indirect speech Epicharis' reflections, the *quia* clause is Tacitus' explanation of *occasiones.*

apud: Tacitus often uses this construction as a substitute for the locative. Cf. 23,2: 34,1.

3. **plura:** a verb of saying is easily understood from the context. Cf. 17,2: 52,2.

4. **composita:** ' confronted with the informer '.

confutauit: the verb appears only here in Tacitus, and adds emphasis to the statement.

haud falsa f.: ' that what was not proven was not necessarily false ': a typically Tacitean epigram to close the chapter.

Chapter 52

1. **crebro uentitabat:** the apparently superfluous adverb adds emphasis. Cf. *A.* 14,52.

omissis ... mole: ' dispensing with guards and the cumbrous trappings of his position '.

inuidiam ... si: another abbreviated conditional sentence. See 36,4 n.

praetendens: ' putting forward as an excuse '.

sacra mensae: guests were sacrosanct, and libations were made to gods during meals.

diique hospitales: the household gods, and perhaps Jupiter Hospitalis (Cic. *Fin.* 3,20,66).

qualiscumque: ' of whatsoever kind ' i.e. ' however bad '.

cruentarentur: the subjunctive is virtual oblique, representing part of Piso's excuse.

in illa ... domo: the Golden House (42,1 n.). It could hardly have been habitable yet, and in fact (55,1) Nero was currently residing elsewhere. The details of his domestic arrangements at this time are not clear from Tacitus' narrative, and they are mentioned mainly to illustrate an excuse of Piso's.

2. **haec in commune**: see 2,3 n. and 51,3 n.

ceterum: ' but in reality '.

L. Silanus: a nephew of D. Silanus (35,1 n.), and so a potential claimant of the Principate. Apart from Nero himself, he was the only male descendant of Augustus left alive. He was also, it is implied, a more admirable and ' Roman ' character than either Nero or Piso.

C. Cassii: a soldier and provincial governor, a distinguished jurist and an austere administrator (*A.* 12,11–12: 13,48) – the kind of man to appeal to Tacitus, who mentions him several times.

prompte daturis f.: ' those being likely to offer (the Principate) readily who were outside the conspiracy and who would pity Nero on the grounds that he had been criminally murdered '. This is all part of Piso's *timor occultus*, presented dramatically in indirect speech. For *tamquam* see 44,5 n.

3. **ad libertatem oreretur**: ' should rise towards (i.e. lead a movement to establish) a republic '. The meaning ' political freedom ' is often particularised to ' republican constitution ', and the word has great emotive quality for Romans.

sui muneris: ' within his own gift ': the gen. expresses sphere of reference.

super: ' in relation to ' i.e. ' Nero used that charge to . . . ' See 68–9.

Chapter 53

1. **circensium ludorum die**: the festival of Ceres was celebrated from 12 to 19 April (Ovid, *Fast.* 4,393,680), and the chief games were on the last day. For the use of the Circus, see 40,2 n.

rarus egressu: ' rare in his going out ' i.e. ' who rarely went out '.

hortis: not necessarily the *horti Seruiliani* (55,1), but any grounds surrounding any of his residences.

promptiores f.: ' opportunities for approaching were easier, because of the cheerful atmosphere of the show '.

2. **ut**: ' namely that . . . ' The subjunctives which follow indicate purpose.

subsidium rei familiari: ' help for his finances '. The scheme was obviously based on that used successfully in the murder of Julius Caesar (Suet. *Jul.* 82).

deprecabundus: the word is found here only in extant Latin literature. It is a standard formation, but its rarity and its position help to emphasise the content of the sentence.

animi ualidus et corpore ingens: with *deprecabundus*, this brackets the proposed action of Lateranus. The variety of construction adds emphasis, as does the Virgilian allusion: for at *Aen.* 11,641 *ingentem corpore* is used of an epic hero who is defeated and killed.

ut . . . habuisset: ' as each had of daring ' i.e. ' according to their individual boldness '.

Salutis f.: the uncertainty about the source of the dagger (cf. 55,2: 74,1) is complicated by textual difficulties. The MSS offer *Salutis in Etruria siue . . . Fortunae f(e)rentano in oppido*: in *Etruria* has long been suspect, because of its imprecision, which is unlike Tacitus' usual method of identifying a site, and it may be removed – it is almost certainly a later explanation of the location of the *oppidum*, which has got into the text. *frentano* (in spite of the ingenious defence of it in *CR* 1967, 264f.) is unlikely to be correct: it too is imprecise (*which* town of the Frentani?), and its possible connection with Scaevinus' family is tenuous (*patria* 55,2 means ' ancestral ', and is part of a desperate defence, not a fact, and 74,1 does not accept it as a fact): the town is almost certainly Ferentinum (Ferento), in Etruria. Finally, the reference is probably to one temple and not two, the doubt being about the deity's name: there was certainly a temple of Salus on the Quirinal in Rome, but 74,1 clearly does not refer to that: the goddess is probably an Etruscan one, variously equated with the Roman Salus or Fortuna.

detraxerat: it had presumably been a dedicatory offering, and its associations with Salus/Fortuna would be an encouraging omen for its intended use.

3. **aedem Cereris:** see 44,1 n.

ferrent in castra: Emperors were often first proclaimed in the Praetorian (49,2 n.) Camp. Nero himself had been (*A.* 12,69), and it was a key point in the Year of the Four Emperors which followed his reign (see, e.g., *H.* 1,17–18, 28, 36).

Antonia: daughter of the Emperor Claudius by his second wife (*A.* 12,2).

C. Plinius: on Tacitus' sources and his attitude to them, see Introd. 1. He here makes a specific citation in order to advance arguments against its validity. The Elder Pliny's ' History of My Times ', in thirty one books, is listed by his nephew in *Ep.* 3,5,6, and mentioned by its author in *N.H. praef.* 20.

4. **quoquo modo traditum:** ' in whatever way handed down ' i.e. ' the story, true or false '.

inanem ad spem: the plot to kill Nero might well have succeeded: but did Piso have a real chance of being proclaimed or accepted as his successor? And would he then have made Antonia his wife? Possibly: human beings, with varied motives, have joined even more unlikely plots.

commodauisse: 'lent her name and danger', a kind of zeugma: 'staked her name and life ' (Grant).

amore uxoris: cf. 59,5.

nisi si: the combination marks an exceptional case ('except if', 'unless of course '). Cf. *A.* 6,25 *uoluntate extinctam, nisi si* . . . Tacitus' comment is presented as a possible universal truth, hence the present indicative: both *cupido* and *dominor* have high emotional content – the (destructive) passion for (absolute) power – and *flagrans* is a fiery metaphor. By his presentation, Tacitus contrives simultaneously to reject the tradition, and to make capital out of its possible truth.

Chapters 54-8   The conspiracy betrayed: interrogations and precautions.

Chapter 54

1. **mirum quam**: the verb ' to be ' is omitted.

diuersi generis f.: ' among (people) of such different types '. The diversity is emphasised by the asyndeton, and by the change of construction from gen. of quality to adjectives.

taciturnitate: the word is strong, and implies deliberate silence. Tacitus uses it only here and of the Emperor Tiberius (*A.* 1,74).

proditio coepit: Plutarch (*Mor.* 6,505) gives a different account, namely that a garrulous conspirator said to a prisoner ' Tomorrow you will bless me ', and the prisoner told Nero. Tacitus' story is precise and circumstantial, his concern is with history not anecdote, and he is generally more reliable than Plutarch: his version is on the face of it more likely to be true.

pridie insidiarum: the gen. with *pridie/postridie*, to be explained as ' the day before/after with reference to . . . ', is first found with *eius diei* only, but extended in Silver Latin. Cf. Val. Max. 9,3,2 *postero comitiorum die*.

multo sermone: an extended and elliptical abl. of attendant circumstances.

dein: Scaevinus' behaviour is so careless as to be almost incredible. Presumably he did not expect treachery, and considered that any gossip would be too late to be dangerous. The staggering fact is that he almost got away with it.

supra: 53,2.

asperari . . . ardescere: ' to be roughened with a stone and to flash into a point '. Friction produces heat, polish and sharpness. The phrase echoes and adapts Luc. 7,139-40 *cautibus asper/exarsit mucro*, and uses poetical language and allusion to underline an action which is in itself commonplace, but here of great significance.

Milicho: the name means 'mild', and belongs to the category of slave name bestowed to indicate character, whether descriptively or hopefully. Cf. Onesimus in the *Epistle to Philemon*, 10-11.

2. **adfluentius:** another rare word, which appears only here in Tacitus.

magnae cogitationis: 'obviously very thoughtful'.

uagis: 'wandering' from subject to subject: 'desultory', 'disconnected'.

3. **siue . . . seu:** the second possible motive is emphasised by the change to *seu*, by the lack of balance within it, and by the weight of authority cited.

4. **nam:** '(whatever his motives, he acted) for . . .' i.e. 'at any rate . . .' The ellipse is not unnatural, and the odd *de consequentibus* which appears in the MSS after *tradidere* is best omitted, as a gloss.

cum . . . reputauit: this is the original indicative construction of circumstantial *cum* clauses, which the normal classical subjunctive largely replaced, but never quite banished. It is probably used by Tacitus as an archaism, in a chapter which has a good deal of literary emphasis. Note the alliteration in the sentence.

ultro metum intentabat: she actually and persistently added fear to his motives. The clause which follows depends on the idea of speaking implicit in *intentabat*.

at praemia: the final motive is greed.

Chapter 55

1. This chapter records the start of action to unravel the conspiracy, and its dramatic story is emphasised by dramatic presentation: historic present, alliteration, asyndeton, vivid vocabulary and dramatic speech all help the rapid narrative.

hortos Seruilianos: their exact location is unknown, but as Nero later (Suet. *Nero* 47) went there when contemplating flight to Ostia, they may be conjecturally placed somewhere between the Palatine and the Porta Ostiensis.

dictitans deductusque: the frequentative verb, and the alliteration of *d* and *t*, suggest insistence: while the series of short phrases mirrors the swift action.

Epaphroditum: he was Nero's private secretary (*a libellis*), who later helped him to suicide (Suet. *Nero* 49) and was himself executed for that by Domitian (Suet. *Dom.* 14). The extensive use of freedmen in positions of responsibility and power in the Imperial Household was developed by Claudius and continued by his successors. They were, for obvious reasons, trusted by the emperors and resented by the senators.

urgens . . . grauis: he tells of 'immediate risk, dangerous conspirators '. The position of the adjectives, and the lack of connection, underlines the urgency.

et cetera: when the last unit of a series sums up the series, it is regularly attached by *et* – cf. *H.* 4,1 *ubique lamenta, conclamationes et fortuna captae urbis.* This produces both the cumulative effect of asyndeton, and an extra emphasis on the last unit.

docet: this is the climax of the sentence, and its essential point.

iussit: the ' order ' is clearly not a real one. It represents an urgent statement, implying ' if you don't believe me, send for him . . . '

2. **defensionem orsus:** Tacitus avoids epic repetition in his narrative. After the detailed description in 54, Milichus is allowed only summary references to the story, and the prosecution's case is left to be inferred from the more dramatically valuable defence.

ferrum: the defence is articulated by the prominent position of the words at the heart of each charge – weapon, will, gifts, feast, dressings.

cuius: ' in respect of which he (understood that he) was being accused '.

olim . . . cultum: he claimed that it was a family relic.

subreptum: this word, which marks the climax of this part of the defence, appears only here in Tacitus.

incustodita . . . obseruatione: ' without taking particular note of days '.

libertates: ' gifts of freedom '. The plural of abstract nouns often so indicates concrete examples of the quality. Cf. *A.* 1,74 *audaciae.*

testamento diffideret: debts had to be settled before legacies could be paid, or slaves' freedom ratified. So gifts before death might be safer. Technically, such gifts and manumissions could also be set aside, if the money were needed for debts, but in practice it might be more difficult to do this.

3. **enimuero f.:** ' indeed he had always kept a good table, his life was comfortable and not entirely acceptable to austere critics '.

fomenta f.: ' the dressings for wounds were none of his ordering '. *nulla* is more emphatic than *non.*

palam: with *uana,* ' obviously without foundation '.

4. **adicit . . . constantiam:** Scaevinus has (belatedly) begun to use his head, and has an answer for every charge. He acts well: and he almost succeeds.

ut labaret . . . nisi: for the condition, see 8,2 n.

uxor: this is the first indication of her presence. Tacitus has compressed an account of complicated proceedings, to produce the important points in swift narrative. Some minor points are in consequence left without precise explanation.

C. Pisonis: see 48,2 n. He was apparently already suspected by Nero (*A.* 14,65).

Chapter 56

1. **tormentorum:** technically, Roman citizens could not be questioned under torture, but in practice it was sometimes employed in such cases of conspiracy. Cf. *A.* 11,22.

2. **arguendi peritior:** he hoped to win favour for himself, by naming as conspirators men Nero wanted to be rid of.

siue . . . siue ut: the evidence for Seneca's involvement in the conspiracy was (and is) inconclusive. Dio (62,24) follows a tradition which names Seneca as a founder member: Fabius Rusticus, who favoured Seneca (*A.* 13,20), is likely to have presented him as innocent. Tacitus, with better historical judgement than Dio, and with no reason to champion Seneca, finds no hard evidence: his presentation suggests that he inclines to think Seneca was not involved (here, the second alternative is given greater length and weight: at 60,2 the lack of evidence is emphasised: in 65 the proposal to replace Piso with Seneca is presented as a *fama*): and nothing that we know of Seneca suggests a desire for open power. It is not impossible that he was involved, but it is on the whole unlikely.

infensus Senecae: see 23,4 n. and 45,3 n.

4. **Lucanus f.:** see 49,3 and 4: 50,1.

matrem suam: she was never prosecuted (71,5). Here, and throughout his account of the conspiracy, Tacitus is emphasising the weakness and self-seeking of many of the conspirators.

Glitium Gallum: cf. 71,3. He was perhaps connected with Corbulo through Corbulo's mother, whose first husband was a P. Glitius Gallus.

Annium Pollionem: probably a brother of Annius Vinicianus (28,3 n.).

Chapter 57

1. **Epicharin:** cf. 51.

at illam non f.: the strong adversative, the prominent pronoun and the anaphora point the difference between her behaviour and that of the 'noble' Romans.

peruicere quin: 'conquered her from denying the charges laid' i.e. 'moved her from her steadfast denial of . . .' For the construction, see 44,2 n.

2. **gestamine sellae:** 'by means of a vehicle consisting of a chair' i.e. '(carried) in a chair'. *gestamen* is mainly poetical (e.g. Virg. *Aen.*

3,286) and its use of forms of transport seems to occur first in Tacitus. Cf. *A.* 2,2: *A.* 14,4.

dissolutis membris: probably dative with *insistere*, cf. *H.* 1,86.

fasciae: a kind of brassière. Cf. Prop. 4,9,49.

arcum sellae: the chair was like a Sedan chair, with a canopy.

ceruicem ... corporis ... conisa: the alliteration points the climax of her story.

clariore exemplo: this points the moral: then come the contrasting elements, not balanced in length or construction, ending in *pro*-compounds whose meanings are significantly different.

protegendo: for the ablative, see 8,2 n.

carissima ... pignorum: ' the dearest of their pledges ' i.e. ' their nearest and dearest '. *pignora* is used of people rather as we may talk of ' hostages to Fortune '.

3. **quamquam ... saepsisset**: the subjunctive with *quamquam*, an obvious analogy with the construction of *quamuis*, becomes fairly common in and after Livy.

Chapter 58

1. **mari et amne**: at Ostia and on the Tiber, to prevent an attack by water.

per fora f.: the anaphora and asyndeton, the variety of construction, and the order of the words, help to portray the rapid and diverse activity.

rura ... municipiorum: ' the country districts and the nearest Italian towns '.

pedites equitesque: these would belong to the Praetorian Guard (49,2 n.). Its cavalry is also mentioned (with the *Germani*) at *A.* 1,24.

Germanis: Batavian horsemen who, from Augustus to Galba, formed a personal bodyguard for the Imperial family.

quasi: see 15,1 n.

2. **continua ... et uincta**: the procession of prisoners was non-stop, and chained. The chains are also mentioned by Suet. *Nero* 36.

ubi ... introissent: for the subjunctive, see 45,3 n.

laetatum erga: ' a smile in the conspirators' direction '. *esse* is understood, and the noun clause, (' that one had smiled ') stands with the nouns as part of the subject of *accipi*.

si ... si ... inissent: the clauses provide variety of construction and therefore emphasis. The subjunct. is virtual oblique, of the charge.

Faenius ... Rufus: see 50,3 n.

3. **Subrio Flauo**: cf. 49,2 and 50,4.

adnuenti: ' nodding (to ask) whether ' i.e. ' making signs to ask whether '.

cognitionem: a recognised legal procedure, but more of an *ad hoc* inquiry than a formal judicial session. It is therefore often used of the Imperial or Senatorial court. Cf. *A.* 1,72 & 75.

Chapter 59   *The consequences of detection: death of Piso.*

Chapter 59

1. pergere ... escendere ... temptare: the infinitive with *hortor* is occasionally found even in classical prose (cf. Cic. *Sest.* 7 *quae me . . . haec minora relinquere hortatur*), but is commoner in the poets and historians.
   castra: see 53,3 n.
   si conatibus f.: their advice is presented in dramatic *obliqua*.
   motae rei: ' of a project under way '.
   2. scaenicus: the stage was no place for a Roman gentleman. Cf. 32; 33,1; 65. The word is derogatory, and appears only here in Tacitus.
   scilicet: a scathing addition. A ' performer ' could not lead an army, and his immediate followers were no better.
   3. sperare: the subject *eum* (i.e. Piso) is understood.
   dum amplectitur: the present indicative is retained for vividness and clarity. It gives the effect of direct speech, and indicates the precise meaning of *dum* – especially necessary when the pair that follow mean ' provided that '.
   The themes of positive action, of service to the state, and of a noble death, are presented as a climax to the arguments. Piso's reaction (*immotus his*) again suggests Tacitus' opinion of him.
   4. donec.... adueniret: see 11,1 n.
   stipendiis recentes: ' fresh in respect of service ' – not absolutely new recruits, but not veterans either.
   tamquam: see 44,5 n.
   5. obiit: Piso's death is (apart from that of Epicharis 57,2) the first one recorded by Tacitus after the discovery of the conspiracy. It is presented as craven and selfish, and accords with the character sketched in 48. For possible sources of information about this and the other deaths, see Introd. 1.
   adulationibus: this was to try and ensure that the estate was not wholly confiscated.
   dedit: ' he made as a concession to ... '
   degenerem: probably ' of low birth '. She and Domitius are known only from this passage.
   patientia: ' complaisance '. The *infamia* of Piso's adultery was increased by the attitudes of the others involved.

Chapters 60–5   Death of Seneca: was he a conspirator?

Chapter 60

1. **Plautii Laterani**: see 49,3 n.

consulis designati: Tacitus carefully, in this chapter, reminds his readers about Lateranus, Statius and Silvanus, who were mentioned in 49 and 50, and whose status could by now have been forgotten.

illud f.: ' the (usual) quick choice of death '.

locum . . . sepositum: outside the Esquiline Gate (Suet. *Claud.* 25).

Statii: cf. 50,3.

2. **sequitur caedes**: the death of Seneca (cf. 23,4 n.: 45,3 n.) is presented centrally, at length, and unequivocally as murder. He has been a recurring and important figure in the history of the period: he is a literary man, a statesman and a Stoic, and one of Nero's chief ' victims '. Tacitus' portrait of him in *A.* 13–15 is not always sympathetic or flattering, but he recognises Seneca's importance and quality, and for this account of his end, he may well have gone to Seneca's friend, Fabius Rusticus (61,3 and Introd. 1).

non quia: normally, *non quo(d)/quia* with the subjunctive repudiates a suggested reason, while *non quod/quia* with the indicative accepts the reason as factually possible, but denies its present validity – contrast Cic. *Acad.* 2,125 *me accusas, non quod tuis rationibus non assentiar, sed quod nullis* with Cic. *Planc.* 78 *quo magis sum miser . . . non quia multis debeo (leue enim est onus beneficii gratia), sed quia . . .* This would here imply that, although Seneca was involved in the conspiracy, Nero's reason for satisfaction was quite other. But this does not make sense. And in fact, from Livy on, we find *non quia* with the indicative used simply to reject a reason – cf. Livy 33,27,6 *id a Quinctio facile impetratum, non quia satis dignos eos credebat, sed quia . . .* Tacitus is therefore implying that Nero had no real evidence. Cf. 56,2 n.

coniurationis: ' clearly (guilty) of conspiracy ': an extension of the gen. used with verbs of accusing and condemning.

quando uenenum: cf. 45,3. Here it is stated as a fact.

3. **sermones . . . conducere**: this is certainly true, and may even have been said. The rest of the alleged statement (*salutem . . . inniti*) *could* be a polite if exaggerated formula: but its dangerous ambiguity must have been evident, and it is perhaps unlikely that the cautious Seneca used it. He is represented as scorning the possibility, in 61,1.

4. **Gauius Siluanus**: see 50,3 n.

nosceret: ' whether he recognised ' (and so would admit to be true).

forte an: like *incertum an* (64,1) and *dubium an*, this develops a purely adverbial meaning (' perhaps '), which has no effect on the construction.

ad eum diem: ' on that day '. *ad* with the acc. expresses a terminus.
ex Campania: where, perhaps, he had gone for his health (45,3).
suburbano rure: abl. of place without a preposition: see 9,1 n.
Pompeia Paulina: probably the daughter of Pompeius Paulinus,
a Roman *eques* from Arles (Pliny *N.H.* 33,143) and a sister of Paulinus
(18,3 n.).

Chapter 61

1. **missum . . . conquestum . . . Pisonis:** Seneca's confirmation of
the first part of Natalis' story (60,3 and n.) is implicit in his repetition of
key words. But the position of *missum* and the use of *nomine* suggests the
cautious lawyer's emphasis that the interview was not of his seeking, and
that he can vouch only for what Natalis *said*.

excusauisse: for the meaning ' offer in excuse ' cf. Livy 26,22,5
oculorum ualetudinem excusauit.

cur salutem f.: this could be evasion, but is more probably rhetorical
argument. Only the Emperor's welfare could be of more concern to him
than his own.

gnarum: this passive meaning (' known ') is found first and almost
exclusively in Tacitus. Cf. 62,2 *ignaram = ignotam.*

Senecae: the name is more emotive than *suam* would be. Cf. Germanicus' dying speech in *A.* 2,71 *flebunt Germanicum etiam ignoti*, and
Catullus' use of his own name in 8,1 and 19.

2. **quod erat f.:** ' who were the Emperor's most confidential advisers
in his brutalities '. For the gender of the relative pronoun, see 2,1 n.
For the more regular *consilium principis*, see 25,2 n.

an: so used to introduce a single indirect question, it is found in early
Latin, and from Livy on. Cf. §3 and Livy 40,14,7 *te quaerere ex eis . . . an
ferrum habuissent.*

3. **tradit Fabius Rusticus:** see Introd. 1.

non . . . reditum: ' the return journey was by a different route '. The
indicative verb probably indicates no more than a periphrasis: see 6,2 n.

flexisse: the intransitive use of *flecto* is mainly poetical and post-
Augustan. Cf. *H.* 2,70.

fatali omnium ignauia: as often in Tacitus, the sting is in the tail
and the abl. abs.

4. **intromisit:** his action is emphasised by the verb, which appears
only here in Tacitus.

necessitatem ultimam: variations of this phrase are used by Tacitus
to indicate enforced suicide. Cf. *H.* 1,72 *Tigellinus accepto . . . supremae
necessitatis nuntio.*

Chapter 62

1. **testamenti tabulas**: he wished to add a codicil to his existing will. Cf. 64,4.

quando f.: Seneca's conversation in his final scene is carefully and dramatically managed. There is fairly summary indirect speech here and at 63,1, which briskly cites philosophical points, more rhetorical but still indirect speech at the end of this chapter, and direct, highly emotional speech to his wife in 63,2. For his final and more formal utterance, and Tacitus' comment upon it, see 63,3 and n.

quod unum: ' the only gift he had, and yet the finest '.

testatur: the verb is neatly used to imply both solemn statement and legacy.

bonarum artium: see 45,2 n. ' They would win a reputation for good character as the reward of steadfast friendship '.

2. **modo intentior**: the emphasis is increased by the variation in construction and length.

rogitans ubi f.: frequentative verb, repeated *ubi*, omission of the verb ' to be ' (49,1 n.), and rhetorical questions, add further intensity.

sapientiae: of the Stoic philosophy. Stoics believed that the man who lived in harmony with reason had a true happiness which was unaffected by the accidentals of life.

cui . . . fuisse: see 6,2 n.

ignaram: for the passive meaning, see 61,1 n., and contrast 64,1.

post . . . interfectos: see 1,1 n. Nero had also (*A.* 14,64) killed his wife Octavia: but this was after Seneca's withdrawal from public life (*A.* 14,56), whereas he had to some extent condoned the deaths of Agrippina (*A.* 14,11) and Britannicus (*A.* 13,17). There is therefore some logic in connecting his own death with theirs.

educatoris praeceptorisque: the double description reinforces the point of his relationship with Nero.

Chapter 63

1. **uelut in commune**: ' more or less publicly ', addressed to the whole group.

paululum . . . mollitus: ' a little softened in contrast to his immediate fortitude '. The text has been suspected, but will perhaps stand. For *aduersus* cf. 19,2.

temperaret: for the omission of *ut*, see 11,3 n.

uitae ... actae: his own life, lived according to Stoic doctrine (62,1 n.).

percussoris: this might refer to the doctor who actually cut the veins (cf. 69,2). But considering the context, *eodum ictu* . . . *exoluunt* §2, and the usual meaning of *percussor*, it is more probably part of a grand gesture: ' she demanded the executioner's stroke '.

2. **tum Seneca**: his motives are described very differently by Dio (62,25,1). For possible sources of information about Seneca's end, see Introd. 1.

uitae f.: the short, sharp phrases, with balance and contrast, reflect Seneca's own style. But they are unlikely to be an exact quotation: see n. on *inuertere* §3.

claritudinis plus: because her death was voluntary.

brachia: i.e. the veins in their arms. The method of suicide was so statutory that Tacitus can take a verbal short cut.

3. **tenuatum**: for *ex-* or *at-tenuatum*: see 14,1 n. For his diet, cf. 45,3.

poplitum: behind the knees.

cruciatibus: from loss of blood? or from the cuts?

impatientiam: loss of self-control.

suadet . . . abscedere: the infinitive after *suadeo* is occasionally found even in classical prose. Cf. Cic. *De Or.* 1,251 *nemo suaserit . . . elaborare*.

et nouissimo quoque f.: Tacitus, though presenting Seneca's death sympathetically, cannot resist a wry comment on his last recorded activity. Seneca may have been distracting his mind from suffering: or trying to complete his current book (Dio 62,25,2): or simply producing the statutory ' last words '.

inuertere supersedeo: both words appear only here in Tacitus, and help to point the comment. Ancient historians seldom quoted another's words *verbatim*: if they wanted to use them, they adapted words and sentiments to their own style (*inuertere*: cf. Manilius 2,898 *inuersus titulus*, and *uertere* in Quint. 10,5,5 *qui uertere orationes Latinas uetant*). Genuine quotation is rare, and specific (see 67,3 and n.).

Tacitus obviously considers Seneca's action ostentatious, and is perhaps deliberately declining to help the publicity.

Chapter 64

1. **ac ne**: again, the change of construction emphasises the second reason.

glisceret: see 10,4 n.

iubet: a verb of instruction is clearly missing, and this, from its resemblance to the beginning of *inhiberi*, is the one most likely to have been lost.

hortantibus f.: the series of short phrases, in different constructions and referring to different people and actions, combined with the asyndeton, mirrors the frenzied and varied activity.

incertum an: ' while she was perhaps unconscious '. For the adverbial phrase, see 60,4 n.

2. **nam f.**: Tacitus may be dissociating himself from uninstructed opinion while also using it to make an insinuation against Paulina. But it is clear from e.g. Dio that a tradition unfavourable to Seneca (and possibly all connected with him) existed.

cui: i.e. *uitae*.

laudabili ... memoria: probably abl. of quality (cf. Cic. *Phil.* 13,47 *adulescens summa ... memoria parentis sui*), as are the following abl. phrases.

ostentui: is there a suggestion of ostentation by Paulina in the use of the word? Cf. 29,3.

3. **tractu**: see 37,2 n.

Statium Annaeum: he is otherwise unknown, but his name (which includes Seneca's family name) suggests that he may be a dependant of his. Doctors in Rome were often foreign, or of inferior status.

uenenum ... Atheniensium: hemlock.

extinguerentur: the subjunctive shows that this is part of Seneca's request, and supports the idea that he saw himself as a second Socrates: cf. Plato, *Phaedo* 117f. and Sen. *Dial.* I, 3,12.

frigidus ... artus: the poison, to take effect, had to circulate in the bloodstream: Seneca had already lost a lot of blood, and what was left was moving sluggishly.

artus is acc. of respect, a poetical construction imitated from the Greek, and first introduced into prose by Tacitus.

4. **calidae aquae**: warmth would stimulate circulation, and so assist both the bleeding and the poisoning processes.

libare ... Ioui liberatori: that Thrasea uses the same phrase (*A.* 16,35) at his suicide, and uses it of his blood, suggests that *liquor* here must at least include blood, and not be simply bath water.

The end of dinner was marked by libations of wine, and Seneca's ' libation ' marks the ending of his life. *Jupiter liberator* is clearly *Zeus eleutherios* (Thuc. 2,71), and is appropriately recognised as Seneca is freed from life and Nero.

praediues et praepotens: the assonance helps the emphasis.

supremis: his funeral.

Chapter 65

fama fuit: see 56,2 n.

Subrium Flauum: cf. 49,2.

destinauisse ut: a rare construction, but a reasonable one.

quasi insontibus: ' chosen, by men apparently innocent, for his noble virtue '.

dedecori: the dative is one of advantage. ' It did not help the disgrace if . . . '

citharoedus . . . tragoedus: the technical terms (only here in Tacitus) are emotive when applied to present and prospective Roman emperors, and their assonance points the sarcasm.

tragico ornatu: he appeared in tragic costume as a leading tragic character, and dramatically recited part of the character's story. Nero did this too (Suet. *Nero* 21 lists *Oedipodem excaecatum* and *Herculem insanum* among his themes), and so did Thrasea (*A.* 16,21). It would hardly by itself have disqualified Piso from the principate, but it makes a neat point in the context.

Chapters 66–8   Deaths of the army officers involved.

Chapter 66

1. **quoque . . . non:** this is occasionally found for *ne . . . quidem*, when a more precise emphasis is required, and where the negative does not qualify the emphasised word. Cf. Livy 22,42,8 *cum . . . pulli quoque auspicio non addixissent.*

Faenium: cf. 58,2.

inquisitorem: the solitary technical term (cf. 65) adds point.

Scaeuinus: cf. 56,3.

ultro f.: ' to do a voluntary favour to a good Emperor '. For the omission of *ut*, see 11,3 n.

2. **non uox f.:** Faenius' downfall is emphasised by anaphora, variety of construction and alliteration.

Ceruario Proculo: cf. 50,1.

Cassio milite f.: this kind of reference suggests that Tacitus had some quite detailed information about the conspiracy and its discovery.

Chapter 67

1. **Subrius Flauus tribunus:** cf. 65 and 49,2. Note that his official position is emphasised again in this story of his end. The whole account is an implicit comment on the difference between his behaviour and that of the more ' noble ' conspirators.

neque se: this depends on the statement implied in *trahens*. ' He was a soldier, and would not join civilians (or worse) in such a criminal project.'

2. **urgebatur:** for the tense, see 37,3 n.

sacramenti: his military oath of loyalty to the Emperor.

oderam . . . nec: ' I hated you: and yet . . . ' Flavus is giving the reasons for his developing hatred. For *nec* so used cf. Cic. *Tusc.* 2,60 *plurimos autem annos in philosophia consumpsi, nec ferre possum (dolorem)*.

parricida: the word is used to describe the murderer of any close kin, and also a traitor (cf. 73,3). The order of *parricida* to *incendiarius* is chronological rather than climactic, but the accumulative effect is still considerable.

3. **ipsa rettuli uerba:** because of the literary tradition of ' inverting ' (63,3 n.) speeches, Tacitus' specific statement that the words are Flavus' own should be taken seriously. The version in Dio 62,24,2 is not quite the same: but it is not so vouched for, and it exists only in epitome. Tacitus' source of information is not clear, but he appears to think it accurate. His use and explanation of the words is characteristically complex: they help to characterise Flavus, his fellow-conspirators and Nero, and also provide an oblique comment on Seneca's highly polished style.

incomptos et ualidos: they were not expressed in formal rhetorical style, but had force.

audiendi . . . insolens: ' unaccustomed within the sphere of hearing ' i.e. ' not accustomed to be told '.

4. **tribuno:** the fact that the executioner was a brother officer is emphasised.

increpans: Flavus retains his humour and his professionalism to the end.

ex disciplina: ' in accordance with training '. He complains that they cannot even dig a regulation grave.

utinam . . . ferias: Flavus' final words are emphasised by alliteration.

sesquiplaga: the word seems to occur only here in Latin literature. Similar *sesqui-* formations are, however, quite common. It may be a soldier's word, and it certainly helps, by its presence, position and oddity, to emphasise the fate of Flavus.

dicendo: for the abl., see 8,2 n.

Chapter 68

1. **non aliter f.:** a comparison with Dio 62,24 and Suet. *Nero* 36 makes it clear that Asper means that death alone can help one so far advanced in wickedness.

ceteri: Scaurus and Paulus, see 50,3.

at non: Faenius' death follows the pattern of cowardice already established (58,2 : 66,2).

Chapters 68 and 69   Death of the consul.

2. **opperiebatur . . . ut**: a rare but logical construction. Cf. Livy 42,48,10. For Vestinus, see 48,1 and 52,3.

plures quia: the change of construction emphasises the more important reason.

insociabilem: ' unco-operative '.

3. **principis f.**: his contempt is expressed in the alliterative *p*'s.

ferociam: ' outspokenness ', perhaps. The word means, among other things, bold freedom of speech. See H. W. Traub in TAPA 1953, 250f.

quae . . . relinquunt: their sting lay not in their roughness, but in their basic truth.

Statiliam Messalinam: she eventually became (Suet. *Nero* 35) Nero's fourth wife: and is said (Schol. in Juv. 6,434) to have been rich, beautiful and clever.

Chapter 69

1. **non . . . non**: the anaphora emphasises the lack of justification for Nero's action. The whole chapter is written in forceful style, the short, sharp clauses gaining extra point from their juxtaposition, and from the figures, alliteration, significant vocabulary and variety of construction which they contain.

speciem . . . induere: Tacitus is particularly fond of such metaphors, which imply dissimulation and deceit.

dominationis: always a charged word in Tacitus. It properly indicates the power of a master over a slave.

Gerellanum: otherwise unknown.

immittit f.: ' sent in with orders to . . . ', as if to deal with an already existing crisis. The use of a senior officer and some five hundred Praetorians on such a mission requires justification, and so Nero's orders employ strong military metaphors to suggest a serious military situation. Vestinus' ' fortress ' (the *uelut* indicates both exaggeration and contempt) and his ' special force ' are to be dealt with, and the verbs ordering the required action stand emphatically at the start of each clause.

quia f.: this is Tacitus' explanation of the orders just given.

imminentis: its ambivalence (' overlooking ' and ' threatening ') is emphasised by its position.

decora . . . et pari aetate: they were ' handsome . . . and all young '.

2. **cuncta f.**: the scene is set in quiet, smooth description.

dissimulando metu: the abl. describes attendant circumstances. It is akin to the modal abl. of the gerund explained in 8,2n.

clauditur f.: haste is conveyed by short clauses, action by emphatic initial verbs: then (*uigens adhuc*) interest shifts to Vestinus and the description of his end.

mersatur: the verb occurs only here in Tacitus, and draws attention to the death inflicted on the consul. For the use of the bath, see 64,4 n.

nulla . . . miseraretur: Vestinus is sympathetically presented as a victim of Nero's tyranny, and as dying a noble death.

3. **ex mensa**: 'immediately after their dinner'. Cf. *G.* 22 *statim e somno . . . lauantur.*

et imaginatus et inridens: Nero's attitude is pointed by the position and balance of the participles, by the alliteration, and by the 'solitary' *imaginatus.*

Chapter 70   Death of Lucan.

Chapter 70

1. **Lucani**: see 49,3 and n.

profluente sanguine: for this death scene, Tacitus depicts the act allusively and subjectively. This suits the subject (a poet), and provides a contrast to the military vigour of the last scene.

frigescere: another Tacitean 'solitary'. The verb is not very common in literature, but appears in Celsus, a medical writer of the first century A.D. *extrema* = 'extremities' has a similar history. They are probably therefore clinical terms, which in this context and presentation have an extra harshness.

carmen: if the passage referred to is Lucan, *Bell. Ciu.* 3,635–46, or any other section of that epic, then *carmen* is used to mean 'part of a poem'. But there is no certainty that we possess the poem or passage recited.

per . . . imaginem: 'by a similar form of death'. Cf. *H.* 3,28 *omni imagine mortium.* The phrase is strongly reminiscent of Virg. *Aen.* 2,369, and so links Lucan with Virgil, and the Pisonian conspiracy with the Fall of Troy. It is fitting, too, that Lucan should die reciting some of the poetry which was the cause of his unpopularity with Nero (49,3).

2. **Senecio etc.**: cf. 49,4: 50,1: 56,4.

ex: 'in accordance with', cf. 72,1. The fact of their brave end is recorded, but not emphasised as was their cowardice (56,4).

nullo . . . memorando: abl. abs. expressing attendant circumstances: 'without memorable act or word'.

Chapters 71–4   Rewards and sufferings, various.

Chapter 71

1. This final chapter about the conspiracy, in appearance so brisk and businesslike and full of detail, starts with an elaborate and emotional

sentence, containing historic infinitives, chiasmus, anaphora and significant vocabulary. The spate of names which follows helps to produce an impression of great numbers involved.

funeribus ... uictimis: the ' victims ' are sacrificial victims, offered in thanksgiving, and the juxtaposition is pointed.

alius ... alius: the alliterative chiasmus is sharply focused on the loss of immediate family, then the phrase is extended to include others. ' With son, brother, relative or friend done to death, they offered thanks ... '

ornare f.: this was a mark of rejoicing. Cf. Juv. 10,65.

ipsius: ' himself ', ' the master '. Cf. 74,2 and Cat. 3,7.

festinata indicia: see 56,2 and 66,2.

remuneratur: this, like *dito* and *conseruator* in the next sentence, appears only here in Tacitus. They may be part of a pattern of ironic emphasis.

Milichus: see 54–5.

conseruatoris f.: ' assumed the name of Saviour, in its Greek form ' (i.e. Soter). The Latin *conseruator* is used of the Emperor (e.g. *CIL* II, 2038), and would therefore be a dangerous name for a freedman to assume. Soter, however, could be so used (*CIL* V, 88). Tacitus appears to be avoiding the Greek word in his sentence.

2. **tribunis**: see 50,3 and n.

uanitate exitus: the details of his ' vainglorious end ' are unknown.

Pompeius: one of his names is clearly missing from the text. None of these men is otherwise known: they were presumably military tribunes of the Praetorian Guard.

quasi: ' on the grounds (15,1 n.) not indeed that they hated the Emperor, but that they were thought (to do so) '. Praetorians had to be like Caesar's wife, or they could not be trusted.

3. **Nouio Prisco**: consul in A.D. 78 (*CIL* VI, 1, 2056).

Glitio ... Pollioni: see 56,4 n. and 28,3 n.

Gallum Egnatia Maximilla: they went to Andros, where an inscription (Smallwood 245) records them as benefactors – which may explain *post ademptis*.

utraque: the fact of her wealth, and of its later confiscation.

4. **Crispinus**: he had once been Prefect of Praetorians, but was removed – for loyalty – by Agrippina (*A.* 12,42).

Verginium Flauum: a teacher of rhetoric, cf. Quint. 7,4,40.

Musonium Rufum: an *eques*, a Stoic (*H.* 3,81), and a friend of the younger Pliny (*Ep.* 3,11,5).

Cluuidieno ... Altino: known only from this passage.

uelut in agmen et numerum: ' to complete the procession and the list '. For the final use of *in* cf. 44,5 *in saeuitiam*.

permittuntur: 'were allowed', perhaps the term of the official decree.

5. **Caesennius:** also a philosopher, and friend of Seneca's (Sen. *Ep.* 87,2).

experti: they discovered that they had been on trial only when informed of the sentence.

Acilia: see 56,4. The charge made against her by Lucan was ignored.

sine ... sine: the anaphora emphasises her ambivalent position.

Chapter 72

1. **bina ... uiritim manipularibus:** all three words emphasise the individual gifts.

ex modo annonae: 'in accordance with (70,2 n.) the way of the corn supply' i.e. 'at the market price'. Soldiers then, as now, had certain deductions against basic pay, and payment for rations was one of these: see Webster, 258. This concession therefore represented an increase in pay for the Praetorians.

quasi ... expositurus: see 10,2 n.

triumphale decus: by this time, triumphs were celebrated only by the emperor, who was C-in-C all forces, or (occasionally) by members of his immediate family. But the triumphal *insignia* (see §2 n.), which allowed the recipient certain privileges (e.g., of having his statue in a public place, and of wearing triumphal dress at festivals) were sometimes awarded. They were originally given to the general who in the field had conducted a successful campaign, but by now were often simply part of the 'Honours List'.

Petronio . . . Neruae: Petronius had been consul in A.D. 61 (*A.* 14,29), and soon afterwards (*A.* 14,39) governor of Britain. Nerva, who in A.D. 96 was for a short time emperor, was just now taking the first major step towards a public career. Precisely how these men had helped Nero is not clear, but they may have been members of his *consilium* (25,2 n.).

apud Palatium: a rare honour. Cf. Suet. *Otho* 1,3.

2. **consularia insignia:** this grant, like that of the triumphal *insignia* (§1), gave some of the social privileges of consular rank, without the rank itself. The holder was, e.g., entitled to wear the dress appropriate to the rank, and to sit among the consulars at festivals. But he had no seat in the Senate.

Nymphidio . . . quia: the MSS readings are either nonsense or ungrammatical: also, we should expect, in such a character sketch, some mention of Nymphidius' surname Sabinus. There is something missing from the text, but although the general drift is clear, the exact supplement remains uncertain.

Nymphidius was the grandson of one of Claudius' freedmen (Plut. *Galba* 9). After Nero's death, he attempted to plot against Galba.

pars . . . erit: ' will (be shown to) be involved in Rome's downfall '. The use of *pars* for a person is not common, and may be poetical: cf. Sil. 5,329 *Italae pars magna ruinae | Appius.*

igitur: see 37,2 n.

principum: probably ' imperial house ' rather than ' Emperors '.

ex G. Caesare: Plutarch (*Galba* 9) says that Nymphidius was born before Gaius knew his mother, and that his real father was a gladiator.

procerus . . . toruo: Gaius' height and grim expression are also mentioned by Suet. *Gaius* 50.

siue: an afterthought, indicating the circumstances in which Nymphidius' claim might just possibly be true.

scortorum . . . cupiens: the construction indicates a permanent characteristic: cf. 6,4 n.

inlusit: cf. *A.* 13,17 *tradunt . . . illusum isse pueritiae Britannici Neronem.*

It is fairly certain that the end of the chapter is missing. Tacitus would not have ended his sketch of Nymphidius at this point.

Chapter 73

1. **uocato senatu:** the repetition (cf. 72,1) is probably resumptive after the digression on Nymphidius.

conlata . . . adiunxit: the trial had not been an open one (55-6), so Nero is now publishing his evidence in justification of his actions. Such material could be no more trustworthy than some of the political ' confessions ' with which the modern world is familiar, and the next sentence shows that this possibility (that the Conspiracy never existed) was recognised. But when Nero is covering up a crime (e.g. *A.* 13,17 Britannicus: *A.* 14,11 Agrippina: *A.* 14,62 Octavia) his technique is different: it is also difficult to believe that so much detailed evidence was fabricated: and a sufficient range of responsible people had been present to guarantee basic authenticity. The considered opinion of Tacitus must also have some value: it is significant that he presents the story as *uulgi rumor.*

tamquam: see 44,5 n.

2. **ceterum:** Tacitus produces sound reasons for his belief in the existence and importance of the conspiracy.

reuictam: probably ' suppressed ', the three participles representing the life history of the conspiracy.

fatentur: the present tense, in obvious contrast to *dubitauere*, suggests that they or their writings were available to Tacitus.

post interitum Neronis: when they would have had nothing to gain from any support of any ' official line '.

3. **ut cuique f.**: ' as each had most sorrow ' – those who had suffered most were first in fawning upon Nero. *adulatio* is a loaded word: Tacitus is throughout his writings very bitter about the servility of senators: he is concerned for the dignity of the body to which he was proud to belong, and feels that it is possible to serve without being servile.

Gallionem: born Annaeus Novatus, he was Seneca's elder brother, but was later adopted by Junius Gallio (*A.* 6,3). When governor of Achaea in A.D. 51/2, he declined to listen to the Jews' charges against St Paul (*Acts* 18,12–16).

Salienus Clemens: otherwise unknown.

parricidam: see 67,2 n.

neu: they were afraid that he might ' drag back to fresh cruel action things settled or wiped out by the Emperor's clemency '. This sounds like a précis of their statements in the House: otherwise, *mansuetudo* has a very odd ring. See n. on *commentarii senatus*, 74,3.

Chapter 74

1. **dona f.**: the alliteration points the bitter statement.

uetus aedes apud circum: the Sun was the charioteer *par excellence*. The cult is said (Varro. *L.L.* 5,68) to be Sabine in origin. For *apud*, see 51,2 n. Tertullian (*Spect.* 8,1) says that the temple was *medio spatio*.

in quo ... parabatur: see 53,1.

occulta coniurationis: ' secrets consisting of the conspiracy ': ' the secret conspiracy '.

retexisset: the subjunctive is virtual oblique, reflecting the reason given. The god's rôle is emphasised by the position of the verb, itself found only here in Tacitus, and by the echo of Virg. *Aen.* 1,356 *caecumque ... scelus omne retexit.*

utque: dependent on *decretum* (*est*), understood from *decernuntur*.

circensium Cerealium: see 53,1 and n.

Neronis cognomentum: it did not establish itself as did the names honouring Julius Caesar and Augustus.

ex quo: but, according to one version, the dagger had come *from* a temple of Salus (53,2): perhaps a temple to the Roman Salus is now being built. This difficulty of meaning, together with the linguistic fact that *ex quo ... prompserat* requires a more specific antecedent than it has got, makes it fairly certain that something is missing from the text.

2. **ipse**: see 71,1 n.

arma: ' the armed rebellion '.

Iulii Vindicis: in A.D. 68 Vindex, then governor of Gallia Lugdunensis, started a great rebellion against Nero (Dio 63,22 f.), which was eventually crushed by Verginius Rufus (23,1 n.).

ad auspicium f.: ' were interpreted as . . . ', Tacitus' tone does not suggest that he thought much of the interpretation.

3. **reperio in commentariis senatus:** on Tacitus' use of the *acta senatus* as an historical source, see Introd. 1. The precise citation here is perhaps made as a guarantee of the truth of his somewhat staggering statement that a consul designate, speaking in the Senate, proposed the building of a temple to Nero as a god, in Rome, in Nero's lifetime. Living Emperors *were* worshipped in the East, where it was politic to establish their inheritance of the attributes of the Hellenistic kings: in the Western provinces, cult centres (22,1 n.) for the worship of 'Rome and Augustus' encouraged the spread of Romanisation: and in Italy, the emperor's Genius was honoured as that of the father of the national family. Only after death (and then only if so voted by the Senate) were emperors accorded deification and the worship that involved.

Cerialem: he committed suicide in the following year, and was apparently not much regretted (*A.* 16,17).

pro sententia: ' when asked for his opinion '. Strict protocol governed the order in which senators were asked to speak, and the consul designate normally came first (*A.* 3,22).

tamquam: see 44,5 n.

mortale fastigium egresso: for the acc., see 45,3 n.

sed ipse . . . interpretatione: there is again, at this point, almost certainly a gap in the text. No certainty is possible, but this supplement gives reasonable sense.

omen malum: for the reasons stated, it was not healthy to be *diuus*.

On this fine dramatic note, Tacitus ends his book. He could, clearly, have so organised his material as to end with the end of a year (his account of this year ends at *A.* 16,13), but he is adapting the basic annalistic structure to his own purpose (1,1 n.), and prefers to leave us with the end of the conspiracy, and an aphorism.

Index to Notes

Index of Proper Names

Romans are generally listed under the gentile name (e.g. Plautius Lateranus under Plautius), except where they are more commonly known by another name (e.g. Corbulo, Seneca). References are to chapters of the text.

Vocabulary

The perfects and supines of all verbs of the third conjugation, and of all irregular verbs of other conjugations are given. Otherwise, the figure following a verb denotes that it is a regular example of that conjugation. The omission of a perfect or supine indicates that it is not in normal use.

The comparatives and superlatives of adjectives and adverbs are not listed separately unless formed irregularly.

The symbol ‾ indicates a long vowel: ˘ that it may be long or short.

ā, ab, *prep. with abl.*, by, from

abauus, -ī, *m.*, great-great-grandfather

abdō, -didī, -ditum (3), *tr.*, hide

abeō, -īre, -iī, -itum, *intr.*, go away

abiciō, -iēcī, -iectum (3), *tr.*, throw away

abnuō, -uī, -uitum (3), *tr.*, deny, refuse

aboleō, -ēuī (2), *tr.*, destroy

abripiō, -puī, -reptum (3), *tr.*, tear away

abrumpō, -ūpī, -uptum (3), *tr.*, break off

abruptus, -a, -um, steep

abscēdō, -cessī, -cessum (3), *intr.*, withdraw, depart

abscessus, -ūs, *m.*, departure

abscindō, -scidī, -scissum (3), *tr.*, cut

absentia, -ae, *f.*, absence

absoluō, -uī, -ūtum (3), *tr.*, acquit

absolūtiō, -ōnis, *f.*, acquittal

abstineō, -uī, -tentum (2), *intr.*, abstain from

abstrahō, -xī, ctum (3). *tr.*, pull away

abstrūdō, -ūsī, -ūsum (3), *tr.*, hide

absum, -esse, āfuī, *intr.*, be absent

absūmō, -umpsī, -umptum (3), *tr.*, consume

absurdus, -a, -um, ridiculous

abūsque, *adv.*, all the way from

abūtor, -ūsus (3), *dep.*, abuse

āc, *see* atque

accēdō, -cessī, -cessum (3), *intr.*, be added

accendō, -ndī, -nsum (3), *tr.*, inflame

accidō, -dī (3), *intr.*, happen, fall at

accingō, -nxī, -nctum (3), *tr.*, gird, equip

acciō (4), *tr.*, summon

accipiō, -cēpī, -ceptum (3), *tr.*, receive, hear

accūsātiō, -ōnis, *f.*, indictment
accūsātor, -ōris, *m.*, accuser
ācer, -cris, -cre, sharp, spirited
aciēs, -ēī, *f.*, battle-line, battle
ācriter, *adv.*, eagerly
āctiō, -ōnis, *f.*, performance
ad, *prep, with acc.*, to, in addition
    to, for, at
adaequō (1), *tr.*, make equal
adcurrō, -currī, -cursum (3),
    intr., run up
addō, -didī, -ditum (3), *tr.*, add
addūcō, -dūxī, -ductum (3), *tr.*,
    bring up
adeō, *adv.*, so much, so
adeō, -īre, -iī, -itum, *intr.*,
    approach
adfectus, -ūs, *m.*, emotion, feel-
    ing
adferō, -ferre, attulī, adlātum,
    tr., bring
adficiō, -fēcī, -fectum (3), *tr.*,
    affect
adfluentius, *adv.*, more lavishly
adgnōscō, -nōuī, -nitum (3), *tr.*,
    recognise
adgredior, -gressus (3), *dep.*,
    attack
adgregō (1), *tr.*, attach to
adhibeō (2), *tr.*, summon, employ
adhūc, *adv.*, still, so far
adiaceō, -ēre (2), *intr.*, be near
adiciō, -iēcī, -iectum (3), *tr.*, add
adigō, -ēgī, -actum (3), *tr.*, drive
adimō, -ēmī, -emptum (3), *tr.*,
    take away
adipiscor, adeptus (3), *dep.*,
    obtain

aditus, -ūs, *m.*, approach
adiungō, -nxī, -nctum (3,) *tr.*,
    join to
admīrātiō, -ōnis, *f.*, admiration
admoneō (2), *tr.*, remind, advise
adnotō (1), *tr.*, note
adnuō, -uī, -ūtum (3), *intr.*, nod
    to, agree to
adolēscō, -ēuī, -ultum (3), *intr.*,
    grow
adoptiō, -ōnis, *f.*, adoption
adoptō (1), *tr.*, adopt
adprobō (1), *tr.*, prove
adpūgnō (1), *tr.*, attack
adquīrō, -īsiuī, -īsitum (3), *tr.*,
    get, acquire
adscīscō, -īuī, -ītum (3), *tr.*,
    admit, adopt
adsēnsus, -ūs, *m.*, approval
adsequor, -secūtus (3), *dep.*,
    catch up with
adseuērō (1), *tr.*, assert, maintain
adsimulātiō, -ōnis, *f.*, likeness
adsimulō (1), *tr.*, compare
adsistō, astitī (3), *intr.*, stand
    by
adstō, -stitī (1), *intr.*, stand by
adsum, -esse, -fuī, *intr.*, be
    present
adsūmō, -mpsī, -mptum (3), *tr.*,
    take, accept, receive
adsurgō, -surrēxī, -surrēctum
    (3), *intr.*, rise up
adueniō, -uēnī, -uentum (4),
    intr., arrive
aduentō (1), *intr.*, approach
aduersus, aduersum, *prep. with*
    acc., against

aduersus, -a, -um, opposite, adverse

aduertō, -rtī, -rsum (3), *tr.*, notice

adūlātiō, -ōnis, *f.*, flattery

adūlor (1), *dep.*, fawn upon

adulter, -erī, *m.*, adulterer, lover

aduocō (1), *tr.*, summon

aduoluō, -uī, -ūtum (3), *tr.*, roll towards

aedēs, -is, *f.*, temple; *pl.*, house

aedificium, -ī, *n.*, building

aeger, -gra, -grum, ill

aegrē, *adv.*, reluctantly

aegrēscō, -ere (3), *intr.*, become ill

aegrōtus, -a, -um, ill

aemulus, -ī, *m.*, rival

aequābiliter, *adv.*, evenly, consistently

aequitās, -ātis, *f.*, moderation

aequus, -a, -um, right, equitable

aes, aeris, *n.*, bronze

aestimātiō, -ōnis, *f.*, appraisement

aestimō (1), *tr.*, value

aestus, -ūs, *m.*, heat

aetās, -ātis, *f.*, age

aeternum, *adv.*, for ever

affīgō, -xī, -xum (3), *tr.*, attach to

ager, -grī, *m.*, field, territory

aggerō (1), *tr.*, pile up

agitō (1), *tr.*, accomplish, be engaged in, discuss

agmen, -inis, *n.*, column, army

agō, ēgī, āctum (3), *tr.*, act, do, drive

agrestis, -e, of the country, rustic

āiō, *defect. intr.*, say

āla, -ae, *f.*, wing, auxiliary troops

alacer, -cris, -cre, eager

ālāris, -is, *m.*, auxiliary cavalryman

ālārius, -ī, *m.*, auxiliary cavalryman

albeō, -ēre (2), *intr.*, be white

aliās, *adv.*, at another time

alibī, *adv.*, elsewhere

aliēnigena, -ae, *m.*, foreigner

aliēnus, -a, -um, belonging to another, strange

aliquandō, *adv.*, sometimes

aliquis, -quid, *indef. pro.*, someone, something

aliter, *adv.*, otherwise

alius, -a, -um, other

alō, -uī, -itum (3), *tr.*, feed

alter, -era, -erum, the other (of two)

altitūdō, -inis, *f.*, height

alumnus, -ī, *m.*, nursling

ambedō, -esse, -ēdi, ēsum (3), *tr.*, devour

ambiguus, -a, -um, doubtful

ambiō (4), *intr.*, go round

ambitiō, -ōnis, *f.*, desire, ambition

ambitus, -ūs, *m.*, canvassing

amīcitia, -ae, *f.*, friendship

amīcus, -a, -um, friendly

amīcus, -ī, *m.*, friend

āmittō, -mīsī, -missum (3), *tr.*, lose

amnis, -is, *m.*, river

amō (1), *tr.*, love

amoenitās, -ātis, *f.*, charm

amoenus, -a, -um, pleasant

amor, -ōris, *m.*, love
amplector, -plexus (3), *dep.*, embrace
amputō (1), *tr.*, cut off
an, *adv.*, or, whether
anceps, -ipitis, uncertain
angō, -nxī, -nctum (3), *tr.*, distress
angustiae, -ārum, *f.*, narrowness, shortage
angustus, -a, -um, narrow, constricted
animaduertō, -rtī, -rsum (3), *tr.*, notice
animal, -ālis, *n.*, animal
animus, -ī, *m.*, mind, temper, courage
annōna, -ae, *f.*, corn supply
annus, -ī, *m.*, year
annuus, -a, -um, annual
ante, *adv. & prep. with acc.*, before
anteeō, -īre, -iī, -itum, *tr.*, surpass, outstrip
anteferō, -ferre, -tulī, -lātum, *tr.*, prefer
antepōnō, -posuī, -positum (3), *tr.*, place before
antequam, *conj.*, before
antīquitās, -ātis, *f.*, antiquity, men of old
antīquitus, *adv.*, of old
antīquus, -a, -um, ancient
aperiō, -uī, -rtum (4), *tr.*, open, reveal
apiscor, aptus (3), *dep.*, acquire
appellō (1), *tr.*, call, name
apud, *prep. with acc.*, among, in, with

aqua, -ae, *f.*, water
aquila, -ae, *f.*, eagle, legionary standard
āra, -ae, *f.*, altar
arbiter, -trī, *m.*, governor
arbitrium, -ī, *n.*, choice
arbitror (1), *dep.*, think
arceō, -cuī, -ctum (2), *tr.*, prevent
arcus, -ūs, *m.*, arch
ārdeō, ārsī, ārsum (2), *intr.*, blaze
ārdēscō, ārsī (3), *intr.*, be inflamed, glitter
arduus, -a, -um, difficult
ārea, -ae, *f.*, vacant space
arēna, *see* harēna
ārēns, -ntis, dry
arguō, -uī, -ūtum (3), *tr.*, reprove, accuse
arma, -ōrum, *n.*, arms
armō (1), *tr.*, arm
arripiō, -uī, -reptum (3), *tr.*, seize
ars, artis, *f.*, art
artus, -a, -um, narrow
artus, -ūs, *m.*, limb
aruum, -ī, *n.*, field
arx, arcis, *f.*, citadel
aspectus, -ūs, *m.*, appearance
asper, -era, -erum, rough, harsh
aspernor (1), *dep.*, reject
asperō (1), *tr.*, roughen, sharpen
aspiciō, -spēxī, -spectum (3), *tr.*, see
at, *conj.*, but
atque, ac, *conj.*, and
atrox, -ōcis, fierce, dreadful

atterō, -trīuī, -trītum (3), *tr.*, exhaust

attineō, -uī, -tentum (2), *tr.*, detain

attollō, -ere (3), *tr.*, lift up, exaggerate

auāritia, -ae, *f.*, greed

auctor, -ōris, *m.*, author, sponsor

auctōritās, -ātis, *f.*, authority

audācia, -ae, *f.*, boldness, courage

audentia, -ae, *f.*, boldness, daring

audeō, ausus (2), *semi-dep.*, dare

audiō (4), *tr.*, hear

āuertō, -rtī, -rsum (3), *tr.*, avert

auferō, -ferre, abstulī, ablā-tum, *tr.*, remove

augeō, auxī, auctum (2), *tr.*, increase

augurāle, -is, *n.*, place of augury, commander's tent

auidē, *adv.*, eagerly

āuius, -a, -um, remote

aula, -ae, *f.*, court

aureus, -a, -um, golden

auriga, -ae, *c.*, charioteer

auris, -is, *f.*, ear

aurum, -ī, *n.*, gold

auspex, -icis, *m.*, soothsayer

auspicium, -ī, *n.*, auspices, token

auspicor (1), *dep.*, begin auspiciously

aut, *conj.*, or; **aut . . . aut,** either . . . or

auxilium, ī, *n.*, aid, help; *pl.*, auxiliary troops

ballista, -ae, *f.*, catapult

balneae, -ārum, *f.*, baths

balneum, -ī, *n.*, bath

barbarus, -ī, *m.*, barbarian, stranger

bellum, -ī, *n.*, war

biceps, -cipitis, two-headed

bīnī, -ae, -a, two each

blandīmentum, -ī, *n.*, allurement, charm

bonum, -ī, *n.*, benefit

bonus, -a, -um, good

brachium, -ī, *n.*, arm

breuis, -e, short, brief

breuitās, ātis, *f.*, shortness

breuiter, *adv.*, briefly

būcina, -ae, *f.*, trumpet

cadō, cecidī, cāsum (3), *intr.*, fall

caedēs, -is, *f.*, slaughter, murder

caedō, cecidī, caesum (3), *tr.*, cut down, kill

caelum, -ī, *n.*, sky

calidus, -a, -um, warm

camēlus, -ī, *m.*, camel

campus, -ī, *m.*, plain

candidātus, -ī, *m.*, candidate

canis, -is, *m.*, dog

canō, cecinī, cantum (3), *intr.*, sing, play

cantus, -ūs, *m.*, song, singing

capessō, -īuī, -ītum (3), *tr.*, take eagerly

capiō, cēpī, captum (3), *tr.*, take, capture

captiuus, -a, -um, captive

capulus, -ī, *m.*, handle, hilt

caput, -itis, *n.*, head

cāritās, -ātis, *f.*, affection

carmen, -inis, *n.*, poem

cārus, -a, -um, dear
castellum, -ī, n., fort
castra, -ōrum, n., camp
cāsus, -ūs, m., event
catapulta, -ae, f., catapult (for arrows)
caueō, cāuī, cautum (2), intr., give security
causa, -ae, f., reason
cēdō, cessī, cessum (3), intr., give way
celeber, -bris, -bre, crowded, famous
celebrō (1), tr., praise, celebrate
celeritās, -ātis, f., speed
cēnseō, -uī, -nsum (2), tr., express opinion, move that
centum, indecl., hundred
centuriō, -ōnis, m., centurion
cernō, crēuī, crētum (3), tr., decide
certāmen, -inis, n., contest, battle
certātim, adv., eagerly
certō (1), intr., struggle
certus, -a, -um, certain, sure, reliable
ceruīx, -īcis, f., neck
cessō (1), intr., stop
cēterī, -ae, -a, the rest
cēterum, adv., however
cieō, cīuī, citum, (2) tr., move
cingō, -nxī, -nctum (3), tr., surround
circensis, -e, of the circus
circumdō, -dedī, -datum (1), tr., surround
circumiciō, -iēcī, -iectum (3), tr., place round

circumsedeō, -sēdī, -sessum (2), tr., besiege
circumsistō, -stetī (3), tr., stand around
circumstō, -stetī (1), intr., stand around
circumueniō, -uēnī, -uentum (4), tr., surround
circus, -ī, m., race course
cithara, -ae, f., lyre
citharoedus, -ī, m., lyre-player
cīuis, -is, c., citizen
cīuitās, -ātis, f., state, city
clādēs, -is, f., disaster
clāmitō (1), intr., shout
clārēscō, clāruī (3), intr., grow bright
clāritūdō, -inis, f., renown
clārus, -a, -um, brilliant
classiāriī, -ōrum, m., naval forces
classis, -is, f., fleet
cl(a)ūdo, cl(a)ūsi, cl(a)ūsum (3), tr., close, enclose
clēmentia, -ae, f., mercy
clūdo, see claudo
cōdicillī, -ōrum, m., note
coepī, coeptus, defect. intr., begin
coerceō (2), tr., restrain
cōgitātiō, -ōnis, f., thought, reflection
cognitiō, -ōnis, f., trial
cognōmentum, -ī, n., surname
cognōscō, -nōuī, -nitum (3), tr., get to know
cohibeō (2), tr., restrain
cohors, -rtis, f., cohort
collis, -is, m., hill

colō, -luī, cultum (3), *tr.*, cultivate

colōnia, -ae, *f.*, colony

comētēs, -ae, *m.*, comet

cōmis, -e, affable

cōmitās, -ātis, *f.*, affability

comitia, -ōrum, *n.*, elections

comitor (1), *dep.*, accompany

commeātus, -ūs, *m.*, provisions, leave

commendō (1), *tr.*, commend

commentāriī, -ōrum, *m.*, notes, record

commīlitō, -ōnis, *m.*, fellow-soldier

comminus, *adv.*, hand to hand

commodō (1) *tr.*, lend

commoueō, -mōuī, -mōtum (2), *tr.*, move

commūniō (4), *tr.*, fortify

commūniō, -ōnis, *f.*, sharing

commūnis, -e, general, common

compellō, -pulī, -pulsum (3), *tr.*, force

comperiō, -perī, -pertum (4), *tr.*, discover

complector, -plexus (3), *dep.*, embrace, encompass

compleō, -ēuī, -ētum (2), *tr.*, fill

complexus, -ūs, *m.*, embrace

compōnō, -posuī, -positum (3), *tr.*, settle, arrange, compose, confront

compos, -otis, in control

compositē, *adv.*, properly

cōnātus, -ūs., m., attempt

concēdō, -cessī, -cessum (3), *intr.*, agree, concede, withdraw

concieō, -cīuī, -citum (2), *tr.*, stir up

conciliō (1), *tr.*, win over

concilium, -ī, *n.*, council

condō, -didī, -ditum (3), *tr.*, found, establish

condūcō, -dūxī, -ductum (3), *tr. & intr.*, collect, be useful for

cōnectō, -nexuī, -nexum (3), *tr.*, join, connect

cōnferō, -ferre, -tulī, -lātum, *tr.*, bring, collect

cōnfessiō, -ōnis, *f.*, confession

cōnficiō, -fēcī, -fectum (3), *tr.*, complete, wear out, accomplish

cōnfirmō (1), *tr.*, affirm

cōnflagrō (1), *intr.*, be burned, go up in flames

cōnflictō (1), *tr.*, harass, afflict

cōnfluō, -xī (3), *intr.*, run together

cōnfūtō (1), *tr.*, silence

congestus, -ūs, *m.*, accumulation

congressus, -ūs, *m.*, social encounter

congruō, -uī (3), *intr.*, coincide

coniectō (1), *tr.*, conjecture

cōnitor, -nīsus (3), *dep.*, struggle, strain

coniugium, -ī, *n.*, marriage

coniunx, -iugis, *f.*, wife

coniūrātiō, -ōnis, *f.*, conspiracy

coniūrātus, -ī, *m.*, conspirator

conlābor, -lāpsus (3), *dep.*, collapse

conloquium, -ī, *n.*, conference

conloquor, -locūtus (3), *dep.*, converse with

conqueror, -questus (3), *dep.*, complain

conquīrō, -quisīuī, -quisītum (3), *tr.*, search for

cōnsalūtātiō, -ōnis, *f.*, mutual greeting

cōnscelerātus, -a, -um, wicked

cōnscientia, -ae, *f.*, conscience, guilt

cōnscius, -ī, *m.*, accomplice

cōnscrībō, -psī, -ptum (3), *tr.*, enrol

cōnsēnsus, -ūs, *m.*, agreement

cōnsentiō, -sēnsī, -sensum (4), *intr.*, conspire

cōnseruātor, -ōris, *m.*, saviour

cōnsīdō, -sēdī, -sessum (3), *intr.*, settle

cōnsilium, -ī, *n.*, plan, policy, advice, council

cōnsociō (1), *tr.*, share

cōnsonō, -uī (1), *intr.*, resound

cōnspīrātiō, -ōnis, *f.*, conspiracy

cōnspīrō (1), *intr.*, conspire

cōnstāns, -ntis, firm

cōnstanter, *adv.*, firmly, steadily

cōnstantia, -ae, *f.*, firmness

cōnstat, -stitit (1), *impers.*, it is well known

cōnstituō, -uī, -ūtum (3), *tr.*, set, place

cōnsul, -ulis, *m.*, consul

cōnsulāris, -e, consular

cōnsulātus, -ūs, *m.*, consulship

cōnsulō, -luī, -ultum (3), *tr. & intr.*, consult, take care of

cōnsultum, -ī, *n.*, decree

contāminātus, -a, -um, polluted, perverted

contegō, -xī, -ctum (3), *tr.*, cover

contemnō, -mpsī, -mptum (3), *tr.*, despise, defy

contemplātiō, -ōnis, *f.*, contemplation

contemptiō, -ōnis, *f.*, scorn, contempt

contendō, -dī, -tum (3), *intr.*, struggle

conterminus, -a, -um, bordering upon

contiguus, -a, -um, adjoining

contineō, -uī, -tentum (2), *tr.*, hold

continuō (1), *tr.*, make continuous

continuus, -a, -um, uninterrupted

contiō, -ōnis, *f.*, assembly

contrā, *adv. & prep. with acc.*, on the contrary, contrary to

contrahō, -xī, -ctum (3), *tr.*, assemble

contrārius, -a, -um, opposite

contubernium, -ī, *n.*, shared tent

contumēlia, -ae, *f.*, insult

conuertō, -tī, -sum (3), *tr.*, turn

conuincō, -uīcī, -uictum (3), *tr.*, convict

conuīuium, -ī, *n.*, feast

cōpia, -ae, *f.*, abundance, number, opportunity; *pl.*, military forces, supplies

cōram, *adv. & prep. with abl.*, on the spot, in the presence of

corōna, -ae, *f.*, crown, wreath

corpus, -oris, *n.*, body

corrigō, -rēxī, -rēctum (3), *tr.*, correct

corripiō, -uī, -reptum (3), *tr.*, seize

corrumpō, -rūpī, -ruptum (3), *tr.*, spoil, corrupt

crēber, -bra, -brum, frequent

crēbrō, *adv.*, frequently

crēditor, -ōris, *m.*, creditor

crēdō, -didī, -ditum (3), *tr.*, believe

crēdulitās, -ātis, *f.*, credulity

cremō (1), *tr.*, cremate

crepidō, -inis, *f.*, bank, edge

crimen, -inis, *n.*, charge

crīminātiō, -ōnis, *f.*, accusation, attack

cruciātus, -ūs, *m.*, torture

crūdēlitās, -ātis, *f.*, cruelty

cruentō (1), *tr.*, make bloody

crūs, crūris, *n.*, leg

crux, -cis, *f.*, cross

cubiculum, -ī, *n.*, bedroom

culpa, ae, *f.*, fault

cum, *prep. with abl.*, with

cum, *conj.*, when, although; cum ... tum, both ... and

cunctātiō, -ōnis, *f.*, delay

cunctātor, -ōris, *m.*, delayer

cunctor (1), *dep.*, delay, hesitate

cunctus, -a, -um, all

cupīdō, inis., *f.*, desire

cupiō, -īuī, -ītum (3), *tr.*, desire

cupītor, -ōris, *m.*, one who longs for

cūr, *adv.*, why

cūra, -ae, *f.*, concern, carefulness

curriculum, -ī, *n.*, racing chariot

cursō (1), *intr.*, run about

cursus, -ūs, *m.*, race

curūlis, -e, curule, official

custōdia, -ae, *f.*, custody, guard

custōs, -ōdis, *m.*, guard

damnātiō, -ōnis, *f.*, condemnation

damnō (1), *tr.*, condemn

damnum, -ī, *n.*, loss

dē, *prep. with abl.*, from, about

dea, -ae, *f.*, goddess

dēcēdō, -cessī, -cessum (3), *intr.*, depart, withdraw

dēcernō, -crēuī, -crētum (3), *tr. & intr.*, decree

dēcertō (1), *intr.*, fight

decet, -uit (2), *impers.*, it is fitting

decimus, -a, -um, tenth

dēclīnō (1), *tr. & intr.*, turn aside

decor, -ōris, *m.*, elegance

decōrus, -a, -um, handsome

dēcurrō, -currī, -cursum (3), *intr.*, sail down

decus, -oris, *n.*, glory

dēdecus, -oris, *n.*, disgrace

dēdō, -didī, -ditum (3), *tr.*, surrender

dēdūcō, -dūxī, -ductum (3), *tr.*, conduct, withdraw

dēfectiō, -ōnis, *f.*, revolt

dēfendō, -dī, -sum (3), *tr.*, defend

dēfensiō, -ōnis, *f.*, defence

dēfensor, -ōris, *m.*, defender

dēferō, -ferre, -tulī, -lātum, *tr.*, report

dēfessus, -a, -um, exhausted
dēficiō, -fēcī, -fectum (3), *tr. &*
　intr., desert, revolt from, fail
dēformis, -e, disgraceful
dēfungor, -fūnctus (3), *dep.,*
　die
dēgener, -eris, low born
dēgenerō (1), *intr.,* be degenerate
dehinc, *adv.,* after this, next
dēiciō, -iēcī, -iectum (3), *tr.,*
　throw down
dein, deinde, *adv.,* then
dēlābor, -lāpsus (3), *dep.,* slip
　down
dēlēnimentum, -ī, *n.,* solace
dēlictum, -ī, *n.,* crime, offence
dēligō, -lēgī, -lectum (3), *tr.,*
　choose
dēlinquō, -līquī, -lictum (3),
　intr., do wrong
dēlūbrum, -ī, *n.,* shrine
dēmereor, -itus (2), *dep.,* oblige
dēmittō, -mīsī, -missum (3),
　tr., let sink
dēmoror (1), *dep.,* delay
dēmoueō, -mōuī, -mōtum (2),
　tr., remove
dēmum, *adv.,* at length
dēnegō (1), *tr.,* refuse, deny
dēnique, *adv.,* finally
dēnūbo, -psī, -ptum (3), *intr.,*
　marry
dēnūntiō (1), *tr.,* intimate offi-
　cially
dēpellō, -pulī, -pulsum (3), *tr.,*
　drive away, expel
dēprecābundus, -a, -um, en-
　treating

dēprēndō, -ndī, -nsum (3), *tr.,*
　detect
dēprimō, -pressī, -pressum
　(3), *tr.,* sink
dērogō (1), *tr.,* detract from
dēscendō, -dī, -sum (3), *intr.,*
　descend, sink to
dēserō, -ruī, -rtum (3), *tr.,*
　desert
dēsīderium, -ī, *n.,* longing, grief
dēsīgnātus, -a, -um, elect
dēsiliō, -luī, -ultum (4), *intr.,*
　leap down
dēsinō, -siī, -situm (3), *intr.,*
　cease
dēspērātiō, -ōnis, *f.,* despair
dēspiciō, -pexī, -pectum (3),
　tr., despise
dēstinātiō, -ōnis, *f.,* determina-
　tion
dēstinō (1), *tr.,* determine
dēstringō, -nxī, -ctum (3), *tr.,*
　draw
dēsum, -esse, -fuī, *intr.,* be
　lacking
dēterior, -ius, worse, meaner
dēterreō (2), *tr.,* discourage
dētorqueō, -torsī, -tortum (2),
　tr., twist, distort
dētrahō, -trāxī, -tractum (3),
　tr., remove
dētrectō (1), *tr.,* refuse
dētrūdō, -ūsī, -ūsum (3), *tr.,*
　push away
deus, -ī, *m.,* god
dext(e)ra, -ae, *f.,* right hand
diadēma, -atis, *n.,* crown
diciō, -ōnis, *f.,* authority

dicō (1), *tr.*, set apart

dīcō, -xī, -ctum (3), *tr.*, say, speak

dictitō (1), *tr.*, say often

dictum, -ī, *n.*, word, saying

diēs, -ēī, *m. & f.*, day

diffāmō (1), *tr.*, malign

differō, -ferre, distulī, dilātum, *tr.*, postpone, put off

diffīdō, -fīsus (3), *semi-dep.*, distrust

dignus, -a, -um, worthy

dīgredior, -gressus (3), *dep.*, depart

dīlacerō (1), *tr.*, tear apart

dīligō, -lexī, -lectum (3), *tr.*, love

dīmētior, -mēnsus (4), *dep.*, measure out

dīmittō, -mīsī, -missum (3), *tr.*, dismiss, let go

dīruō, -ruī, -rutum (3), *tr.*, demolish

dis, dītis, rich

disceptō (1), *tr.*, dispute, discuss

disciplīna, -ae, *f.*, training, upbringing

discordia, -ae, *f.*, disagreement

discrīmen, -inis, *n.*, danger

discumbō, -cubuī, -cubitum (3), *intr.*, recline at table, dine

dispergō, -rsī, -rsum (3), *tr.*, scatter

disserō, -ruī, -rtum (3), *tr.*, discourse

dissimilitūdō, -inis, *f.*, difference

dissimulō (1), *tr.*, hide, ignore

dissoluō, -uī, -ūtum (3), *tr.*, loosen

dissolūtus, -a, -um, dissolute

distīnctiō, -ōnis, *f.*, discrimination

distinguō, -nxī, -nctum (3), *tr.*, decorate

distō, -āre (1), *intr.*, be distant

dītō, -āre (1), *tr.*, enrich

diū, *adv.*, for a long time, by day

dīuersitās, -ātis, *f.*, difference

dīuersus, -a, -um, opposite, different, separate

dīuidō, -uisī, -uīsum (3), *tr.*, divide

diurnus, -a, -um, daily

dīuus, -a, -um, divine

dō, dedī, datum (1), *tr.*, give

doceō, -cuī, -ctum (2), *tr.*, teach

doctrīna, -ae, *f.*, learning

documentum, -ī, *n.*, proof, warning

dolor, -ōris, *m.*, grief, pain

dolus, -ī, *m.*, trick, treachery

domesticus, -a, -um, private, domestic

domINātiō, -ōnis, *f.*, tyranny

dominor (1), *dep.*, rule

dominus, -ī, *m.*, owner

domus, -ūs, *f.*, house, home

dōnec, *conj.*, until, as long as

dōnō (1), *tr.*, present, bestow

dōnum, -ī, *n.*, gift

dōs, dōtis, *f.*, dowry

dubitō (1), *tr. & intr.*, hesitate, doubt

ducentī, -ae, -a, two hundred

dūcō, -xī, -ctum (3), *tr.*, construct, lead

dulcēdō, -inis, *f.*, sweetness

dum, *conj.*, while

duo, -ae, -o, two

duodecimus, -a, -um, twelfth

dūrō (1), *intr.*, last

dūrus, -a, -um, harsh

dux, -cis, *m.*, general

ē, ex, *prep. with abl.*, from, out of, according to

ebur, -oris, *n.*, ivory

ēdictum, -ī, *n.*, edict

ēdō, -didī, -ditum (3), *tr.*, utter, produce, elevate

ēducātor, -ōris, *m.*, tutor

ēdūcō (1), *tr.*, bring up, educate

effēminātus, -a, -um, effeminate

efferō, -ferre, extulī, ēlātum, *tr.*, bring out, exalt

efficiō, -fēcī, -fectum (3), *tr.*, complete

effigiēs, -ēī, *f.*, statue

effodiō, -ōdī, -ossum (3), *tr.*, dig out

effugium, -ī, *n.*, escape

effundō, -ūdī, -ūsum (3), *tr.*, pour out

egēnus, -a, -um, needy

ēgerō, -gessī, -gestum (3), *tr.*, carry out, carry off

egŏ, meī, *pro.*, I

ēgredior, -gressus (3), *dep.*, depart from

ēgregius, -a, -um, good, distinguished

ēgressus, -ūs, *m.*, departure

elephantus, -ī, *m.*, elephant

ēliciō, -uī, -itum (3), *tr.*, entice out

ēloquentia, -ae, *f.*, eloquence

ēlūdō, -lūdī, -lūsum (3), *tr.*, cheat

ēmendō (1), *tr.*, correct

ēmētior, -mēnsus (4), *dep.*, traverse

ēmittō, -mīsī, -missum (3), *tr.*, discharge, emancipate

ēmolumentum, -ī, *n.*, advantage

enim, *conj.*, for

enimuĕrō, indeed

ēnormis, -e, irregular

ēnumerō (1), *tr.*, enumerate

eō, *adv.*, to that place, for that reason

eō, īre, iī, itum, *intr.*, go, proceed

epistula, -ae, *f.*, letter

epulae, -ārum, *f.*, banquet

epulor (1), *dep.*, dine

eques, -itis, *m.*, horseman, knight

equitātus, -ūs, *m.*, cavalry

equus, -ī, *m.*, horse

ergā, *prep. with acc.*, to, towards

ergō, *adv.*, therefore

ērigō, -rēxī, -rēctum (3), *tr.*, erect

ēripiō, -puī, -eptum (3), *tr.*, snatch, rescue

ērumpō, -rūpī, -ruptum (3), *intr.*, break out

ēruptiō, -ōnis, *f.*, sally

ēscendō, -dī, -sum (3), *tr. & intr.*, climb, mount

et, *conj.*, and, even, also

etenim, *conj.*, for

etiam, *adv.*, also, even

ēuādō, -sī, -sum (3), *intr.*, go out, escape

ēueniō, -uēnī, -uentum (4), *intr.*, happen

ēuertō, -tī, -sum (3), *tr.*, turn upside down

ēuinciō, -nxī, -nctum (4), *tr.*, bind round

ēuincō, -īcī, -ictum (3), *tr.*, conquer

exanimō (1), *tr.*, kill

excēdō, -cessī, -cessum (3), *intr.*, depart

excidium, -ī, *n.*, destruction

excindō, -idī, issum (3), *tr.*, destroy

exciō, -iī, -itum (4), *tr.*, summon

excipiō, -cēpī, -ceptum (3), *tr.*, receive, except

excubiae, -ārum, *f.*, guard

excūsō (1), *tr.*, excuse, give as excuse

execūtiō, -ōnis, *f.*, administration

exemplār, -āris, *n.*, pattern

exemplum, -ī, *n.*, example, precedent

exequor, -secūtus (3), *dep.*, follow through, fulfil

exerceō (2), *tr.*, practise

exercitus, -ūs, *m.*, army

exilium, -ī, *n.*, exile

exim, *adv.*, next

eximius, -a, -um, distinguished

exīstimō (1), *tr.*, think

existō, -titī, -titum (3), *intr.*, emerge, appear

exitiābilis, -e, deadly

exitium, -ī, *n.*, destruction

exitus, -ūs, *m.*, end, death

exolētus, -a, -um, degenerate

exoluō, -uī, -ūtum (3), *tr.*, discharge (a vow), open

exorior, -ortus (4), *dep.*, start

expectō (1), *tr.*, await

expediō (4), *tr.*, prepare, make easy

expellō, -pulī, -pulsum (3), *tr.*, drive out

experimentum, -ī, *n.*, proof

experior, -pertus (4), *dep.*, try, discover

expers, -rtis, free from

expiō (1), *tr.*, expiate, atone for

expleō, -plēuī, -plētum (2), *tr.*, fulfil, satisfy

expōnō, -posuī, -positum (3), *tr.*, explain

exposcō, -poposcī (3), *tr.*, demand

expostulō (1), *tr.*, demand, expostulate

exprimō, -pressī, -pressum (3), *tr.*, extort

exprobrō (1), *tr.*, reproach, cast in the teeth

expūgnātiō, -ōnis, *f.*, siege

exsurgō, -surrēxī, -surrēctum (3), *intr.*, rise

externus, -a, -um, foreign

exterreō (2), *tr.*, frighten

extimulō (1), *tr.*, goad, stimulate

extinguō, -nxī, -nctum (3), *tr.*, destroy

extollō, -ere (3), *tr.*, exalt, exaggerate

extrahō, -xī, -ctum (3), *tr.*, draw out

extrēmus, -a, -um, farthest, final, end

extruō, -xī, -ctum (3), *tr.*, construct

exturbō (1), *tr.*, drive out

exuō, -uī, -ūtum (3), *tr.*, strip

exūrō, -ussī, -ustum (3), *tr.*, burn up

fabricor (1), *dep.*, build

facētiae, -ārum, *f.*, wit, pleasantry

faciēs, -ēī, *f.*, face, appearance

facile, *adv.*, easily

facilis, -e, easy

facilitās, -ātis, *f.*, easiness, ease

facinus, -oris, *n.*, deed, crime

faciō, fēcī, factum (3), *tr.*, do, make

factum, -ī, *n.*, deed

facultās, -ātis, *f.*, opportunity

fācundia, -ae, *f.*, eloquence

fallō, fefellī, falsum (3), *intr.*, escape notice

falsus, -a, -um, false

fāma, -ae, *f.*, reputation, rumour

famēs, is, *f.*, hunger

familia, -ae, *f.*, family

familiāris, -e, intimate, friendly; **res familiāris,** family property

familiāritās, -ātis, *f.*, friendship

fānum, -ī, *n.*, sanctuary, shrine

fās, *indecl. n.*, right

fascia, -ae, *f.*, breast-band

fastigium, -ī, *n.*, dignity, rank

fātālis, -e, fatal

fateor, fassus (2), *dep.*, admit, acknowledge

fatigō (1), *tr.*, harass, persecute

fauor, -ōris, *m.*, support

fax, -cis, *f.*, torch

fēcunditās, -ātis, *f.*, fertility

fēlix, -īcis, fortunate

fēmina, -ae, *f.*, woman

fera, -ae, *f.*, wild beast

feriō, -īre, (4) *tr.*, strike

fermē, *adv.*, almost

ferō, ferre, tulī, lātum, *tr.*, bear, bring, declare

ferōcia, -ae, *f.*, spirit, ferocity

ferōciter, *adv.*, fiercely

ferrum, -ī, *n.*, weapon, sword

feruidus, -a, -um, glowing

fessus, -a, -um, worn out

festīnanter, *adv.*, speedily

festīnō (1), *intr.*, hurry

fidēlis, -e, loyal

fidēs, -ēī, *f.*, faith, loyalty, conviction

fīdō, fīsus (3), *semi-dep.*, trust

fīdūcia, -ae, *f.*, confidence

fīdus, -a, -um, trustworthy

fīlia, -ae, *f.*, daughter

fīlius, -ī, *m.*, son

fingō, -nxī, -ctum (3), *tr.*, feign, invent

fīniō (4), *tr.*, end, complete, define

fīnis, -is, *m.*, end; *pl.*, territory

fīnitimus, -a, -um, neighbouring

fīo, fierī, factus, *intr.*, become, be made

firmitūdō, -inis, *f.*, strength of mind

firmō (1), *tr.*, confirm, strengthen

flāgitium, -ī, *n.*, shameful act, crime

flagrō (1), *intr.*, blaze

flamma, -ae, *f.*, flame

flammeum, -ī, *n.*, bridal veil

flammō (1), *tr.*, set on fire

flectō, -xī, -xum (3), *tr. & intr.,* turn

flētus, -ūs, *m.*, weeping

flexus, -a, -um, winding

flūmen, -inis, *n.*, river

fluō, -xī, -xum (3), *intr.*, flow, proceed

fluuius, -ī, *m.*, river

fluxus, -a, -um, perishable, transistory

foedō (1), *tr.*, defile

foedus, -a, -um, abominable

foedus, -eris, *n.*, treaty

fōmentum, -ī, *n.*, poultice, dressing

fōns, -ntis, *m.*, spring, source

foris, -is, *f.*, door

fōrma, -ae, *f.*, form, manner, beauty

formīdō, -inis, *f.*, fear

fors, -rtis, *f.*, chance

forte, *adv.*, by chance, accidentally

fortis, -e, brave

fortiter, *adv.*, bravely

fortitūdō, -inis, *f.*, courage, strength of mind

fortuitus, -a, -um, accidental

fortūna, -ae, *f.*, state, condition, fortune

forum, -ī, *n.*, public square

fossa, -ae, *f.*, ditch, canal

foueō, fōuī, fōtum (2), *tr.,* foster, encourage

frāter, -tris, *m.*, brother

fraus, -dis, *f.*, trickery, deceit

frequentia, -ae, *f.*, crowd

frequentō (1), *tr.*, frequent

frigēscō, frixī (3), *intr.,* grow cold

frīgidus, -a, -um, cold

frondōsus, -a, -um, leafy

frōns, -ntis, *f.*, front

frūctus, -ūs, *m.*, reward

frūmentārius, -a, -um, of provisions

frūmentum, -ī, *n.*, corn, provisions

frūstrā, *adv.*, in vain

frūstror (1), *dep.*, frustrate

fuga, -ae, *f.*, flight

fugiō, fūgī, -itum (3), *intr.*, flee

fugō (1), *tr.*, put to flight, rout

fulgeō, fulsī (2), *intr.*, glitter

fulgur, -uris, *n.*, lightning

fulmen, -inis, *n.*, lightning

fungor, fūnctus (3), *dep.*, perform

fūnus, -eris, *n.*, funeral

gaudium, -ī, *n.*, joy

gemma, -ae, *f.*, jewel

gener, -erī, *m.*, son-in-law

generō (1), *tr.*, produce, create

geniālis, -e, bridal

gēns, -ntis, *f.*, tribe, nation

genū, -ūs, *n.*, knee

genus, -eris, *n.*, family, race

gerō, gessī, gestum (3), *tr.,* wage, act, accomplish

gestāmen, -inis, n., vehicle
gestō (1), tr., carry, wear
gestus, -ūs, m., gesture
gignō, genuī, genitum (3), tr., bring forth, produce
gladiātor, -ōris, m., gladiator
gladiātōrius, -a, -um, gladiatorial
gladius, -ī, m., sword
gliscō, -ere (3), intr., grow
globus, -ī, m., troop
glōria, -ae, f., glory, honour
gnārus, -a, -um, knowing, known
gradus, -ūs, m., step, stage, degree
grassor (1), intr., proceed, rage
grātēs, f., defect., thanks
grātia, -ae, f., favour, influence; pl., thanks
grātulor (1), dep., congratulate
grauidus, -a, -um, pregnant
grauis, -e, troublesome, serious
grauitās, -ātis, f., weight, seriousness
grex, -gis, m., company
gubernātor, -ōris, m., pilot
gymnasium, -ī, n., gymnasium

habeō (2), tr., have, hold, consider
habilis, -e, fit
habitus, -ūs, m., dress, appearance
hāctenus, adv., so far
(h)arēna, -ae, f., sand, arena
haruspex, -icis, m., soothsayer
hasta, -ae, f., spear
haud, not
hauriō, hausī, haustum (4), tr., draw, consume

herbidus, -a, -um, grassy
hērēditās, -ātis, f., inheritance
hīberna, -ōrum, n., winter quarters
hībernācula, -ōrum, n., winter quarters
hībernō (1), intr., spend the winter
hīc, haec, hōc, this
hiemps, -mis, f., winter
hinc, adv., on this side
histriō, -ōnis, m., actor
homŏ, -inis, c., human being, man
honestus, -a, -um, respectable
honor, -ōris, m., honour, office
horreum, -ī, n., granary
hortor (1), dep., encourage, exhort
hortus, -ī, m., garden
hospitālis, -e, of hospitality
hostia, -ae, f., sacrifice
hostīlis, -e, hostile
hostis, -is, c., enemy
hūc, adv., in this direction, this way
hūmānus, -a, -um, human
humilis, -e, low, shallow

iaceō (2), intr., lie, be situated
iaciō, iēcī, iactum (3), tr., throw, discuss
iactō (1), tr., boast
iactus, -ūs, m., throw
iam, adv., now, already
iānitor, -ōris, m., doorkeeper
ibĭ, adv., there
ictus, -ūs, m., stroke
īdem, eadem, idem, the same
ideō, adv., for that reason

igitur, *conj.*, therefore

ignārus, -a, -um, unknown, unconscious

ignāuia, -ae, *f.*, laziness. cowardice

ignis, -is, *m.*, fire

ignōminia, -ae, *f.*, disgrace

ignōrō (1), *tr.*, be ignorant of

ignōscō, -nōuī, -nōtum (3), *tr.*, pardon

ignōtus, -ī, *m.*, stranger

ille, -a, -ud, that, he

illīc, *adv.*, there

illicitus, -a, -um, forbidden

illō, *adv.*, to that place

illūc, *adv.*, in that direction, that way

imāginātiō, -ōnis, *f.*, fancy, thought

imāginor (1), *dep.*, picture to oneself, imagine

imāgō, -inis, *f.*, likeness, phantom

imbēcillitās, -ātis, *f.*, weakness

imbēcillus, -a, -um, weak

imbellis, -e, unwarlike

imbuō, -uī, -ūtum (3), *tr.*, infect

immēnsus, -a, -um, vast

immineō, -ēre (2), *intr.*, threaten, overhang

immītis, -e, harsh

immittō, -mīsī, -missum (3), *tr.*, send in

immō, *adv.*, indeed, in fact

immodicus, -a, -um, uncontrolled

immolō (1), *tr.*, sacrifice

immōtus, -a, -um, unmoved

impār, -aris, unequal

impatientia, -ae, *f.*, want of endurance

impedīmentum, -ī, *n.*, hindrance

impediō (4), *tr.*, hinder

impellō, -pulī, -pulsum (3), *tr.*, induce

imperātor, -ōris, *m.*, emperor

imperātōrius, -a, -um, of the emperor, imperial

imperitō (1), *tr. & intr.*, rule

imperium, -ī, *n.*, empire, power

imperō (1), *tr. & intr.*, order

imperuius, -a, -um, impervious

impetus, -ūs, *m.*, violence, impulse

impingō, -pēgī, -pactum (3), *tr.*, dash against

implācābilis, -e, implacable

impleō, -plēuī, -plētum (2), *tr.*, fulfil

impōnō, -posuī, -positum (3), *tr.*, place upon

impudīcitia, -ae, *f.*, depravity

impūnitās, -ātis, *f.*, safety from punishment

īmus, -a, -um, lowest, foot

in, *prep. with acc. & abl.*, in, into

inānis, -e, empty

incautus, -a, -um, off guard

incēdō, -cessī, -cessum (3), *intr.*, advance, occur

incendiārius, -ī, *m.*, incendiary, fire-raiser

incendium, -ī, *n.*, fire

incendō, -dī, -sum (3), *tr.*, kindle

incertus, -a, -um, uncertain
incipiō, -cēpī, -ceptum (3), tr.
& intr., begin
inclīnō (1), intr., sink
incolumis, -e, unharmed
incolumitās, -ātis, f., safety
incōmptus, -a, -um, artless,
blunt
incorruptus, -a, -um, undamaged
incrēdibilis, -e, incredible, impossible
increpō, -uī, -itum (1), tr.,
scold, blame
incūriōsus, -a, -um, heedless
incursō (1), tr., attack, invade
incūsō (1), tr., accuse
incustōdītus, -a, -um, unprotected
inde, adv., from that side, from
there, on that side, then
index, -icis, c., informer
indicium, -ī, n., information,
charge
indīcō, -xī, -ctum (3), tr.,
announce
indigēns, -ntis, needy
indignus, -a, -um, shameful
indiscrētus, -a, -um, not separated
indō, -didī, -ditum (3), tr., put
upon, put in
indomitus, -a, -um, unruly
indulgeō, -sī, -tum (2), intr.,
indulge in
induō, -uī, -ūtum (3), tr., clothe,
put on
indūtiae, -ārum, f., truce

ineō, -īre, -iī, -itum, intr., enter
inermis, -e, unarmed
infāmia, -ae, f., disgrace
infāmis, -e, notorious
infāmō (1), tr., disgrace
infāns, -ntis, c., infant
infaustus, -a, -um, unfortunate
infēlix, -īcis, unfortunate
infēnsus, -a, -um, hostile
inferior, -ius, lower
inferō, -ferre, -tulī, -lātum, tr.,
bring into
infīgō, -xī, -xum (3), tr., impress,
implant
infirmō (1), tr., weaken
infitiae, -ārum, f., denial
inflammō (1), tr., set fire to
infōrmis, -e, shapeless
infrequentia, -ae, f., small number
infringō, -frēgī, -frāctum (3),
tr., break
ingenium, -ī, n., nature, natural
ability; pl., men of genius
ingēns, -ntis, huge
ingenuus, -a, -um, free born
ingredior, -gressus (3), dep.,
enter
ingressus, -ūs, m., entry
ingruō, -uī (3), tr., attack
inhibeō (2), tr., check
inhonestus, -a, -um, dishonourable
iniciō, -iēcī, -iectum (3), tr.,
put on
initium, -ī, n., beginning
iniūria, -ae, f., injury, wrong
inligō (1), tr., entangle, impede

inlūdo, -sī, -sum (3), *intr.*, mock at, fool away, amuse oneself with

inlūstris, -e, distinguished

innītor, -nīsus (3), *dep.*, rest on, depend on

inopia, -ae, *f.*, shortage

inops, -opis, needy

inquam, *defect. intr.*, say

inquīsītor, -ōris, *m.*, examiner

inrīdeō, -rīsī, -rīsum (2), *intr.*, jeer

inrīsus, -ūs, *m.*, derision

inritus, -a, -um, useless, empty-handed

inrumpō, -rūpī, -ruptum (3), *tr. & intr.*, invade

inscītia, -ae, *f.*, ignorance

inscrībō, -psī, -ptum (3), *tr.*, inscribe

insectātiō, -ōnis, *f.*, criticism

insector (1), *dep.*, censure

inserō, -sēuī, -situm (3), *tr.*, implant

insideō, -sēdī, -sessum (2), *tr. & intr.*, occupy, sit on

insidiae, -ārum, *f.*, trap, treachery

insigne, -is, *n.*, badge

insignis, -e, remarkable, famous

insistō, -stitī (3), *intr.*, stand upon, pursue

insociābilis, -e, unsociable, independent

insolēns, -ntis, unaccustomed

insōns, -ntis, innocent

instīnctus, -ūs, *m.*, impulse

instō, -stitī, -statum (1)., *intr.*, press upon, threaten

insula, -ae, *f.*, island, block of flats

insum, -esse, -fuī, *intr.*, be in

insuper, *adv.*, over and above, besides

intāctus, -a, -um, intact, untouched

integer, -gra, -grum, undiminished, untouched, fresh

intellegō, -lexī, -lectum (3), *tr.*, perceive, understand

intentē, *adv.*, eagerly

intentō (1), *tr.*, stretch out

intentus, -a, -um, eager, intent

inter, *prep. with acc.*, among

intercipiō, -cēpī, -ceptum (3), *tr.*, cut off

intereā, *adv.*, meanwhile

intereō, -īre, -iī, -itum, *intr.*, die

interficiō, -fēcī, -fectum (3), *tr.*, kill

interiaceō, -ēre (2), *intr.*, lie between

intericiō, -iēcī, -iectum (3), *tr.*, intervene

interim, *adv.*, meanwhile

interitus, -ūs, *m.*, ruin, death

internūntius, -ī, *m.*, go-between

interpretātiō, -ōnis, *f.*, interpretation

interpretor (1), *dep.*, explain

interritus, -a, -um, undaunted

interrogō (1), *tr.*, question

interscindō, -scidī, -scissum (3), *tr.*, cut

intestābilis, -e, abominable

intimus, -a, -um, internal, intimate

intolerandus, -a, -um, intolerable

intrā, *prep. with acc.,* within

intrō (1), *tr. & intr.,* enter

introeō, -īre, -iī, -itum, *intr.,* enter

intromittō, -mīsī, -missum (3), *tr.,* send in

intus, *adv.,* within

inuādō, -uāsī, -uāsum (3), *tr. & intr.,* invade

inualidus, -a, -um, weak

inuertō, -tī, -sum (3), *tr.,* paraphrase

inuictus, -a, -um, invincible

inuideō, -uīdī, -uīsum (2), *tr.,* grudge

inuidia, -ae, *f.,* grudge, unpopularity

inuīsus, -a, -um, hated

inuocō (1), *tr.,* call upon

ipse, -a, -um, self

īra, -ae, *f.,* anger

is, ea, id, that, he

ita, *adv.,* in this way

iter, -ineris, *n.,* journey, march, route

iterum, *adv.,* again, a second time

iubeō, iussī, iussum (2), *tr.,* order

iūdex, -icis, *m.,* judge, critic

iūdicium, -ī, *n.,* judgement

iugum, -ī, *n.,* yoke, ridge

iūmentum, -ī, *n.,* pack animal

iungō, iūnxī, iūnctum (3), *tr.,* join

iūs, iūris, *n.,* justice, right

iūs iūrandum, -ris -dī, *n.,* oath

iussum, -ī, *n.,* order

iussus, -ūs, *m.,* order

iūstus, -a, -um, lawful, right

iuuenis, -is, *m.,* young man

iuuentūs, -ūtis, *f.,* youth, young people

iuuō, iūuī, iūtum (1), *tr.,* help

iuxtā, *adv. & prep. with acc.,* near, nearby

Kalendae, -ārum, *f.,* Kalends, first day of the month

labefaciō, -fēcī, -factum (3), *tr.,* shake one's loyalty

labō (1), *intr.,* fall to pieces

labor, -ōris, *m.,* work, effort

lacer, -era, -erum, mangled

lacerō (1), *tr.,* abuse

lacessō, -iuī, -ītum (3), *tr.,* provoke, challenge

lacrima, -ae, *f.,* tear

lacus, -ūs, *m.,* lake

laetitia, -ae, *f.,* joy

laetor (1), *dep.,* rejoice

laetus, -a, -um, happy

lāmentātiō, -ōnis, *f.,* lamentation

lāmentum, -ī, *n.,* wailing

languidus, -a, -um, languid

laniātus, -ūs, *m.,* mangling, laceration

lapis, -idis, *m.,* stone, milestone

laqueus, -ī, *m.,* noose

largior (4), *dep.,* bestow

largītiō, -ōnis, *f.,* bribery, gift

largus, -a, -um, abundant

lātē, *adv.*, widely
lātitūdō, -inis,*f.*, width
latrōcinium, -ī, *n.*, robbery, brigandage
lātus, -a, -um, wide
latus, -eris, *n.*, side
laudābilis, -e, praiseworthy
laudō (1), *tr.*, praise
laurus, -ūs,*f.*, laurel
laus, -dis,*f.*, praise
lēgātiō, -ōnis,*f.*, legation
lēgātus, -ī, *m.*, envoy
legiō, -ōnis,*f.*, legion
legiōnārius, -a, -um, legionary
lēnitās, -ātis,*f.*, gentleness
lentitūdō, inis,*f.*, slowness
lentus, -a, -um, slow
leuis, -e, light
leuitās, -ātis,*f.*, frivolity
lēx, lēgis,*f.*, law
libellus, -ī, *m.*, petition
līber, -era, -erum, free
liber, -brī, *m.*, book
līberālis, -e, generous
līberātor, -ōris, *m.*, liberator
līberī, -ōrum, *m.*, children
līberō (1), *tr.*, free
lībertās, -ātis, *f.*, freedom, republicanism
lībertīnus, -a, -um, freed
lībertus, -ī, *m.*, freedman, exslave
libīdō, -inis,*f.*, lust, wantonness
lībō (1), *tr.*, make a libation
licenter, *adv.*, without restraint
licentia, -ae,*f.*, licence
licitus, -a, -um, permissible
ligāmentum, -ī, *n.*, bandage

liquefaciō, -fēcī, -fectum (3), *tr.*, melt
litterae, -ārum,*f.*, letter
lītus, -oris, *n.*, shore
locō (1), *tr.*, place
locus, -ī, *m.*, place
lōcusta, -ae,*f.*, locust
longē, *adv.*, far
longinquus, -a, -um, distant
longitūdō, -inis,*f.*, length
longus, -a, -um, long
luctus, -ūs, *m.*, grief
lūdibrium, -ī, *n.*, laughing stock, mockery
lūdicrum, -ī, *n.*, show
lūdus, -ī, *m.*, game
lūmen, -inis, *n.*, light
luō, -uī (3), *tr.*, undergo
lupānar, -āris, *n.*, brothel
lūstrō (1), *tr.*, purify by sacrifice
lūx, -cis,*f.*, daylight
luxus, -ūs, *m.*, luxury

māchināmentum, -ī, *n.*, siege engine
māchinātor, -ōris, *m.*, engineer
maeror, -ōris, *m.*, sorrow
maestus, -a, -um, sorrowful
magis, *adv.*, more
magister, -trī, *m.*, architect
magistrātus, -ūs, *m.*, magistrate
magnificentia, -ae,*f.*, splendour
magnificus, -a, -um, splendid
magnitūdō, -inis,*f.*, might, size
magnus, -a, -um, large, great
maior, māius, greater; *pl.*, ancestors
malitia, -ae,*f.*, spite

mālō, mālle, māluī, *intr.*, prefer

malus, -a, -um, unlucky, evil

mancipium, -ī, *n.*, slave

mandō (1), *tr.*, order, entrust

maneō, -nsī, -nsum (2), *intr.*, stay

manifestus, -a, -um, obvious, clear

manipulāris, -is, *m.*, ordinary soldier

manipulus, -ī, *m.*, company of soldiers

mānsuētūdō, -inis, *f.*, kindness

manus, -ūs, *f.*, band, hand, legal power

mare, -is, *n.*, sea

maritimus, -a, -um, of the sea

marītus, -ī, *m.*, husband

māter, -tris, *f.*, mother

mātrimōnium, -ī, *n.*, marriage

mātrōna, -ae, *f.*, married woman

mātūrē, *adv.*, soon

mātūrō (1), *tr.*, hurry on

maximē, *adv.*, particularly

medicīnus, -a, -um, medical

medicus, -ī, *m.*, doctor

meditāmentum, -ī, *n.*, preparation

meditor (1), *dep.*, reflect upon

medius, -a, -um, middle

megistānes, -um, *m.*, magnates

melior, -ius, better

membrum, -ī, *n.*, limb

meminī, -isse, *defect.*, remember

memor, -oris, mindful

memoria, -ae, *f.*, memory, recollection

memorō (1), *tr.*, mention

mēns, -ntis, *f.*, mind, intellect

mēnsa, -ae, *f.*, table

mēnsis, -is, *m.*, month

mercimōnium, -ī, *n.*, merchandise

mereō (2), *tr.*, deserve

meritō, *adv.*, deservedly

meritum, -ī, *n.*, service

mersō (1), *tr.*, immerse

-met, *suff.*, -self

metuō, -uī, -ūtum (3), *tr.*, fear

metus, -ūs, *m.*, fear

mīles, -itis, *m.*, soldier

mīlitāris, -e, military

mīlitia, -ae, *f.*, military service

mille, mīlia, thousand(s)

minae, -ārum, *f.*, threats

minister, -trī, *m.*, assistant

minitor (1), *dep.*, threaten

minor, -us, inferior, less

minuō, -uī, -ūtum (3), *tr.*, reduce

mīrāculum, -ī, *n.*, marvel

mīrus, -a, -um, remarkable

misceō, -cuī, -xtum (2), *tr.*, join

miserātiō, -ōnis, *f.*, pity, compassion

misericordia, -ae, *f.*, pity

miseror (1), *dep.*, bewail

missilis, -e, missile

mītis, -e, gentle

mittō, mīsī, missum (3), *tr.*, send

moderātiō, -ōnis, *f.*, restraint

moderor (1), *dep.*, set bounds to

modestia, -ae, *f.*, correct behaviour

modicus, -a, -um, moderate

modo, *adv.*, lately, recently, only; modo ... modo, now ... again

modus, -ī, *m.*, moderation, manner

moenia, -ium, *n.*, walls

mōlēs, -is, *f.*, weight, might

molliō (4), *tr.*, soften

mollitia, -ae, *f.*, softness, effeminacy

mōmentum, -ī, *n.*, moment

moneō (2), *tr.*, advise, warn

mōns, -ntis, *m.*, mountain, hill

mōnstrō (1), *tr.*, show

monumentum, -ī, *n.*, memorial

mora, -ae, *f.*, delay

morior, mortuus (3), *dep.*, die

mors, -rtis, *f.*, death

mortālis, -e, mortal

mōs, mōris, *m.*, custom; *pl.*, behaviour, character

mōtus, -ūs, *m.*, movement, emotion

moueō, mōuī, mōtum (2), *tr.*, move

mox, *adv.*, presently, soon

mucrō, -ōnis, *m.*, sharp point

muliebris, -e, of a woman

mulier, -eris, *f.*, woman

multiplicō (1), *tr.*, multiply

multitūdō, -inis, *f.*, mass

multus, -a, -um, much, many

mūnia, -ōrum, *n.*, duties

mūnicipium, -ī, *n.*, town

mūnimentum, -ī, *n.*, fortification

mūniō (4), *tr.*, guard

mūnus, -eris, *n.*, duty, service, show, gift

mūrus, -ī, *m.*, wall

mūtō (1), *tr.*, change

mūtuus, -a, -um, mutual

nam, namque, *conj.*, for

narrō (1), *tr.*, relate

nāscor, nātus (3), *intr.*, be born

nātiō, -ōnis, *f.*, tribe

nātūra, -ae, *f.*, nature

nāuālis, -e, naval

nauarchus, -ī, *m.*, commander

nāuigābilis, -e, navigable

nāuigium, -ī, *n.*, ship

nāuis, -is, *f.*, ship

nāuō (1), *tr.*, accomplish

nē, *conj.*, that ... not; nē ... quidem, not even

nec, *see* neque

necdum, *conj.*, and not yet

necessitās, -ātis, *f.*, necessity

necessitūdō, -inis, *f.*, relationship

nēdum, *conj.*, not to speak of

neglegō, -exī, -ectum (3), *tr.*, neglect

nēmŏ, -inis, *c.*, no one

nemus, -oris, *n.*, wood

neque, nec, *conj.*, and not, neither, nor

nequeō (4), *intr.*, be unable

neruus, -ī, *m.*, sinew

nescius, -a, -um, unaware

neu, *conj.*, and that ... not

neuter, -tra, -trum, neither (of two)

nex, -cis, *f.*, murder, violent death

nihil, *indecl.*, *n.*, nothing

nimius, -a, -um, excessive

nisi, *conj.*, unless
nōbilis, -e, noble
nōbilitās, -ātis, *f.*, noble birth
noceō (2), *intr.*, hurt
noctū, *adv.*, by night
nocturnus, -a, -um, nocturnal
nōmen, -inis, *n.*, name, title
nōminō (1), *tr.*, name
nōn, not
nōndum, *adv.*, not yet
nōnnihil, *indecl. n.*, something
nōs, nostrī, *pro.*, we
nōscō, nōuī, nōtum (3), *tr.*,
  recognise
noster, -tra, -trum, our
nōtitia, -ae, *f.*, knowledge
nōtus, -a, -um, well known
nouissimus, -a, -um, extreme,
  last
nouus, -a, -um, new
nox, noctis, *f.*, night
noxa, -ae, *f.*, harm
nūdus, -a, -um, bare
nūllus, -a, -um, no, none
nūmen, -inis, *n.*, divine power
numerō (1), *tr.*, count, reckon
numerus, -ī, *m.*, number
nummus, -ī, *m.*, sesterce
numquam, *adv.*, never
nunc, *adv.*, now
nūntiō (1), *tr.*, announce
nūntius, -a, -um, announcing
nūntius, -ī, *m.*, messenger, news
nūper, *adv.*, recently
nuptiālis, -e, bridal
nūtus, -ūs, *m.*, nod

ob, *prep. with acc.*, because of

obeō, -īre, -iī, -itum, *intr.*, die
obiciō, -iēcī, -iectum (3), *tr.*,
  charge
obligō (1), *tr.*, tie up
oblitterō (1), *tr.*, blot out
oblīuiō, -ōnis, *f.*, forgetful-
  ness
obnītor, -nīxus (3), *dep.*, struggle
  against
obnoxius, -a, -um, vulnerable
oboediō, (4), *intr.*, obey
obsaepiō, -psī, -ptum (4), close
  up
obscēnus, -a, -um, obscene
obscūrus, -a, -um, obscure
obsequium, -ī, *n.*, obedience,
  allegiance
obsequor, -secūtus (3), *dep.*,
  obey
obseruātiō, -ōnis, *f.*, observation,
  notice
obses, -sidis, *m.*, hostage
obsideō, -sēdi, -sessum (2), *tr.*,
  besiege
obsidiō, -ōnis, *f.*, siege
obsidium, -ī, *n.*, siege
obsīgnō (1), *tr.*, sign, seal
obstinātus, -a, -um, determined,
  inflexible
obstringō, -nxī, -ictum (3), *tr.*,
  bind, oblige
obtemperō (1), *tr.*, obey
obtendō, -dī, -tum (3), *tr.*,
  proffer
obterō, -trīuī, -trītum (3), *tr.*,
  crush
obtineō, -tinuī, -tentum (2), *tr.*,
  hold

obtundō, -tudī, -tūsum (3), *tr.*, blunt

obuersor (1), *dep.*, float before, appear to

obuius, -a, -um, in the way, meeting

occāsiō, -ōnis,*f.*, opportunity

occidō, -cīdī, -cīsum (3), *tr.*, kill

occultō (1), *tr.*, conceal

occultus, -a, -um, secret

occupō (1), *tr.*, seize, occupy

occurrō, -currī, -cursum (3), *intr.*, meet

occursus, -ūs, *m.*, meeting

octingentī, -ae, -a, eight hundred

oculus, -ī, *m.*, eye

ōdī, -isse, *defect. tr.*, hate

odium, -ī, *n.*, hatred

offendō, -dī, -sum (3), *tr. & intr.*, come upon, give offence

offerō, -ferre, obtulī, oblātum, *tr.*, offer

ōlim, *adv.*, formerly, long ago

ōmen, -inis, *n.*, omen

omittō, -mīsī, -missum (3), *tr.*, let go, drop, omit

omnis, -e, all

onus, -eris, *n.*, load, burden

onustus, -a, -um, loaded

opera, -ae,*f.*, work

operiō, -uī, -rtum (4), *tr.*, cover

opīniō, -ōnis,*f.*, idea, opinion

opperior, -pertus (4), *dep.*, await

oppidānus, -ī, *m.*, townsman

oppidum, -ī, *n.*, town

opprimō, -pressī, -pressum (3), *tr.*, crush

oppūgnātiō, -ōnis,*f.*, siege

ops, opis,*f.*, resources, wealth

optimus, -a, -um, best

opus, -eris, *n.*, need, deed

ōrātiō, -ōnis,*f.*, speech

ōrātor, -ōris, *m.*, orator

orbis, -is, *m.*, world

orbus, -a, -um, childless

ōrdior, ōrsus (4), *dep.*, begin

ōrdō, -inis, *m.*, rank, row, order

oriēns, -ntis, *m.*, the East

orīgō, -inis,*f.*, source

orior, ortus (4), *dep.*, arise, begin

ōrnātus, -ūs, *m.*, dress

ōrnō (1), *tr.*, decorate

ōrō (1), *tr.*, pray for

ōs, ōris, *n.*, mouth

ōsculum, -ī, *n.*, kiss

ostendō, -dī, -sum (3), *tr.*, show

ostentātiō, -ōnis,*f.*, display

ostentō (1), *tr.*, demonstrate

ostentus, -ūs, *m.*, display, demonstration

ōstium, -ī, *n.*, (river) mouth

ōtium, -ī, *n.*, leisure, peace

pābulum, -ī, *n.*, fodder, foraging ground

pacīscor, pactus (3), *dep.*, agree

paelex, -icis, *f.*, concubine, mistress

palam, *adv.*, openly

pallor, -ōris, *m.*, pallor

palūs, -ūdis,*f.*, marsh

pango, pepigī, pactum (3), *tr.*, contract

pār, paris, equal

parātus, -ūs, *m.*, preparation

parcō, pepercī, parsum (3), *intr.*, spare
parcus, -a, -um, frugal
parēns, -ntis, *c.*, parent
pāreō (2), *intr.*, obey
paries, -etis, *m.*, wall
pariō, peperī, partum (3), *tr.*, produce, acquire
pariter, *adv.*, equally
parō (1), *tr.*, prepare
parricīda, -ae, *c.*, murderer of kin, traitor
pars, -rtis, *f.*, part; *pl.*, party, side
parsimōnia, -ae, *f.*, thrift
particeps, -ipis, *m.*, partner
partiō (4), *tr.*, divide
partus, -ūs, *m.*, birth
parum, *adv.*, too little, not
passim, *adv.*, everywhere
passus, -ūs, *m.*, pace, step
patefaciō, -fēcī, -factum (3), *tr.*, reveal
pateō, -uī (2), *intr.*, be obvious, be open
pater, -tris, *m.*, father; *pl.*, senators
paternus, -a, -um, of a father, paternal
patiēns, -ntis, patient
patientia, -ae, *f.*, complaisance
patria, -ae, *f.*, native land
patrius, -a, -um, ancestral
patrō (1), *tr.*, accomplish
patrōnus, -ī, *m.*, patron
patulus, -a, -um, open
paucī, -ōrum, few
paueō, pāuī (2), *tr. & intr.*, fear
pauidus, -a, -um, afraid

paulātim, *adv.*, gradually
paululum, *adv.*, a little
pauor, -ōris, *m.*, fear
pauper, -eris, poor
pāx, -cis, *f.*, peace
peccō (1), *tr. & intr.*, transgress
pectus, -oris, *n.*, breast, heart
pecūnia, -ae, *f.*, money
pedes, -itis, *m.*, foot soldier, one on foot
peditātus, -ūs, *m.*, infantry
pelagus, -ī, *n.*, sea
pellō, pepulī, pulsum (3), *tr.*, beat, drive
penātēs, -ium, *m.*, household gods, household
penes, *prep. with acc.*, in the power of
penetrō (1), *tr.*, penetrate, reach
penitus, *adv.*, deeply
per, *prep. with acc.*, through, by means of
percellō, -culī, -culsum (3), *tr.*, overthrow
percontātiō, -ōnis, *f.*, questioning
percontor (1), *dep.*, ask
percrēbēscō, -buī (3), *intr.*, become prevalent
percursō, -āre (1), *tr.*, range through
percussor, -ōris, *m.*, assassin
pereō, -īre, -iī, -itum, *intr.*, die
perferō, -ferre, -tulī, -lātum, *tr.*, endure
perficiō, -fēcī, -fectum (3), *tr.*, complete, accomplish
perfidia, -ae, *f.*, treachery

pergō, -rrēxī, -rēctum (3), *tr.*
& *intr.*, proceed with, proceed to
perīculum, -ī, *n.*, danger
perinde, *adv.*, just as, as much as
perītus, -a, -um, skilful
permeō (1), *tr.*, pass through,
traverse
permisceō, -cuī, -ixtum (3), *tr.*,
mingle
permittō, -mīsī, -missum (3),
tr., entrust, allow
perpetior, -pessus (3), *dep.*,
endure
perpetrō (1), *tr.*, complete
perrumpō, -rūpī, -ruptum (3),
tr., break through
perseuērus, -a, -um, very strict
persimplex, -icis, very simple
perspergō, -rsī, -rsum (3), *tr.*,
sprinkle
pertaesus, -a, -um, wearied
peruādō, -sī, -sum, (3) *tr.* &
intr., spread
peruagor (1), *dep.*, overrun
peruāstō (1), *tr.*, devastate utterly
peruertō, -tī, -sum (3), *tr.*,
overthrow
peruigilium, -ī, *n.*, vigil, watch
peruincō, -uīcī, -uictum (3),
tr., conquer, achieve
peruius, -a, -um, passable
pēs, pedis, *m.*, foot
petō, -īuī, -ītum (3), *tr.*, look for,
seek, ask, make for
piāculum, -ī, *n.*, appeasing sacrifice
piget, -uit (2), *impers.*, it irks,
repents

pignus, -oris, *n.*, pledge, guarantee, relation
pīlum, -ī, *n.*, javelin
pīlus, -ī, *m.*, division of the Roman
army
pīrāticus, -a, -um, of pirates
plācāmentum, -ī, *n.*, appease-
ment
placeō (2), *intr.*, please; *impers.*,
it seems good
plānus, -a, -um, flat
plēbēs, -eī, *f.*, common people
plēbs, -bis, *f.*, common people
plēnus, -a, -um, full
plērīque, -aeque, -aque, many,
most
plūrimus, -a, -um, most
plūs, plūris, more; *pl.*, more,
several
poena, -ae, *f.*, punishment
polliceor, pollicitus (2), *dep.*,
promise
pōmum, -ī, *n.*, fruit
pondus, -eris, *n.*, weight
pōnō, posuī, positum (3), *tr.*,
set aside, pitch (camp),
place
pōns, -ntis, *m.*, bridge
poples, -itis, *m.*, knee-ham
populāris, -e, popular, of the
people
populor (1), *dep.*, ravage
populus, -ī, *m.*, people
porticus, -ūs, *f.*, portico, colon-
nade
portus, -ūs, *m.*, harbour
poscō, poposcī (3), *tr.*, demand
possessiō, -ōnis, *f.*, possession

possum, posse, potuī, *intr.*, be able

post, *adv. & prep. with acc.*, after

posteā, *adv.*, afterwards

posterus, -a, -um, later, following

posthāc, *adv.*, after this

postquam, *conj.*, after

postrēmō, postrēmum, *adv.*, finally

potēns, -ntis, powerful

potentia, -ae, *f.*, power, authority

potestās, -ātis, *f.*, power

potius, *adv.*, rather

prae, *prep. with abl.*, because of

praebeō (2), *tr.*, provide

praeceps, -itis, dangerous, impetuous

praeceptor, -ōris, *m.*, teacher

praeceptum, -ī, *n.*, order, maxim

praecipuus, -a, -um, outstanding, special

praeda, -ae, *f.*, booty

praedīues, -itis, very rich

praedium, -ī, *n.*, estate

praeeō, -īre, -iī, -itum, *tr. & intr.*, precede

praefectūra, -ae, *f.*, district

praefectus, -ī, *m.*, commander

praeferō, -ferre, -tulī, -lātum, *tr.*, present, display

praeferōx, -ōcis, very fierce

praeficiō, -fēcī, -fectum (3), *tr.*, appoint to command

praefluō, -ere (3), *intr.*, flow past

praefor (1), *dep.*, say beforehand, preface

praemineō, -ēre (2), *tr.*, surpass

praemittō, -mīsī, -missum (3), *tr.*, send ahead

praemium, -ī, *n.*, reward

praenūntius, -a, -um, foreboding

praepediō (4), *tr.*, entangle

praepōnō, -posuī, -positum (3), *tr.*, set over

praepotēns, -ntis, very powerful

praeripiō, -puī, -reptum (3), *tr.*, snatch away

praesāgium, -ī, *n.*, portent

praescrībō, -psī, -ptum (3), *tr.*, instruct

praesēns, -ntis, present, powerful

praesidium, -ī, *n.*, protection, garrison

praestāns, -ntis, outstanding

praestō, *adv.*, ready, at hand

praetendō, -dī, -tum (3), *tr.*, put forward

praeter, *prep. with acc.*, beyond, above

praetor, -ōris, *m.*, praetor

praetōrium, -ī, *n.*, praetorian guard

praetōrius, -a, -um, praetorian

praetūra, -ae, *f.*, praetorship

praeualeō, -uī (2), *intr.*, be superior

praeualidus, -a, -um, very powerful

praeueniō, -uēnī, -uentum (4), *tr. & intr.*, precede, get start, anticipate

prāuus, -a, -um, bad

premō, pressī, pressum (3), *tr.*, press, check, crush

pretium, -ī, n., reward, price

prex, -cis, f., prayer, entreaty

prīdem, adv., long ago

prīdiē, adv., the day before

prīmōrēs, -um, m., chief men, leaders

prīmum, prīmō, adv., at first

prīmus, -a, -um, first

prīnceps, -ipis, m., emperor

prīncipium, -ī, n., beginning

prior, -ius, earlier

prīscus, -a, -um, ancient

prīuātus, -a, -um, private

prō, prep. with abl., in front of, along, instead of, on behalf of, in proportion to

probō (1), tr., prove, approve

probrōsus, -a, -um, offensive

prōcēdō, -cessī, -cessum (3) intr., advance, succeed

prōcērus, -a, -um, tall

prōcidō, -cidī (3), intr., fall down

procul, adv., far away

prōcūrātor, -ōris, m., procurator, governor

prōdigentia, -ae, f., extravagance

prōdigium, -ī, n., portent

prōdigus, -a, -um, lavish

prōditiō, -ōnis, f., betrayal

prōdō, -didī, -ditum (3), tr., disclose, betray

proelium, -ī, n., battle

profectiō, -ōnis, f., departure

prōfluō, -xī, -xum (3), intr., flow, run

profugus, -a, -um, fugitive

prōgredior, prōgressus (3), dep., advance

prohibeō (2), tr., hinder, prevent

proindē, adv., just so, so much

prōlātō (1), tr., postpone

prōmiscus, -a, -um, indiscriminate, public

prōmittō, -mīsī, -missum (3), tr., promise

prōmō, -mpsī, -mptum (3), tr., produce

prōmoueō, -mōuī, -mōtum (2), tr., move forward

prōmptē, adv., readily

prōmptus, -a, -um, ready

prōmunturium, -ī, n., promontory, cape

prŏpāgō (1), tr., increase

prōpalam, adv., openly

prōpatulum, -ī, n., open place

prope, adv., near, almost

properē, adv., quickly

properō (1), tr. & intr., hurry

propinquō (1), intr., approach

propinquus, -a, -um, near

propinquus, -ī, m., relation

propitiō (1), tr., appease

proprius, -a, -um, one's own, special

propter, prep. with acc., near

prōpūgnō (1), tr., defend

prōrsus, adv., certainly

prōrumpō, -rūpī, -ruptum (3), intr., burst forth

prōruō, -uī, -ūtum (3), tr., demolish

prōspectus, -ūs, m., prospect, view

prosper, -era, -erum, prosperous

prosperē, *adv.*, prosperously

prōsternō, -strāuī, -strātum (3), *tr.*, knock down

prōsum, prōdesse, prōfuī, *intr.*, benefit

prōtegō, -xī, -ctum (3), *tr.*, protect

prōtendō, -dī, -sum (3), *tr.*, stretch out

prōturbō (1), *tr.*, drive away

prōuehō, -xī, -ctum (3), *tr.*, promote, prolong

prōuideō, -uīdī, -uīsum (2), *tr.*, provide

prōuidus, -a, -um, provident

prōuincia, -ae, *f.*, province

prōuinciālis, -e, provincial

prōuīsus, -ūs, *m.*, provision

proximus, -a, -um, next, nearest

prūdēns, -ntis, cautious

pūblicus, -a, -um, public

pudendus, -a, -um, scandalous

pueritia, -ae, *f.*, youth, childhood

puerperium, -ī, *n.*, childbirth

pugiō, -ōnis, *m.*, dagger

pūgna, -ae, *f.*, fight, battle

pulcher, -chra, -chrum, attractive

pulchritūdō, -inis, *f.*, beauty

puluīnar, -āris, *n.*, couch

pūrgō (1), *tr.*, clean, clear

quā, *adv.*, where

quadrāgintā, *indecl.*, forty

quaerō, -sīuī, -sītum (3), *tr.*, seek

quaestiō, -ōnis, *f.*, investigation

quālis, -e, what kind of

quāliscumque, quālecumque, of whatsoever kind

quam, *adv.*, than, how

quamquam, *conj.*, although

quamuīs, *conj.*, although

quandō, *conj.*, since

quantus, -a, -um, how great, how much

quārtus, -a, -um, fourth

quasi, *conj.*, as if, as

quattuor, *indecl.*, four

quattuordecim, *indecl.*, fourteen

-que *conj.*, and

querimōnia, -ae, *f.*, complaint

queror, questus (3), *dep.*, complain

questus, -ūs, *m.*, complaint

quī, quae, quod, *rel. pro., interr. & indef. adj.*, who, what, any

quia, *conj.*, because

quīcumque, quae-, quod-, *pro.*, whoever, whatever

quīdam, quae-, quod-, certain, some

quidem, *adv.*, indeed

quiēs, -ētis, *f.*, peace

quīn, *adv. & conj.*, indeed, in fact, but that

quīnam, quaenam, quodnam, who, which (precisely)

quīntadecimānī, -ōrum, *m.*, soldiers of the fifteenth legion

quīntus, -a, -um, fifth

quippe, *adv. & conj.*, for, indeed

quis, quid, *indef. pro.*, anyone

quisnam, quae-, quid-, who, what (precisely)

quisquam, quae-, quic-, *pro.*, anyone

quisque, quae-, quod-, *indef. pro.*, each

quisquis, quidquid, *pro.*, whoever, whatever

quod, *conj.*, because

quondam, *adv.*, formerly, once

quoniam, *conj.*, since

quoque, *conj.*, also

quotiēs, *adv.*, as often as

rapiō, -puī, -ptum (3), *tr.*, lead rapidly, snatch

raptim, *adv.*, quickly

raptus, -ūs, *m.*, plunder

rārus, -a, -um, scattered, rare

ratiō, -ōnis, *f.*, account, reason, conduct

ratis, -is, *f.*, raft

recēns, -ntis, recent, fresh

recēns, *adv.*, recently

reciperō (1), *tr.*, recover

reconciliō (1), *tr.*, reconcile

recordātiō, -ōnis *f.*, recollection

recordor (1), *dep.*, recollect

recūsō (1), *tr.*, refuse

reddō, -didī, -ditum (3), *tr.*, render

redeō, -īre, -iī, -itum, *intr.*, return

reditus, -ūs, *m.*, return

redūcō, -dūxī, -ductum (3), *tr.*, lead back

referō, -ferre, rettulī, relātum, *tr.*, relate, bring back, propose

rēfert, -tulit, *impers.*, it matters

refoueō, fōuī, fōtum (2), *tr.*, revive

rēgia, -ae, *f.*, palace

regimen, -inis, *n.*, rule

regiō, -ōnis, *f.*, region

rēgius, -a, -um, royal

rēgnum, -ī, *n.*, kingdom

regō, rēxī, rēctum (3), *tr.*, rule, direct

regredior, -gressus (3), *dep.*, return

religiō, -ōnis, *f.*, religious observance, scruple

relinquo, -īquī, -ictum (3), *tr.*, leave, abandon

reliquiae, -ārum, *f.*, remains, relics

reliquus, -a, -um, remaining

remedium, -ī, *n.*, cure

remeō (1), *intr.*, return

rēmex, -igis, *m.*, rower

remittō, -mīsī, -missum (3), *tr.*, send back

remūneror (1), *dep.*, reward

renīdeō, -ēre (2), *intr.*, smile

renuō, -uī (3), *intr.*, decline

reor, rātus (2), *dep.*, think

reparō (1), *tr.*, restore

repēns, -ntis, recent

repentē, *adv.*, suddenly

repentīnus, -a, -um, sudden

reperiō, repperī, repertum (4), *tr.*, find

repetō, -iuī, -ītum (3), *tr.*, return to, repeat

repetundae (pecuniae), *f.*, extortion

reprimō, -pressī, -pressum (3), *tr.*, check, crush

reputō (1), *tr.*, calculate

rēs, reī, *f.*, affair, event, circumstance, fact

rescrībō, -psī, -ptum (3), *tr.*, write back

respectō, -āre (1), *tr.* & *intr.*, look back

respergō, -sī, -sum (3), *tr.*, sprinkle

respondeō, -ndī, -nsum (2), *tr.*, reply

respōnsum, -ī, *n.*, answer

rēspūblica, reīpūblicae, *f.*, state

restinguō, -nxī, -nctum (3), *tr.*, extinguish

restrictus, -a, -um, stingy

restringō, -nxī, -ctum (3), *tr.*, tie tightly

resūmō, -mpsī, -mptum (3), *tr.*, take back

resurgō, -surrēxī, -surrēctum (3), *intr.*, rise again

retegō, -xī. -ctum (3), *tr.*, uncover

reticeō, -cuī (2), *tr.* & *intr.*, keep secret

retineō, -uī, -tentum (2), *tr.*, keep

retrahō, -xī, -ctum (3), *tr.*, drag back

retrō, *adv.*, back

reuerentia, -ae, *f.*, respect

reuertō, -tī, -sum (3), *intr.*, return

reuincō, -uīcī, -uictum (3), *tr.*, subdue

reuīsō, -ere (3), *tr.*, revisit

reuocō (1), *tr.*, recall

reus, -ī, *m.*, defendant

rēx, rēgis, *m.*, king

rīpa, -ae, *f.*, bank

rīte, *adv.*, properly, duly

rīuus, -ī, *m.*, stream

rōbur, -oris, *n.*, strength

rogātiō, -ōnis, *f.*, (legal) bill

rogitō (1), *tr.*, ask repeatedly or insistently

rogō (1), *tr.*, ask

rōstra, -ōrum, *n.*, speaker's platform

rudis, -e, inexperienced

rūdus, -eris, *n.*, rubbish

ruīna, -ae, *f.*, ruin

rūmor, -ōris, *m.*, rumour, reputation

rūrsum, rūrsus, *adv.*, on the other hand, again

rūs, rūris, *n*, country, fields

sacer, -cra, -crum, sacred

sacerdōs, -ōtis, *m.*, priest

sacerdōtium, -ī, *n.*, priesthood

sacrāmentum, -ī, *n.*, military oath

sacrificium, -ī, *n.*, sacrifice

sacrilegium, -ī, *n.*, sacrilege

sacrō (1), *tr.*, consecrate

saepe, *adv.*, often

saepiō, -psī, -ptum (4), *tr.*, enclose

saeuiō (4), *intr.*, rage

saeuitia, -ae, *f.*, ferocity

saeuus, -a, -um, fierce

sagitta, -ae, *f.*, arrow

salūbritās, -ātis, *f.*, health

salūs, -ūtis, *f.*, safety

salūtāris, -e, advantageous

sanciō, -nxī, -nctum (4), *tr.*, decree

sanguīs, -inis, *m.*, blood

sapientia, -ae, *f.*, philosophy

satis, *adv.*, enough, sufficiently

saucius, -a, -um, wounded

saxum, -ī, *n.*, stone

scaena, -ae, *f.*, stage

scaenicus, -ī, *m.*, actor

scāla, -ae, *f.*, ladder

scelus, -eris, *n.*, crime

scientia, -ae, *f.*, knowledge

scīlicet, *adv.*, of course

sciō (4), *tr.*, know

scīscitor (1), *dep.*, inform oneself

scītum, -ī, *n.*, statute

scortum, -ī, *n.*, prostitute

scrībō, scrīpsī, scrīptum (3), *tr.*, write

scrīptor, -ōris, *m.*, writer, secretary

scrobis, -is, *m.*, trench

scurrīlis, -e, scurrilous

sē, suī, *pro.*, himself, themselves

sēcessus, -ūs, *m.*, retirement

sēcrētus, -a, -um, secret

sector (1), *dep.*, escort

secundus, -a, -um, favourable

sēcūritās, -ātis, *f.*, unconcern

sed, *conj.*, but

sēdēs, -is, *f.*, seat

sedīle, -is, *n.*, seat

sēgnis, -e, slow

sella, -ae, *f.*, chair

sellisternium, -ī, *n.*, formal religious banquet

sēmifactus, -a, -um, half-finished

semper, *adv.*, always

sēmūstus, -a, -um, half-burned

senātor, -ōris, *m.*, senator

senātōrius, -a, -um, senatorial

senātus, -ūs, *m.*, senate

senīlis, -e, elderly

seniōrēs, -um, *m.*, elders

sēnsus, -ūs, *m.*, feeling, expression

sententia, -ae, *f.*, opinion

sēpōnō, -posuī, -positum (3), *tr.*, set apart

septem, *indecl.*, seven

sequor, secūtus (3), *dep.*, follow

sermō, -ōnis, *m.*, conversation

seruīlis, -e, of a slave

seruitium, -ī, *n.*, slavery, servility; *pl.*, slaves

seruō (1), *tr.*, save

seruus, -ī, *m.*, slave, servant

sēsquiplāga, -ae, *f.*, blow and a half

sēstertius, -ī, *m.*, sesterce

seu, *see* sīue

seuēritās, -ātis, *f.*, strictness

sexcentiēs, *adv.*, six hundred times

Sextīlis, -e, August

sextus, -a, -um, sixth

sexus, -ūs, *m.*, sex

sī, *conj.*, if

sīc, *adv.*, so

sīdus, -eris, *n.*, star

signō (1), *tr.*, sign

sīgnum, -ī, *n.,* military standard, sign

silentium, -ī, *n.,* silence

silua, -ae, *f.,* wood

similis, -e, like

simul, *adv.,* at the same time

simulācrum, -ī, *n.,* semblance, image

simulō (1), *tr.,* pretend

simultās, -ātis, *f.,* rivalry, quarrel

sine, *prep. with abl.,* without

singulī, -ae, -a, one each, individual

sistō, stitī, statum (3), *tr.,* place, stop

sitis, -is, *f.,* thirst

situs, -a, -um, placed

sīue, seu, *conj.,* or; **sīue . . . sīue,** whether . . . or

societās, -ātis, *f.,* alliance

sociō (1), *tr.,* unite

socius, -a, -um, allied

socius, -ī, *m.,* ally

sodālitās, -ātis, *f.,* friendship

sōl, sōlis, *m.,* sun

sōlācium, -ī, *n.,* consolation

soleō, solitus, (2), *semi-dep.,* be accustomed

solidō (1), *tr.,* strengthen

sōlitūdō, -inis, *f.,* wilderness, solitude

solium, -ī, *n.,* throne

sollemne, -is, *n.,* ceremony

sollemnis, -e, formal

sollicitūdō, -inis, *f.,* trouble, worry

solum, -ī, *n.,* ground

sōlus, -a, -um, alone

somnus, -ī, *m.,* sleep, sloth

sōns, -ntis, guilty

sors, -rtis, *f.,* lot

sortior (4), *dep.,* draw lots

spatium, -ī, *n.,* distance, interval

speciēs, -ēī, *f.,* display, appearance

spectāculum, -ī, *n.,* show

spectō (1), *tr.,* look at

spernō, sprēuī, sprētum (3), *tr.,* scorn

spērō (1), *tr.,* hope

spēs, -eī, *f.,* hope

spīritus, -ūs, *m.,* breath

spolia, -ōrum, *n.,* spoils

spoliō (1), *tr.,* despoil

squālēns, -ntis, desert, rough

stāgnum, -ī, *n.,* pool

statim, *adv.,* immediately

statuō, -uī, -ūtum (3), *tr.,* decide

status, -ūs, *m.,* state, condition

sternō, strāuī, strātum (3), *tr.,* stretch out

stimulus, -ī, *m.,* goad

stīpendium, -ī, *n.,* pay

stō, stetī, statum (1), *intr.,* stand

strāgēs, -is, *f.,* slaughter

struō, -xī, -ctum (3), *tr.,* construct, arrange

studium, ī, n., support

suādeō, suāsī, suāsum (2), *tr. & intr.,* advise, persuade

sub, *prep. with acc.,* about, near, under

subdō, -didī, -ditum (3), *tr.*, place under, substitute

subeō, -īre, -iī, -itum, *intr.*, submit to

subiciō, -iēcī, -iectum (3), *tr.*, place at

subiectus, -a, -um, low lying, subject

subigō, -ēgī, -āctum (3), *tr.*, subdue

subitārius, -a, -um, emergency, hasty

subitus, -a, -um, unexpected

subripiō, -ripuī, -reptum (3), *tr.*, steal

subsidium, -ī, *n.*, help, assistance

subsistō, -stitī (3), *intr.*, stop, halt

subuectō (1), *tr.*, convey

subuectus, -ūs, *m.*, conveying

subuehō, -xī, -ctum (3), *tr.*, convey

subueniō, -uēnī, -uentum (4), *intr.*, help, assist

suburbānus, -a, -um, suburban, near Rome

succēdō, -cessī, -cessum (3), *intr.*, follow, succeed

succurrō, «currī, -cursum (3), *intr.*, help

suētus, -a, -um, customary, accustomed

suffrāgium, -ī, *n.*, vote

suggredior, -gressus (3), *dep.*, approach

sum, esse, fuī, *intr.*, be

summa, -ae, *f.*, whole, sum

summus, -a, -um, highest

sūmō, -mpsī, -mptum (3), *tr.*, take, undertake

sūmptus, -ūs, *m.*, expense

super, *prep. with abl.*, about, over and above

superbia, -ae, *f.*, pride

superō (1), *tr.*, surmount, double (a point)

superpōnō, -posuī, -positum (3), *tr.*, place upon

supersedeō, -sēdī, -sessum (2), *intr.*, refrain

superstitiō, -ōnis, *f.*, superstition

supersum, -esse, -fuī, *intr.*, survive, be left

suppeditō (1), *intr.*, be in abundance

supplex, -icis, submissive

supplicātiō, -ōnis, *f.*, public prayer

supplicium, -ī, *n.*, (capital) punishment

supplicō (1), *tr.*, pray to

suprā, *adv.*, above

suprēma, -ōrum, *n.*, last rites

suprēmus, -a, -um, last

suscipiō, -cēpī, -ceptum (3), *tr.*, undertake

suspectō (1), *tr.*, suspect

suspīciō, ōnis, *f.*, suspicion

sustentō (1), *tr.*, sustain, restrain

sustineō, -nuī, -tentum (2), *tr.*, support

sūtrīnus, -a, -um, of a shoemaker

suus, -a, -um, one's own

taberna, -ae, *f.*, shop

tabula, -ae, *f.*, writing tablet

taciturnitās, -ātis, *f.*, silence
tālis, -e, such
tam, *adv.*, so
tamen, *adv.*, none the less
tamquam, *adv.*, as if
tandem, *adv.*, finally
tantum, *adv.*, only
tantus, -a, -um, so great
tarditās, -ātis, *f.*, slowness
tēctum, -ī, *n.*, roof, building
tēlum, -ī, *n.*, weapon
temeritās, -ātis, *f.*, foolhardiness
temperanter, *adv.*, moderately
temperō (1), *tr. & intr.*, abstain
tempestās, -ātis, *f.*, storm, time
templum, -ī, *n.*, temple
temptō (1), *tr.*, attempt
tempus, -oris, *n.*, time
tenebrae, -ārum, *f.*, darkness
tenuis, -e, thin, poor
tenuō (1), *tr.*, make thin
tenus, *prep. with abl.*, as far as
tergum, -ī, *n.*, back, pelt
ternī, -ae, -a, three (each)
terra, -ae, *f.*, earth, land
terreō (2), *tr.*, frighten
terror, -ōris, *m.*, fright, fear
tertius, -a, -um, third
testāmentum, -ī, *n.*, will
testificor (1), *dep.*, bear witness
testis, -is, *c.*, witness
testor (1), *dep.*, testify
tetrarchēs, -ae, *m.*, tetrarch, petty prince
theātrum, -ī, *n.*, theatre
timeō, -uī (2), *intr.*, fear
timor, -oris, *m.*, fear

tīrō, -ōnis, *m.*, new recruit
tolerō (1), *tr.*, bear, endure
tollō, sustulī, sublātum (3), *tr.*, raise
tormentum, -ī, *n.*, rack, torture
torqueō, torsī, tortum (2), *tr.*, torture
torus, -ī, *m.*, bed
toruus, -a, -um, grim
tot, *indecl.*, so many
totidem, *indecl.*, just as many
totiēs, *adv.*, so often
tōtus, -a, -um, whole
trabs, -bis, *f.*, beam, timber
tractus, -ūs, *m.*, drawing out
trādō, -didī, -ditum (3), *tr.*, hand over, relate
tragicus, -a, -um, tragic
tragoedus, -ī, *m.*, tragic actor
trahō, trāxī, tractum (3), *tr.*, draw, pull
trāiectus, -ūs, *m.*, crossing
trāmittō, -mīsī, -missum (3), *tr.*, cross, pass over
trāns, *prep. with acc.*, across
trānseō, -īre, -iī, -itum, *tr. & intr.*, cross
trānsferō, -ferre, -tulī, -lātum, *tr.*, transfer
trānsgredior, -gressus (3), *dep.*, cross
trānsgressus, -ūs, *m.*, crossing
trānsitus, -ūs, *m.*, crossing
tremō, -uī (3), *intr.*, shake, tremble
trepidātiō, -ōnis, *f.*, confusion, alarm
trepidō (1), *intr.*, be alarmed

trepidus, -a, -um, fearful, frightened
trēs, tria, three
tribūnal, -ālis, n., platform
tribūnātus, -ūs, m., tribunate
tribūnus, -ī, m., tribune, officer
tribuō, -uī, -ūtum (3), tr., bestow
tribūtum, -ī, n., tribute
trīduum, -ī, n., three days
trīginta, indecl., thirty
trirēmis, -is, f., trireme, warship
trīstis, -e, gloomy, unfortunate
triumphālis, -e, triumphal
triumphus, -ī, m., triumph
tropaeum, -ī, n., trophy
trucīdō (1), tr., murder
tū, tuī, pro., you (s.)
tueor, tuitus (2), dep., protect
tugurium, -ī, n., hut
tum, adv., then
tumultuārius, -a, -um, hastily raised
tunc, adv., then
turbō (1), tr., disturb
turma, -ae, f., squadron, troop
turris, -is, f., tower
tūtēla, -ae, f., protection
tūtus, -a, -um, safe
tuus, -a, -um, your (s.)

uacuus, -a, -um, empty, free from
uāgīna, -ae, f., sheath
uagus, -a, -um, roaming, vague
ualeō, -uī (2), intr., be strong
ualētūdō, -inis, f., health

ualidus, -a, -um, strong
uallum, -ī, n., rampart
uānitās, -ātis, f., vainglory
uānus, -a, -um, empty, useless
uapor, -ōris, m., heat, steam
uarius, -a, -um, different
uāstātiō, -ōnis, f., ravaging
uāstō (1), tr., lay waste
ubi, conj., when, where
ubīque, adv., everywhere
-ue, conj., or
uectīgal, -ālis, n., tax
uel, conj., or
uēlōcitās, -ātis, f., speed
uelut, adv., as if, as it were
uēna, -ae, f., vein
uenēnum, -ī, n., poison
uenerātiō, -ōnis, f., worship
ueneror (1), dep., worship
uenia, -ae, f., pardon
ueniō, uēnī, uentum (4), intr., come
uentitō (1), intr., come often
uentus, -ī, m., wind
uēr, uēris, n., spring
uerber, -eris, n., whip
uerbum, -ī, n., word
uersor (1), dep., stay
uersus, -ūs, m., verse
uertō, -tī, -sum (3), tr. & intr., turn
uērum, conj., but
uērus, -a, -um, true
uespera, -ae, f., evening
uester, -tra, -trum, your (pl.)
uestīgium, -ī, n., track, trace
uestis, -is, f., clothing
uetō, -tuī, -titum (1), tr., forbid

uetus, -eris, old
uetustās, -ātis, *f.*, old age
uetustus, -a, -um, ancient
uexillum, -ī, *n.*, standard, detachment
uia, -ae, *f.*, street, road
uīcēnī, -ae, -a, twenty (each)
uicis, -is, *f.*, alteration, misfortune, recompense; in uicem, *adv.*, by turns
uictima, -ae, *f.*, sacrifice, victim
uictor, -ōris, *m.*, victor
uictōria, -ae, *f.*, victory
uictus, -ūs, *m.*, livelihood, food
uīcus, -ī, *m.*, village, block
uideō, uīdī, uīsum (2), *tr.*, see; *pass.*, seem
uigeō, -ēre (2), *intr.*, be lively
uigilia, -ae, *f.*, night watch
uīlla, -ae, *f.*, country house
uinciō, -nxī, -nctum (4), *tr.* bind
uinclum, -ī, *n.*, chain, bond
uincō, uīcī, uictum (3), *tr.*, defeat
uindicta, -ae, *f.*, revenge
uiolenter, *adv.*, violently
uiolentia, -ae, *f.*, violence
uiolentus, -a, -um, violent
uir, -rī, *m.*, man
uirgō, -inis, *f.*, virgin
uirītim, *adv.*, individually
uirtūs, -ūtis, *f.*, courage, good qualities
uīs, vim, *f.*, strength, force, power; *pl.*, military forces, resources
uīsō, -sī, -sum (3), *tr.*, survey visit

uīsus, -ūs, *m.*, sight
uīta, -ae, *f.*, life
uītālis, -e, vital
uitium, -ī, *n.*, vice, depravity
uītō (1), *tr.*, avoid
uitulus, -ī, *m.*, calf
uīuidus, -a, -um, vigorous
uīuō, uīxī, uīctum (3), *intr.*, live
uix, *adv.*, scarcely
ulcīscor, ultus (3), *dep.*, take vengeance on, punish
ūllus, -a, -um, any
ultiō, -ōnis, *f.*, revenge
ultrā, *adv.*, farther; *prep. with acc.*, beyond
ultrō, *adv.*, voluntarily
umbra, -ae, *f.*, shadow, shade
ūmidus, -a, -um, wet
unde, *adv.*, from where
undique, *adv.*, from all sides
ūnicē, *adv.*, especially
ūnus, -a, -um, one
uocābulum, -ī, *n.*, name
uōciferor (1), *dep.*, shout
uocō (1), *tr.*, call, summon
uolitō (1), *intr.*, flit about
uolō, uelle, uoluī, *intr.*, wish, desire
uolŭcris, -is, *f.*, bird
uoluntārius, -a, -um, voluntary
uoluptās, -ātis, *f.*, pleasure
uōtum, -ī, *n.*, prayer, vow
uoueō, uōuī, uōtum (2), *tr. & intr.*, vow, promise
uōx, -cis, *f.*, voice, utterance
urbs, -bis, *f.*, city
urgeō, ursī (2), *tr.*, press

ūrō, ussī, ustum (3), *tr.*, burn
usquam, *adv.*, anywhere
ūsque, *adv.*, all the way (to)
ūsurpō (1), *tr.*, use, employ, take
  possession of
ūsus, -ūs, *m.*, use, necessity,
  experience, purpose
ut, *adv. & conj.*, that, so that, as
ūtēnsilia, -ium, *n.*, necessities
uterque, -traque, -trumque,
  each of two
uterus, -ī, *m.*, womb

ūtilis, -e, useful
ūtilitās, -ātis, *f.*, utility, prac-
  ticality
utinam, *adv.*, if only
ūtor, ūsus (3), *dep.*, use
utrimque, *adv.*, on both sides
uulgō (1), *tr.*, make common
uulgus, -ī, *n.*, mass of people
uulnerō (1), *tr.*, wound
uulnus, -eris, *n.*, wound
uultus, -ūs, *m.*, expression, face
uxor, -ōris, *f.*, wife